THE CATHOLIC ANSWER BOOK 3

REVEREND PETER M.J. STRAVINSKAS PH.D., S.T.D.

Our Sunday Visitor Publishing Division
Our Sunday Visitor, Inc.
Huntington, Indiana 46750

Our Sunday Visitor Publishing Division
Our Sunday Visitor, Inc.
200 Noll Plaza
Huntington, IN 46750

ISBN: 08973-933-9
LCCN: 98-66242

Cover design by Monica Watts
PRINTED IN THE UNITED STATES OF AMERICA
933

Contents

Key to Abbreviations of Biblical Books
(In Alphabetical Order)

Old Testament

Am / Amos
Bar / Baruch
1Chr / 1 Chronicles
2 Chr / 2 Chronicles
Dn / Daniel
Dt / Deuteronomy
Eccl / Ecclesiastes
Est / Esther
Ex / Exodus
Ez / Ezra
Gn / Genesis
Hb / Habakkuk
Hg / Haggai
Hos / Hosea
Is / Isaiah
Jb / Job
Jdt / Judith
Jer / Jeremiah
Jgs / Judges
Jl / Joel
Jon / Jonah
Jos / Joshua

1 Kgs / 1 Kings
2 Kgs / 2 Kings
Lam / Lamentations
Lv / Leviticus
Mal / Malachi
1 Mc / 1 Maccabees
2 Mc / 2 Maccabees
Mi / Micah
Na / Nahum
Neh / Nehemiah
Nm / Numbers
Ob / Obadiah
Prv / Proverbs
Ps(s) / Psalms
Ru / Ruth
Sg / Song of Solomon
Sir / Sirach
1 Sm / 1 Samuel
2 Sm / 2 Samuel
Tb / Tobit
Wis / Wisdom
Zec / Zechariah
Zep / Zephaniah

New Testament

Acts / Acts of the Apostles
Col / Colossians
1 Cor / 1 Corinthians
2 Cor / 2 Corinthians
Eph / Ephesians
Gal / Galatians
Heb / Hebrews
Jas / James
Jn / John
1 Jn / 1 John
2 Jn / 2 John
3 Jn / 3 John
Jude / Jude
Lk / Luke

Mk / Mark
Mt / Matthew
Phil / Philippians
Phlm / Philemon
1 Pt / 1 Peter
2 Pt / 2 Peter
Rom / Romans
Rv / Revelation
1 Thes / 1 Thessalonians
2 Thes / 2 Thessalonians
Ti / Titus
1 Tm / 1 Timothy
2 Tm / 2 Timothy

Documents of Vatican Council II
(In Chronological Order)

Sacrosanctum Concilium: Constitution on the Sacred Liturgy

Inter Mirifica: Decree on the Means of Social Communication

Lumen Gentium: Dogmatic Constitution on the Church

Orientalium Ecclesiarum: Decree on the Catholic Eastern Churches

Unitatis Redintegratio: Decree on Ecumenism

Christus Dominus: Decree on the Pastoral Office of Bishops in the
Church

Perfectae Caritatis: Decree on the Up-to-Date Renewal of Religious
Life

Optatam Totius: Decree on the Training of Priests

*Gravissimum Educationi*s: Declaration on Christian Education

Nostra Aetate: Declaration on the Relations of the Church to Non-
Christian Religions

Dei Verbum: Dogmatic Constitution on Divine Revelation

Apostolicam Actuositatem: Decree on the Apostolate of Lay People

Dignitatis Humanae: Declaration on Religious Liberty

Ad Gentes: Decree on the Church's Missionary Activity

Presbyterorum Ordinis: Decree on the Ministry and Life of Priests

Gaudium et Spes: Pastoral Constitution on the Church in the Modern
World

THE CATHOLIC ANSWER BOOK III
Preface

One of the great realities of our time is that we live in an Age of Information. Information is the new wealth, and we have more of it than at any time in our history. Moreover, we're getting more of it every moment of every day as our tools of communication become ever more powerful and pervasive.

At the same time, we have *less meaning* than ever before. We confuse information-processing with thinking; we confuse data with purpose. It's probably safe to say that Americans in the late 1990s have more knowledge and less direction than at any time in our memory as a people.

This is why our Catholic Faith is so important. It gives our lives a sure and loving guide in the person of Jesus Christ, who speaks to us today through His Church. Any tool that builds up the Church therefore deserves our respect and support — but some tools do such a vital job that they call for special recognition. *The Catholic Answer*, edited by Father Peter M.J. Stravinskas, has been offering encouragement, meaning, and truth to Catholics for more than decade. It's an outstanding magazine, and the book you are about to read is entirely consistent with that excellence. It is my hope that, in reading it, you will draw strength from the words of John the Evangelist: "You will know the truth, and the truth will make you free."

✠Charles J. Chaput, O.F.M. Cap.
Archbishop of Denver

Catholic Practices

School funding

Q. I have been told that the American system of funding education violates parental freedom of choice and is unique in the free world in that regard. However, aren't we also bound by the constitutional doctrine of separation of church and state?

Are Catholics really right in trying to get something different from all other American citizens?

A. You are right in observing that the American approach to educational funding violates parental freedom of choice and, yes, it is unique among the world's democracies — 95 percent of which, incidentally, have some type of "separation of church and state." I have studied this issue since my high school days and, in fact, wrote my doctoral dissertation in education on this topic fifteen years ago; the only conclusion that can be honestly drawn is that what we have lived with and under for well over a century (this was not the case for the first century of our republic's life) has its roots in anti-Catholicism, pure and simple.

As far as Catholics wanting preferential treatment, that is totally off the mark. We want for ourselves — and for all parents — the freedom to choose the most appropriate educational environment for our children, without financial penalty. And over the past decade or so, we have been joined in this battle by a wide array of supporters from Orthodox Jews to Evangelicals to non-believers — all concerned about parental rights, the quality of education, and the need for a plurality of educational forms in a truly pluralistic society.

Finally, I want to recommend most heartily a book on this topic by William Bentley Ball, the premier constitutional lawyer in the nation on this issue and also an outstanding Catholic. His work: *Mere Creatures of the State? Education, Religion and the Courts: A View from the Courtroom*, is available from Crisis Books, Box 1006, Notre Dame, IN 46556.

The book is a behind-the-scenes study of the cases, and Mr. Ball was a key player in most if not all of them.

7

Eucharistic adoration

Q. I have been a Catholic for seventy years. My parish has had the tradition of exposition of the Blessed Sacrament on Wednesdays from 10 a.m. until 6 p.m. for adoration. This is now being canceled, and we have been told that the Church doesn't do this anymore. Is this the norm of the Church now?

A. If anything, modern Church legislation makes this more feasible than ever before in history. If anyone wants to know the mind of the chief legislator in the Church, it is simple enough to discover that Pope John Paul II has repeatedly encouraged such periods of adoration and has instituted this practice in the four major basilicas of Rome.

For further information on eucharistic adoration and the mind (as well as the legislation) of the Church, I would suggest that you write to the international headquarters of Perpetual Eucharistic Adoration, 660 Club View Drive, Los Angeles, CA 90024; or call 310-273-3856.

Amen

Q. We have always said "Amen" at the end of recited prayers. Why is it almost always omitted at the end of the Our Father, especially during the recitation of the Rosary? Should it be included as the conclusion of the prayer?

A. Yes it should. As I have indicated before, "Amen" seems to have been dropped by common consensus because it is not used during the recitation of the Lord's Prayer at Mass, and that practice has then been transferred to other recitations of it, incorrectly.

Polish nationals

Q. I am aware that many Roman Catholic priests have left the Church and are functioning as priests in the Polish National Catholic Church. Is it true that these priests who have left the Catholic Church have been excommunicated?

Furthermore, I understand there is some type of intercommunion between the Polish National Church and the Catholic Church. If so, is it permissible for a member of the PNCC to receive Communion in the Catholic Church and vice versa? All this seems confusing; would you please explain fully?

A. For the second part of your question, kindly see the inquiry handled on pages eleven and twelve on the Eastern Orthodox; the answer is substantially the same, except that the Polish Nationals do not have the same skittishness as the Orthodox on this matter.

Any priest (or any other member of Christ's faithful) who, with full knowledge and consent, leaves the Catholic Church automatically excommunicates himself, but isn't that precisely what he intends to do?

Sad delusion

Q. Enclosed please find a clipping from my local newspaper in which we read of a woman who is considered by her pastor and many parishioners, as well as in her own estimation, to be a priest.

The article mentions that the congregation gave her an alb; she evaluates that action thus: "It was a sign that they recognized me as a pastor and as a minister, even though official recognition hasn't come from the Catholic Church. Up until that time, I had worn regular clothes. That was fine, too. But the wearing of the alb helps identify my role." The author ends this entire disgrace with asking the woman if she thinks she has a shot at ordination to the priesthood. Her answer: "It might happen in my lifetime. I didn't expect the Berlin Wall to come down or to see Mandela and DeKlerk together leading South Africa. Extraordinary things have happened."

What is going on in this Church of ours?

A. If the author of the article had waited less than a month, he would have seen that the star of his story could be waiting for hell to freeze over, for Pope John Paul II issued a declaration in which he says he intends to settle the women's ordination question "definitively" and that no further discussion should occur since it is a theological impossibility.

Of course, the basic problem is allowing people to perform tasks with which they should not be involved, to begin with. In my judgment, this is rather cruel since it sets up false hopes and sends out conflicting signals. Truth be told, that is exactly what some have in mind to do.

The first mistake is the wholesale clericalization of the laity in the United States; the second is the institutionalization of this fact by granting such people titles and ecclesiastical garb. If bishops are going to be true pastors of their flock, they will have to be vigilant that the Pope's directives be obeyed according to both the letter and the spirit. The sad case you have identified fails on both scores.

No "Lone Rangers"

Q. If I am already a baptized Christian, why can't I just come to Mass and be a member of the Catholic Church?

A. The first reason is that being or becoming a Catholic is a communal affair and not just something between you and the Lord. Second, you must take instructions in the Catholic Faith. Third, you must receive any other sacraments of initiation (Confirmation, Holy Communion) which you have not validly received in your former ecclesial community. Fourth, you need to make a profession of faith and be received into full communion with the Catholic Church.

Catholicism does not cotton to "Lone Rangerism," and so, the Church is involved in our entire process of salvation: in the person of the priest and in the community of believers. Granted, in some situations the communal dimension has been so highlighted as to obscure the personal and even so as to make odious the communal, but those exaggerations should never blind us to the basic reality of salvation as an event mediated through a community which is the Body of Christ, His holy Church.

Sabbath and sundown

Q. If we are following Jewish tradition in having our Sabbath begin at sundown, then shouldn't we be consistent? What I mean is that if it is true that we can legitimately celebrate a Sunday liturgy at sundown of Saturday, doesn't it make sense that we can't celebrate a Sunday liturgy after sundown on Sunday, since a new day has begun (namely, Monday)? Please enlighten me.

A. You're almost onto something, but not quite!

While you got the first end of the equation correct, the second is just a hair off. Sunday is the longest liturgical day of the week, beginning with evening prayer (vespers) on Saturday and concluding with night prayer (compline) on Sunday, recited just before retiring. Thus, one can licitly offer a Sunday Mass up to midnight on Sunday. The same holds true for days ranked as solemnities.

Throat blessing

Q. I took my infant to have her throat blessed on Saint Blaise's feast day. After the priest finished blessing my throat, by touching the candles to it, he merely made the sign of the cross on my daughter's forehead —

no recitation of the prayer or touch of the candles. Was her throat properly blessed?

A. I don't know why the priest would have done that, but I am sure that almighty God conferred the same grace on your child that would have come from the proper blessing.

Blessed candles

Q. Is there a serious obligation to have the procession and bless candles on the Feast of the Presentation? If this was done at one Mass by the pastor, would the other priests need to do it at subsequent Masses?

A. The Roman Missal seems to presume that the ceremony will be conducted either solemnly or simply at every Mass celebrated on that day, but I must admit that I do not know of any parish (either pre- or post-conciliar) that ever performed the rite more than once.

Russian Orthodox

Q. Recently I moved from Texas to Alaska to live with my daughter and her family. Most small towns here do not have a resident priest; therefore, there is no daily Mass and sometimes no Sunday Mass. Some places we go do have a Russian Orthodox Church. Please inform me about the Russian Orthodox Church. Do they have valid Orders? Is their Mass valid? Can a Latin-rite Catholic receive Holy Communion at their Mass? Is it better to go to a Russian Orthodox Mass or to a Communion service in our rite? Can one go to confession to a Russian Orthodox priest?

A. You have a number of good questions, but it all makes for a very complex matter. Let's try to sort things out.

(1) All Eastern Orthodox Orders are valid, which means their priests validly confect the Eucharist and confer absolution; in theory, then, it would be possible to receive those sacraments from their clergy under certain circumstances.

(2) The Holy See has identified grave spiritual need and lack of access to a Catholic priest as fulfilling the requirements for approaching the sacraments of a Church not in full communion with Rome, and we would permit it the other way around as well. However, the Orthodox — for the most part — do not accept this idea in either direction. That is, they do not want their people to receive from us nor us from them. Therefore, out of respect for their discipline, which is more restrictive than ours, we should refrain from attempting to receive either Holy

11

Communion or the Sacrament of Penance; their attitude would usually be different if one were in danger of death.

(3) It is always better to participate in the full eucharistic sacrifice than to attend a simple Communion service (especially since priesthood and Eucharist are clearly united in a Mass, and not separated as they are in a Communion service), and I would hold to that principle even in the current discussion, wherein we realize that you will not be able to receive Holy Communion.

May I suggest, as you abstain from Holy Communion and make a spiritual communion, that you would pray for two important intentions: an increase in priestly vocations, so that these Communion services become obsolete as quickly as possible; and full, organic unity with the Eastern Orthodox, so that intercommunion can be restored and the prayer of Christ on Holy Thursday night would be brought to reality.

Lay ministers?

Q. In [a recent] issue of TCA, you mentioned that the notion of a lay minister is a "theological impossibility." I was a lay "eucharistic minister" when they changed the title to "extraordinary minister of the Eucharist." Is a eucharistic minister considered a layman or a part of the clergy or part of the order of ministers or what?
A. Let's try to put this whole question into perspective.

At Vatican II, the Council Fathers were extremely careful, when speaking of lay activity in the Church, never to use the word *ministerium* ("ministry"), but words like *officium* ("office") or *munus* ("duty") and particularly *apostolatus* ("apostolate"). The reason for this approach was to safeguard the traditional significance of "ministry," which, in the Catholic scheme of things, implies participation in the Sacrament of Holy Orders. After the council, especially in the United States, many people became very careless in their terminology and quite indiscriminately began to use "ministry" or "minister" for any Church-related work or person working for the Church.

This kind of theological imprecision was censured at the 1987 Synod on the Laity and by Pope John Paul II in his post-synodal apostolic exhortation *Christifideles Laici* (The Christian Lay Faithful), wherein we read the following: "A critical judgment was voiced [among the Synod Fathers] . . . about a too indiscriminate use of the word 'ministry,' the confusion and the equating of the common priesthood and the ministerial priesthood . . . [and] the tendency toward a 'clericalization' of the lay faithful and the risk of creating, in reality, an ecclesial structure of parallel service to that founded on the Sacrament of Orders." He also reminds all that "a person is not a minister simply in performing a task, but through sacramental ordination" (no. 23).

I think that puts it all most clearly. And so, a layperson can perform certain tasks that properly belong to the ordained, but in a delegated manner. When exercising such roles, that person may be considered a minister — by delegation — but not in any precise or proper use of the word. Therefore, extraordinary ministers of Holy Communion are laity who have been appointed to fulfill a ministerial task because of an extraordinary set of circumstances.

Proper genuflection

Q. I was taught that one should genuflect on the right *knee when entering or leaving the presence of the Blessed Sacrament. Recently I have noticed many people, including an associate pastor in my parish, genuflecting on the* left *knee. Which is proper? Or does it matter?*
A. Yes, it matters, and you are correct: it is the right knee unless, of course, someone has a problem with that knee and then uses his left for that reason. In and of itself, genuflecting on one knee or the other is not heresy or anything of that nature, but not knowing the tradition is most unfortunate, especially for a priest. Besides, genuflection on the left knee is the proper gesture for a formal greeting of a prelate, especially when done in conjunction with kissing his ring as a declaration of one's obeisance to his apostolic authority.

Jesuit bishops

Q. Recently, I came across an appeal for financial support from the Catholic Mission of Northern Alaska whose central office is located in the city of Fairbanks. The printed material asked that checks be made out to the Catholic Bishop of Northern Alaska, who was identified as a Jesuit. It has been my understanding that Jesuits do not aspire to positions of authority in the Church. Can you clarify this?
A. It is true that Jesuits are not to aspire to higher office. However, simply because a man is a bishop does not mean that he sought the office but merely that he accepted what had been offered to him, seeing in that action the will of God. There are presently several Jesuit

bishops in the United States, including auxiliaries of Washington and Chicago.

Eucharistic Congress

Q. What is a Eucharistic Congress? Who started them? How do I find out more about them?

A. A Eucharistic Congress is an assembly of the Catholic faithful intended to show and foster devotion to the Blessed Sacrament. Public manifestations of this are made through the celebration of Holy Mass, eucharistic adoration and outdoor processions; the faith life of those in attendance is enhanced through homilies and lectures.

The first such international gathering was held in Lille, France, in 1881. They are scheduled at regular intervals around the world; two of them have occurred in the United States: at Chicago in 1926 and at Philadelphia in 1976. Our present Holy Father has made a special effort to attend these gatherings whenever possible.

Eucharistic Congresses may also be diocesan in scope. For example, the Diocese of Peoria, Illinois, had such an event a few years back. Given the abysmal ignorance of Catholic eucharistic doctrine today and the ever-increasing irreverence, even among regular Mass-goers, these gatherings have much to recommend them.

Shared titles

Q. Why are some of Christ's titles applied to Mary, for example, Morning Star?

A. Sometimes certain titles, being metaphors, have more than one application. Thus, in the one you cite, while it is true that the New Testament speaks of Jesus as the Morning Star, the Church gives that title to Mary in the Litany of Loreto because Our Lord is also called the Sun of Justice and the Morning Star is the last star visible in the sky before sunrise. Once more, one must be careful not to use terminology that can confuse the poorly catechized or those outside the Church. Context is extremely important in these cases.

Meet the saints

Q. When are we going to get some decent post-conciliar material on the saints, both for children and adults? You would think that with this Pope canonizing people every week, writers would get the idea that sanctity is the goal of the Christian life and so highlight these heroes of our faith.

A. Your hyperbole aside, it is true that this Pope does indeed believe that modern man needs the example of saints, in order to live the Gospel in the trying circumstances of our world.

Ignatius Press has been doing a good amount of hagiography, some new and some reprints of good (that is, not saccharine) works from the past; get hold of one of their catalogues. For youngsters ages nine to fifteen, they have their *Vision Books* series, with the latest item being an excellent biography, entitled *Saint Pius X: The Farm Boy Who Became Pope.* The other day I came across a more theological work by Regis Armstrong, *St. Francis of Assisi: Writings for a Gospel Life*, published by Crossroads. I mention this one because all too often books on St. Francis either offer little but platitudes or make of him a 1960s hippie or rebel; this takes the man seriously and makes superb applications of his teachings to the Christian life today.

Lives of the Saints You Should Know, a book by Margaret and Matthew Bunson, is also very good. It is published by Our Sunday Visitor Books. The Bunsons, a mother-and-son team, also have published numerous lives of the saints for children, including Our Sunday Visitor's *Saints You Should Know* series. For young adults and adults, the Bunsons' latest book, *Our Sunday Visitor's Encyclopedia of Saints* is one of the most comprehensive listings of saints and beati published in one volume.

A clever gimmick for introducing children to the saints has emerged with Holy Traders. Instead of baseball players, these cards have the pictures of saints, with vital statistics on the reverse; the box of forty attractively printed cards costs $7. For more information, call: 800-242-8467.

Religious differences

Q. What is the difference between a religious order and a religious congregation?

A. In common English usage, the two terms have become synonymous, but they really refer to two distinct realities. A religious order is a body of men and/or women bound to a rule by solemn vows (e.g., Benedictines, Franciscans, Dominicans), whereas a Religious is related to a congregation by simple vows (e.g., Vincentians, Marianists, and most communities of women Religious engaged in an active apostolate in the United States).

That having been said, I need to make a disclaimer. The 1983 Code of Canon Law does not employ the above terminology at all and now distinguishes between institutes of consecrated life (orders or congregations with either solemn or simple perpetual vows) and societies of apostolic life (which do not make perpetual vows).

Solemnity explained

Q. I grew up Catholic and was knowledgeable regarding the feasts of the Church calendar. Why is January 1 now the Solemnity of Mary, Mother of God, and no longer the Circumcision of the Lord? Is it not confusing to celebrate the Epiphany on any day other than January 6? Does doing so make the so-called "Twelve Days of Christmas" meaningless? Also, what is the special meaning attributed to a day identified as a "solemnity"?

A. Starting at the back, let us note that a "solemnity" is a liturgical observance of the highest rank, the equivalent of the former designation of "first-class feast." It calls for three readings, a Gloria, and Creed.

When the calendar of the Roman rite was revised, provision was made to transfer certain solemnities to the nearest Sunday for those places where they were not holy days of obligation. The motivation was good (namely, that those mysteries of our Faith would be observed by the faithful since they would probably not be able to attend the weekday celebration), but I think it has failed at a practical level. Certain transfers just don't "work," and Epiphany is one of them, in my opinion, for the very reason you give. Days of special significance and with a long tradition attached to them should not be tampered with.

Regarding January 1, let me say that in my own lifetime that feast has had numerous name-changes; the present name, however, is the most ancient one for the day.

Jackie at peace

Q. I was always brought up to believe that couples who live together without being married are living in mortal sin. When Jackie Kennedy Onassis died, it became known that she had been living with a man who, until then, had been publicly identified as "a friend." Not only that, he himself is still married. Now, don't misunderstand me; I am not being judgmental, but the man was at her side as she received the last rites and actively participated in her funeral Mass. Are we once again up to a Catholic double standard: The wealthy can get away with what the poor cannot?

A. Let's review the whole situation, not to judge (as you yourself correctly note) but to clarify.

First, when Jackie Kennedy decided to marry Aristotle Onassis, that union was invalid because he was previously married; therefore, Jackie was ineligible to receive the sacraments. So, no double standard, right? Same penalty for all.

Second, for years after the death of Onassis, it appears that his widow was not involved in any relationships which could deny her access to the sacraments. Therefore, presuming that she went to confession after his death, she could have resumed a normal sacramental life, like any other repentant sinner. So, once more, no double standard, right?

Third, once this last relationship began, I never heard of her reception of the sacraments until the end of her life. Again, she merely availed herself of the opportunity for which we all pray — the grace of final repentance and reconciliation with Christ and His Church. Allegedly, upon receiving the sacraments on her deathbed, the former First Lady said, "Now I am at peace with God." That sounds very honest and sincere to me.

But what about her former alleged paramour's presence at the bedside and, as you note, so actively involved in the funeral?

As the attending priest, I would have had no difficulty with his presence during her last hours, but in no way would I have countenancéd his involvement in the funeral liturgy. Besides which, the poetry reading routine is rather hackneyed and detracts from the proclamation of God's Word. In coming to that decision, I would have been applying the same standard I have used, for instance, in burying an AIDS victim who wanted his former companion to take an active role at the funeral Mass; while God is forgiving and compassionate, I do not think we can flaunt our immoral and supposedly repented-of behavior or, even worse yet, use the survivor's presence as a potentially political statement about one's guilt, innocence, or pride about objectively wrong acts and relationships.

17

All of the above evaluation, of course, is predicated on the fact that the man in question was indeed a paramour of the former First Lady and that ecclesiastical authorities involved in funeral preparations had full knowledge of that situation.

A good idea

Q. When there is a communal celebration for the Anointing of the Sick, should there not be an opportunity for those receiving that sacrament to go to confession beforehand? Should it not also be brought to the attention of the sick and elderly?

A. Yes, I think it would be a very good idea. Even if these people do not have mortal sins, many of them may not have had access to the Sacrament of Penance for a prolonged period of time, and this would surely be a good opportunity.

Confession time

Q. In my parish, confessions are scheduled for fifteen minutes prior to Mass each Sunday; however, the confessions normally take longer and run well after the Mass has started. I know that confessions should not be heard while Mass is being celebrated, but what can be done?

A. I have worked in many parishes where confessions are heard before Sunday Masses, a practice which I consider to be pastorally beneficial. I do think that the time frame should probably be thirty minutes before, instead of fifteen. I have always instructed ushers to make sure that no one else gets in line at least ten minutes before Mass for a priest who will be celebrating the next Mass and to allow no one to do so five minutes before the hour of Mass for any other priest hearing confessions. Furthermore, when the priest has heard the entrance hymn begin, he should simply say to that penitent at the end of confession, "Kindly tell anyone else in line that you were the last person now."

Scouting-Masonic 'axis'?

Q. Considering the Boy Scouts' past history with the Masons and the strong influence on them of both deism and naturalism, would it not be better for a Catholic parish to have a Columbian Squire Circle instead of a Boy Scout troop? Wouldn't it be better to have an organization that is 100 percent Catholic for young men?

A. I was unaware of any historical connection between the Boy Scouts and the Masons. I think it fair to say, however, that any linkage that may have ever existed surely does not today. Furthermore, there are specifically Catholic programs of scouting, awards and all (for example, Parvuli Dei, Ad Altare Dei). Now, I have nothing against having a unit of Columbian Squires too. Very often these two groups appeal to different kinds of boys and young men, and there is no reason not to offer both options.

Wrong conclusions?

Q. I have recently learned that the Catholic preparatory school I attended is about to begin offering an elective to seniors in "Existentialism." Aware that Pope Pius XII referred to it as an erroneous philosophical system, why would a Catholic institution want to introduce students to such a subject, instead of to the teaching of Augustine or Aquinas?
A. You may be jumping to some unwarranted conclusions.

Back in the 1950s, my Catholic grammar school taught us all about communism, leaving no doubt as to its inherent evil. In the 1960s, my Catholic high school offered us a course in existentialism, again making clear the inadequacies of that system of thought. And today, when I teach a graduate course in educational philosophy in a Catholic university, I always include a unit on existentialism for the simple reason that it is really impossible to understand the evolution of the twentieth century without reference to this phenomenon.

Is that what your old prep school is doing? If so, it is performing a valuable function. And that need not be done to the exclusion of the perennial thought of an Augustine or Aquinas.

Narrow-minded?

Q. I need your help to understand a recent occurrence in my diocese. A priest left the active ministry and, shortly thereafter, was married in a Protestant church. A number of priests in good standing were among the invited guests and attended the ceremony. It seems to me that even such a passive participation was not only inappropriate but giving scandal. Am I being narrow-minded? Please comment.
A. No. I do not think your attitude is narrow; I think the behavior of the clergy was reprehensible. They owe an apology to the entire diocese and the whole presbyterate for their act of defiance, which demoralizes all who attempt to live by Church teaching.

Sweet dreams?

Q. I have sent you a copy of our parish bulletin with an announcement that I cannot understand to be a part of Catholic teaching or belief. Would you comment, please, on the following: "Dreams and Spiritual Growth: This workshop is for anyone who wants to understand the value of their dreams as a communication to them from God. There will be input on dreams and an opportunity to work with individual people's dreams." If this is part of the Catholic Faith, then I must belong to a different Church!

A. Dreams were considered normal means of God's communication with human beings in both the Old and New Testaments. Daniel was even an interpreter of dreams. St. Joseph received some of the most important instructions related to the Holy Family, precisely in the context of dreams (cf. Mt 1:19-21; Mt 2:13; Mt 2:19-20). The Scriptures also warn us to be sure that such events are truly divine communications; on that score, it would be important to consult passages like Isaiah 29:8; Deuteronomy 13:1-5; Sirach 34.

Given the shallow nature of much of what passes for spirituality workshops today and the propensity of some people to name themselves self-appointed experts, I would be cautious in this regard. But the basic notion is not wrong or unbiblical.

Essential parts of Mass

Q. I like to go to Mass during the week, but because of my work schedule I'm not able to make the start of Mass and I generally have to leave after Communion. I was interested in what is considered officially attending Mass. What are the parts of the Mass that are necessary to attend in order to receive Communion?

A. The Mass is a complete work of praise and thanksgiving of the Church to Almighty God. Therefore, the goal should always be full participation in an entire celebration.

Obviously, certain parts are more critical than others. Hence, if we were discussing a Sunday or holy day of obligation, I would list the following: the Scripture readings and the Liturgy of the Eucharist, up to and including Holy Communion. Your situation is different, however, since you are attending Mass out of devotion and not obligation. And so, whatever you can do is, in and of itself, meritorious.

Valid but illicit

Q. My husband and I were recently visiting relatives who have left the Catholic Church. They still claim to be Catholic even though they attend Baptist services and have not been to the Catholic Church in at least nine years. Their eighteen-year-old daughter decided to have her child baptized. She is not married and is not Catholic either. The ceremony, however, was performed by a Catholic deacon who was a friend of the family.

The deacon basically used the Catholic baptismal ceremony but left out specific references to raising the child Catholic, etc. He essentially changed "Catholic" to "Christian." He blessed the water in the backyard pool and placed the child in the water three times as he said, "I baptize you in the name of the Father, the Son, and the Holy Spirit."

Does this ceremony fulfill the requirements for Baptism? May a Catholic deacon perform such a ceremony obviously outside the Catholic Church? My husband and I were disturbed by the whole event and would welcome your comments.

A. The action of the deacon was highly irregular and irresponsible; he is commissioned to be a minister (which means "servant") of the Church and not her master. Therefore, he acts in her name only when fulfilling her will.

The Baptism sounds as though it was valid but most illicit. You would do well to contact your diocesan director of deacons for further investigation.

OK to omit the *Filioque*?

Q. I have been attending the Divine Liturgy of the Byzantine rite for several years. Recently, I was in another Byzantine church and was confused during the recitation of the Creed. At the parish I normally attend, the Filioque *is always included; in this parish, it was omitted. When I asked the pastor about it, he said that their bishop had instructed them to omit the phrase since it was not in their tradition. I thought the Nicene Creed was to be accepted in its entirety by all Catholics. Would you please explain this difference in practice?*

A. There is a long and convoluted history to the *Filioque* (Latin: "and from the Son") clause of the Nicene Creed. The expression refers to the line in the Creed concerned with the procession of the Holy Spirit: In the East, the preference was to speak of this as occurring from the Father *through* the Son, while in the West it was seen as happening from both the Father *and* the Son (hence, *Filioque*).

The long and the short of it all is that in the Eastern rites of the Catholic Church, the recitation of that phrase is optional, with the decision being made by the local bishop. Inasmuch as there is clearly a way to recite the Creed without its inclusion in a completely acceptable manner (doctrinally speaking), its use is not forced by the Holy See; Orthodox Christians have a problem with the phrase, not for doctrinal reasons generally but because it was inserted by papal authority after the Council of Nicaea. It should also be remembered that on Pentecost of 1981, Pope John Paul II, in celebration of the anniversary of the Council of Chalcedon, led the Creed — without the *Filioque*.

How much is too much?

Q. Is exterior mortification, such as flagellation, an approved and proper penitential discipline?

A. For centuries, various spiritual writers and directors promoted the notion of physical mortification (including flagellation) as an appropriate means of personal discipline and growth in one's life in Christ. Today there is less than universal acclaim for such forms of spirituality. While flagellation and related disciplines could be taken to exaggerated and unhealthy lengths, it is also accurate to say that contemporary spirituality often suffers from a lack of any kind of mortification. In all questions of this type, there is no substitute for common sense and good spiritual direction.

Artistic license?

Q. In our parish every spring, there is a performance of "Death in the Cathedral." The sanctuary becomes the stage and the tabernacle is used as a prop. Is this permissible?

A. It is certain that in the Middle Ages the Church earned herself the title of "mistress of the arts" because of her encouragement of artistic development, demonstrated by financially supporting beleaguered artists and by offering her facilities for various performances. As time went on, secular forums were provided for presentations that were not explicitly religious or where alternative sites existed. While I would not be opposed, in principle, to the use of a church for what you describe,

I would have problems with the way the facility is being used if what you describe is the reality.

First Fridays

Q. While I know that some can get carried away in their devotions, isn't it wrong for a priest to brand First Friday and First Saturday devotions as "superstitions"?

A. Yes, especially since the Church actively encourages those devotions, and from her highest teaching authorities.

Corpus removed

Q. Thank you for answering my question in reference to the covering of the crucifix during Lent. Last year, the liturgy committee went one step further. Prior to Ash Wednesday, the corpus was removed and only the bare wooden cross remained for the entire Lenten season. When I asked my pastor about it, he said, "Protestants don't have crucifixes, and they're good people." I fail to see the connection. Is his explanation sufficient reason to relinquish our traditional and distinctly Catholic symbol?

A. His *non sequitur* demonstrates an inability to respond to the substance of your argument. Whether or not Protestants are good (some are and some aren't, just like Catholics!) or whether or not they use crucifixes (some do, by the way) is all beside the point.

Liturgical law requires the presence of a crucifix in the sanctuary when the eucharistic sacrifice is being offered. Yet another logical problem exists, in that if I ever considered removing the corpus from the crucifix, it certainly wouldn't be during Lent! Isn't that precisely the time when we are invited to gaze upon the Crucified One to see what our sins caused and still cause?

Scouting update

Q. There was a question in [a recent] issue of TCA I think I can shed some light on. The person who was concerned about Masonic influences in the Boy Scouts of America may be the product of thinking that was prevalent in the Church in this country until the mid-1930s. The acceptance nationally of the BSA is credited by Scouting to Cardinal George Mundelein of Chicago. Until him, the Church in many dioceses sponsored the Boys' Brigade as an alternative program. The concerns of

Masonic influence related to Scouting's promotion of God without a specific creed and Lord Baden-Powell's personal background. The Boys' Brigade still exists in a few places, including a parish in Queens, New York.

A. Thank you.

Solemnity of Thanksgiving?

Q. My parish priest says that we ought to eliminate most of our holy days of obligation and make Thanksgiving one instead, since that coincides with our American culture and more people come to Mass on that day than do so on Ascension Thursday. What do you think about his idea?

A. His is not an original idea, but I think it's a bad one for a number of reasons.

First, if holy days are not well-attended, that's a fault of poor preaching and catechesis. Second, if more Catholics go to Mass on Thanksgiving than on Ascension Thursday (and I don't think that's true, by the way), that says our people have become more comfortable in blending in with American culture than in being part of the universal Church.

Getting specific about Thanksgiving, it is important to note that the observance (while praiseworthy) should be seen as essentially redundant for a Catholic because we celebrate the eucharistic sacrifice every day, the purpose of which is to offer to the Father the most perfect act of thanksgiving (*eucharistia* in Greek means precisely "thanksgiving") possible. Furthermore, I think that ecumenical services for Thanksgiving make the most sense since that acknowledges the American nature of the feast, especially within the context of a pluralistic society.

And before I receive a hundred letters accusing me of being "down" on Thanksgiving (which I'm not), let me say that all I'm calling for is a more nuanced understanding of the holiday, specifically for Catholics.

The Sunday obligation

Q. In my parish, in the event that there is no priest to celebrate Mass on the Sabbath, the custom is for the lector to conduct a prayer-and-Communion service. The people are told "this will fulfill your obligation." I have always been taught that in addition to keeping holy the Sabbath (in accordance with the Third Commandment), the Catholic Church also obligates us to hear Mass on the Sabbath. The obligation is not binding if it is not possible to go to a neighboring town where Mass is being celebrated, is it? What is the truth concerning these Communion services and the Sabbath Mass obligation?

A. If another church is close enough, I don't know why your parish is having a Communion service to begin with; it seems to me that going to the other church would be the normal thing to do. If the next parish over is too far or cannot accommodate its neighbors, then a Communion service should be offered as an opportunity for the local parish community to gather for worship; that, however, is merely an opportunity and not an obligation. If someone can go to a church for Mass without grave inconvenience, then that should be done. The Sunday Mass obligation, however, cannot be transferred to a Communion service.

Latin resources

Q. We understand that you chair an organization that advocates the use of Latin in the liturgy. Our parish wishes to use more Latin music in our services, but all the old music is out of print! Can you suggest any resources for us?

A. The most comprehensive resource I know of (more than five thousand listings) for out-of-print Latin music for the current liturgy and the pre-conciliar rite is available from Mr. Daniel J. Pross, 143 Duncan Ave. #4, Jersey City, NJ 07306-6028. Send $5 for the current catalog.

Papal Masses

Q. I have heard some "horror" stories about the papal Mass celebrated in Denver, most of them pertaining to the distribution of Holy Communion. Is it true that extraordinary ministers of the Eucharist assisted in the distribution of Holy Communion, while some of the priests did not? I have heard that some of the "ciboria" were cardboard boxes and that some of the young people passed the hosts one to another.

How can one determine if these charges are true? If they are, would it not be better in the future to distribute Holy Communion only to a *small number at such Masses, since otherwise reverence for the Eucharist seems to disappear.*

A. I was out of the country at the time of the event, but I have heard many such reports. I must say, however, that any videos I have seen show only priests or deacons distributing Holy Communion and only from true ciboria. Aside from whether or not any of these things occurred, I have a predisposition against such huge Masses, especially when we attempt to distribute the Eucharist. I have been involved with many papal Masses like this and always come away upset because of the many problems that are almost bound to take place, given difficulties related to time, space, and crowds.

When I was a sophomore in high school, Pope Paul VI came to New York and celebrated Mass at Yankee Stadium. At Communion time, however, only one hundred people received (doing so directly from the Holy Father), while the rest were led in an act of spiritual communion. I see nothing wrong with this approach and wish those with the authority to make liturgical judgments for papal events would take a second look at it.

One thing that did strike me about the papal Masses in Denver (easily observable on the videos) is how poorly behaved many of the participants were: laughing, joking, eating hot dogs, drinking soda. I do not even question their goodwill. I just think that mammoth gatherings breed such problems, especially since control becomes more difficult and those in attendance (especially at a distance) can gradually slip from the grasp of what is going on hundreds of yards away. This happens not only with young people; I have frequently seen this at Masses in St. Peter's Square.

The penitential rite

Q. If venial sins are forgiven in the penitential rite of the Mass, why are lay people allowed to lead this rite in a Communion service?

A. The forgiveness of venial sins in the penitential rite of the Mass is brought about through the ministry of the priest. You may recall that mortal sins require priestly absolution, but venial sins do not and can be forgiven in many ways: prayer, fasting, good works, etc. Therefore, when these prayers are recited during a Communion service, it is no different from your praying them on your own, with the same possible effect.

A sample letter

Q. I take exception to your answer [in a recent] issue of TCA regarding "Why no women priests?"

First, let me tell you that I am eighty years old and a Catholic in good standing with the Church.

Second, I would like to know where in the Bible or any reputable documents of birth it says that Jesus was a man. Did anyone ever see him completely disrobed? Can it be proven that Jesus was male, or being God, was He both male and female? What a shock to the soul of John Paul II if, when he gets to heaven, our Lord Jesus Christ turns out to be female, or both male and female. I also realize that according to the Bible (which was written by men), God the Father called him "My Son."

Third, Holy Orders was specified by men and not by both men and women Church members. In the first days of the Church, women were not educated and were more or less considered as chattel. That is not true today.

Fourth, if we had both male and female priests, perhaps we wouldn't have priests (even bishops) who practice pedophilia and other sexual acts.

Fifth, perhaps if priests were married, as was the case in the early Church, it would be better, and we would have less scandal today.

Sixth, if you answer this letter in TCA, please publish the letter in its entirety or not at all.

A. I publish this letter to let our readers know the kind of material that often comes in. Much of this is angry and silly. Points raised here have been answered in other issues of TCA, except for the fourth and fifth ones which I would like to handle now, since this type of illogical statement surfaces from time to time.

I do not justify in any way the sinful acts of priests or diminish their awful impact on the lives of Catholics and the effectiveness of our priestly witness. That having been said, however, it is important to note that most acts of pedophilia are committed by married parents on their own children! Second, a recent study of evangelical ministers has revealed that 28 percent of them admit to having had extramarital relations with a parishioner, and a like number have also done so with a non-parishioner. In other words, more than half of these ministers are unfaithful to their marriage vows. So much for married clergy being the answer to all our problems, eh?

I do not gloat over the facts I report above. I share them to provide some perspective, which is very simply and sadly to suggest that we live in an extremely sick and perverted society and that this disorder has obviously infected the Church as well. This calls for a deeper commitment to our Christian identity and to our respective vocations (married or priestly) and for the support needed to be faithful.

Vigil Masses

Q. Is it necessary to go to Mass on Easter morning if one has gone to the Easter Vigil liturgy?

A. No, it is not, because the Easter Vigil is a Sunday liturgy, fulfilling the Sunday Mass obligation. Perhaps this would be a good moment to explain once again the rationale behind Saturday evening Masses.

Following Jewish liturgical practice, the Church has always begun a solemn liturgical celebration on the night before. Hence, the event's commemoration starts with the praying of First Vespers (Evening Prayer) after 4 p.m. on the vigil. That is why it is legitimate to attend a Saturday evening Mass, which is in reality a Sunday celebration. That having been said, I think it an abuse of the option if one participates in Saturday evening Masses to the exclusion of Sunday celebrations. My understanding of the thinking behind the legislation was that it is intended, primarily, for those who would find Sunday attendance difficult or impossible. In my pastoral experience, I have found people who have not been to a Sunday morning Mass in more than twenty-five years! And what do they do then on Sunday morning? Sleep, go shopping, or watch Robert Schuller!

When availing oneself of certain freedoms, it is important that one be honest and mature. Otherwise, our observance of our religion devolves into a childish game of trying to get away with as much as possible, rather than an effort to do as much as possible.

Confusion of roles

Q. A dying friend was anointed at home. The priest told the family to invite friends and relatives to the ceremony, and he brought a crew of minstrels with him. It was more like "Entertainment Tonight" than anything I can remember from Last Rites in the old days. Also, he had everyone lay hands on the woman. What are your thoughts on this?

A. All celebrations of the sacraments are essentially communal affairs.

Ideally, then, that dimension should be honored whenever possible. Both spiritually and psychologically, such an approach is particularly worthwhile for the Sacrament of Anointing of the Sick. Explicit mention of this is made in Vatican II's *Sacrosanctum Concilium*, Pope John Paul II's *Salvifici Doloris* (Apostolic Constitution on the Christian Meaning of Suffering) and the new *Catechism of the Catholic Church*. Communal worship, however, is not "Entertainment Tonight," nor should it be. If your description is accurate, it was wrong to have occurred because it violates the sense of the sacred and likewise does not reflect with seriousness and sensitivity on the situation of the sick person.

Having lay people impose hands on the patient is grossly erroneous, adding to the confusion of lay and priestly roles — which development the Holy Father has condemned on numerous occasions, most notably and forcefully in *Christifideles Laici* (Apostolic Constitution on the Vocation and Mission of the Christian Lay Faithful in the Church).

Lefebvre was warned

Q. My friend says you're all wrong about Archbishop Marcel Lefebvre and his alleged excommunication. What proof do you have that he was ever formally excommunicated? And what about lay people who are involved with the movement?

A. As I have said before, the archbishop did not need a hand-delivered bull of excommunication for the penalty to take effect. He had been warned by both the Pope and Cardinal Joseph Ratzinger that going ahead with the episcopal consecrations would put him outside the Church. However, if it is of any assistance to your friend, ask her to consider this excerpt from the decree of Cardinal Bernardin Gantin, prefect of the Congregation of Bishops, dated July 1, 1988:

"Monsignor Marcel Lefebvre . . . having — despite the formal admonition of June 17 last and repeated appeals that he desist from his intention — carried out an act of a schismatic nature in the episcopal consecration of four priests, without a pontifical mandate and against the will of the Sovereign Pontiff, has incurred the penalty envisaged by Canon 1364, Paragraph 1, and by Canon 1382 of the Code of Canon Law.

"I declare that, for all juridical purposes, both the above-mentioned Monsignor Marcel Lefebvre [and the four priests] have incurred *ipso facto* excommunication *latae sententiae,* reserved to the Apostolic See.

" . . . The priests and faithful are warned not to seek to adhere to the schism of Monsignor Lefebvre, because they would incur *ipso facto* the extremely grave penalty of excommunication."

I don't think that could be any clearer. I know that some folks argue that the episcopal ordinations did not fall under the penalty because of a supposed "necessity" that nullifies the Canon (for example, as happened behind the Iron Curtain when bishops consecrated priests to succeed them, even without papal permission), but that is really grasping at straws. Not only was there no true necessity, but the Pope himself enjoined the archbishop not to proceed with the consecrations.

Surely, then, people who remain under the leadership of this movement do so at great personal peril, and no amount of mental gymnastics or canonical sleight-of-hand can change that. Even Martin Luther didn't try to go that route and accepted the excommunication that flowed from his actions.

Prayer or study?

Q. My wife and I, both twenty-seven, have just moved here from the East Coast, where we had wonderful devotions on a regular basis. None of that seems to exist here. The pastor says that he prefers to spend his time offering adult education rather than services like the Stations of the Cross and Benediction. Isn't the focus all off?

A. Christian spirituality is not generally a matter of dichotomies, so that one is faced with either prayer or study. In truth, the greatest saints have more often than not combined both to a marvelous degree. Furthermore, the Fathers of the Second Vatican Council and all the subsequent popes have called for a renewal and bolstering of the Church's devotional life, not its elimination. The Rosary, exposition of the Blessed Sacrament, Stations of the Cross and the like are means by which the liturgy is extended and which lead back to the liturgy, which is precisely what *Sacrosanctum Concilium* (Constitution on the Sacred Liturgy) mandated.

As a parish priest, I frequently scheduled adult-education classes to follow Marian and Lenten devotions, thereby "killing two birds with one stone," in the best sense of that expression.

St. Veronica

Q. My name is Veronica, and I am interested in information on my patroness. I was upset to be told recently that she may only be a legend. Your help would be appreciated.

A. Much of early Christian tradition is shrouded in mystery. That a woman wiped the brow of Our Lord on His way to Calvary makes sense. That Our Lord rewarded her piety by imprinting His holy countenance on the towel is surely within the realm of possibility. Tradition gives the woman the name "Veronica" because that comes from two Greek words meaning, "true image." Consult any standard lives of the saints for more details on this valiant woman.

Latin translations

Q. I know that your St. Gregory Foundation has produced a study document with your own translation of the ordinary of the Mass for the bishops' consideration. Are there any similar attempts for the proper of the Mass?

A. Yes, there are. Two Jesuit priests (Fathers Martin O'Keefe and Paul Distler) worked on all the orations of the Roman Missal and came up with a rather interesting result. It has been published as *Oremus: Speaking with God in the Words of the Roman Rite* and is available for $24.95 from the Institute of Jesuit Sources, 3700 West Pine Blvd. St. Louis, MO 63108.

I see the involvement of so many people in the re-translation process as extremely healthy. First, it bespeaks a tremendous amount of interest in the sacred liturgy. Second, it gives the bishops a number of viable alternatives from which to choose, rather than being hemmed in by a monopoly.

The St. Gregory Foundation translation of the ordinary of the Mass is available for $11, by writing to: 21 Fairview Ave, Mt. Pocono, PA 18344.

Annulment reversed

Q. My former wife and I were married for twenty-three years and suddenly, without giving me a reason, she filed for divorce. We raised and educated five children in Catholic schools. She had an annulment granted and remarried as soon as the law would allow. I fought the annulment all the way to the Vatican, where it was reversed. The Vatican said our marriage vows are still valid and binding.

Since the diocese made the mistake, I feel that I should be granted a special dispensation because the mistake wasn't mine.

What is your opinion? After being a Knights of Columbus member for more than twenty-five years, I dropped my membership and am protesting by leading the life of an inactive Catholic.

A. I'm terribly confused. If the Holy See agreed with your position, then what kind of a dispensation do you want? And with all charity, I must say the sentiments of the last paragraph come off as incredibly childish.

Plenary indulgences

Q. I frequently see writings enclosed with certain religious items in Catholic book stores which state that if a person is devoted in prayer to what the item represents he can gain a plenary indulgence on certain feast days; some grant a plenary indulgence at the time of the person's death. Can you please comment on plenary indulgences granted at the time of death? What conditions need to be present for the plenary indulgence to be valid? What devotion(s) do you recommend for obtaining one at the time of death?

A. The plenary indulgence granted at the time of death is no different from one given at any other time, except that its value is increased to the degree that no further sins would be possible to render its effects less potent.

To gain any plenary indulgence, one must be in the state of grace (actually free of even venial sins), have a spirit of contrition for all one's past sins, perform the work and/or prayer in question, pray for the intentions of the Pope, and receive the Sacraments of Penance and Holy Communion within a week in either direction of the appointed day.

For specific ways to earn any indulgence (plenary or partial), consult the "Enchiridion (Handbook) of Indulgences," which should be available at any Catholic bookstore.

First Penance

Q. In my diocese, children are allowed to receive First Holy Communion in the second grade without receiving the Sacrament of Penance beforehand. When I questioned our DRE about this, she responded that another canon states that a person in the state of mortal sin must go to confession before Communion, but that this cannot possibly apply to seven-year-olds. Therefore, Canon 914 is effectively canceled out! She says the current practice is legitimate because of the conflict between the two canons.

A. Since Canon 914 deals explicitly with First Holy Communion and the needed preparations, it is a bit disingenuous to suggest that there is a conflict between this law and some other. Repeatedly, the Church has said that the experimental procedure of the 1970s on this matter must cease.

Angelus position

Q. What is the best or correct position while praying the Angelus? Everyone seems to have a different answer.

A. Because the Angelus is a devotion and not liturgical prayer, there are no hard-and-fast norms for its recitation; custom prevails, and custom varies from place to place. When I was a boy, the practice was to stand for the prayer and to genuflect at the lines commemorating the Incarnation.

Today, I generally find standing still the posture, with a profound bow replacing the genuflection (to parallel the change for the same line during the Creed when recited in the liturgy). When impeded from standing for any number of possible reasons, any respectful posture would be acceptable. I do think, however, that if we are talking about a communal recitation of this beautiful prayer, there ought to be a unified posture agreed upon in advance.

Learning Latin

Q. I'm a young priest who feels very cheated out of his ecclesial patrimony — no Latin, no Greek, no patristics — which is to say that I find myself an alien to the Tradition I have solemnly sworn to represent. I would like to make a move toward some intelligent self-education, starting with some basic Latin and eventually going on to tackle other gaps in my education. Can you recommend any sources whereby I can teach myself some rudimentary Latin, enough to read the Vulgate and say/chant the more common prayers of the Mass?

A. Your letter, Father, is sadly typical today. You deserve to be applauded, however, not only for recognizing the *lacunae* in your formation but for being willing to do something about it.

As far as Latin goes, I would suggest several things. A very elementary program has just come out, produced by none other than Dr. Ralph McInerny, philosopher at the University of Notre Dame, head of the Fellowship of Catholic Scholars and author of the Father Dowling mystery series. It's called *Let's Read Latin* and includes both a text and an audio cassette ($29.95), available by calling: 1-800-234-2726. Now, don't expect to be reading Virgil at the end, but it is a start.

Another new item on the horizon has come to my attention: "Learning Liturgical Latin." It is a computer-based learning experience for reciting and chanting the *Ordo Missae*, with the option for either internal hard disk drives or for external drives. The total cost for this very attractive program is less than $25. For further information, contact: Mrs. Patricia Feighan, 11009 Edgewater Drive, Cleveland, OH 44102; Phone 216-281-9357; FAX 216-281-0019.

Finally, the St. Gregory Foundation for Latin Liturgy (which I founded several years ago) offers an intensive home study course in Latin, using "Ecclesiastical Latin" of Professor Collins from The Catholic University of America. Assignments are given and corrected; tuition is $100. For details, contact: SGF, 21 Fairview Ave, Mt. Pocono, PA 18344; phone 717-839-2185; Fax 717-839-0405. We also offer a course in New Testament Greek.

Catholic bookstores

Q. I try to live by the Church's teachings and not support those doing otherwise. It is becoming more and more difficult to shop in supposedly "Catholic" bookstores: They have sections on New Age spirituality, women's concerns (which includes a series of worship books geared toward women), and the like. They also have a large selection of decent material. It seems that their only concern is making a profit — not disseminating material that will promote the Catholic Faith. Should I support such an establishment or go elsewhere? Also, is it wrong to deal with schismatics who operate religious gift stores, such as the Orthodox selling icons? Please advise.

A. It seems to me that the first step in the process ought to be to approach the Catholic bookseller himself and share your concerns — which you may have done already. If he is determined to sell questionable or problematic matter, then I would suggest using other options if they are available.

As far as patronizing the Orthodox is concerned, I have no difficulty with that, so long as you were alert regarding any teachings that diverge from Catholic doctrine and not find yourself proselytized; icons and incense do not appear as potential carriers of divergent doctrines!

Holy day observance

Q. I now find holy days of obligation really confusing to explain or defend. I always thought that we attended Mass on those specific days because of the importance of the feast that was being celebrated. Was that idea wrong? If not, how does it square with the current practice of certain days— the Assumption, All Saints', and Mary, the Mother of God — not being obligatory when they fall on Saturday or Monday?

I have always believed the teaching that one who dies in mortal sin goes to hell. Now it seems a little silly to include the Mass obligation as a mortal sin: I can go to hell if this particular holy day falls Tuesday through Friday and I miss Mass, but it doesn't matter on Saturday or Monday! This ruling is a parent's nightmare. Please help me to understand and explain it better.

A. We have treated this topic of holy days many times before. As you know, the universal Church has ten solemnities, all of which are days of obligation. However, Church law has always permitted local conferences of bishops to add to that list or subtract from it. In Ireland, for example, not surprisingly, the feast of St. Patrick is a holy day. In the United States, we never had more than six holy days.

For the past fifteen years, the question of reducing or even almost totally eliminating days of obligation has been hotly debated in the episcopal conference. A compromise was reached at the last such debate, so that all six days would remain, but with the proviso for lifting of the obligation when some of those days fell on Monday or Saturday. I say nothing more or less than what dozens of bishops said during that very spirited discussion when I say: Doing this was certainly legitimate, but pastorally I think it was unwise and confusing.

No intercommunion

Q. At a recent wedding of a friend (not in my home diocese), both spouses received Communion, which surprised me since I knew one was not Catholic. Afterwards, I had explained to me the conditions which must be present in order for a non-Catholic (and not an Orthodox) to receive the Sacraments of Penance, Eucharist, or Anointing in the Catholic Church. The stipulations (as I was told) included that they held a Catholic faith in regard to that sacrament. How can one have a Catholic faith in a particular sacrament if he is outside the Catholic Faith? Does getting the marriage off to a good start necessitate Communion for

both parties? Isn't this playing fast and loose with the sacraments?
A. We really have two questions here which need to be separated before attempting a coherent response.

The first and easiest is that no intercommunion is possible at a wedding only for situations of an emergency nature. Therefore, your surprise at the wedding was correct. It is the very reason, of course, that priests should discourage Nuptial Masses when one party is not Catholic, since the sign value of the Eucharist and of Matrimony are both compromised when only one spouse receives Holy Communion.

Your second concern is valid but calls for a bit more nuance. It is surely possible to understand, and accept, Catholic teaching on a host of doctrines while rejecting one or more others; after all, this was precisely what occurred in the Protestant Reformation. Luther, for example, did not commit himself or his followers to a wholesale repudiation of Catholic truth. In fact, he was really quite circumspect in his approach. As the process devolved, others took Luther's finishing point and made it their own starting point. As a result, the drama unfolded and Catholic truth was gradually unraveled. Most mainline Protestants accept a panoply of Catholic doctrines (Trinity, divinity of Christ, resurrection, etc.), even as they fail to hold to others. It should not shock you, then, to discover that it is indeed possible to adhere to a Catholic understanding of certain sacraments while still outside the bonds of full, visible communion with the Catholic Church. People like Mother Seton, for instance, believed in the Lord's Real Presence in the Eucharist for years before becoming Catholic; in reality, her acceptance of that truth is what ultimately brought her to "buy the whole package." And that should be our prayer for all who are similarly situated.

Offertory prayers

Q. Our pastor does not mingle water with the wine at Mass, nor does he pray what we commonly call the Offertory prayers ("Blessed are You, Lord. . ."). He claims that he says these prayers in the sacristy before Mass. When we have a substitute priest, he sends the server for the water to mix with the wine. Please comment.

Also, is it true that a priest has to pay $1,000 to become a monsignor, bishop, etc.?

A. Your pastor has no authority to say those prayers anywhere except where the Church says they are to be done.

As far as a stipend to become a monsignor or bishop, there is none. The buying and selling of sacred offices was strictly enjoined by the Council of Trent. It is commonplace, however, for a man to make a kind of "thank-offering" to the Holy See upon his elevation; this freewill offering is then generally given to the Holy Father to use for his charities. Sometimes the diocese makes the gift itself for new monsignori, lest the impression be given or taken that these titles are "for sale."

Multiple receptions

Q. May a person receive Holy Communion more than once a day? Please quote the source of authority.

My situation is this: On Saturdays, I receive at the morning weekday Mass and a second time at the Saturday Vigil Mass, but I do not receive when I go again on Sunday morning or if I attend two Sunday morning Masses.

A. Canon 917 says the following: "One who has received the Blessed Eucharist may receive it again on the same day only within a eucharistic celebration in which that person participates. . . ." In other words, one may receive more than once — only if one participates in a complete Mass each time. Reception is not permitted more than twice in one twenty-four hour period, a clarification issued by the Congregation for the Doctrine of the Faith some years after the revised Code appeared. Reception of Viaticum is not affected by this ruling [cf. Canon 921].

For your situation, then, attendance at a Saturday morning Mass and a Sunday Vigil Mass (on Saturday evening) would allow for two receptions. Similarly, participation in two full celebrations on Sunday morning or evening would permit two additional receptions.

Papal blessing

Q. My parents are approaching their fiftieth wedding anniversary, and I would like to do something special for them. As a young child, I remember my grandparents receiving papal acknowledgment, in the form of a certificate, and I would like to do the same for my parents. My problem is that I have no idea to whom I should direct this request. Please help.

A. The easiest way to go about procuring a papal blessing for your parents is to contact your diocesan center or the office of the apostolic nuncio in Washington. The nuncio's address is: U.S. Apostolic Nunciature, 3339 Massachusetts Ave., N.W., Washington, D.C. 20008.

Sell art for poor?

Q. Would the pope ever sell the most valuable art works and other Vatican wealth to feed some starving countries? You know Our Lord's line about selling your possessions and following Him?

A. Every so often someone comes up with this type of question. On the surface, it sounds noble, but below the surface, upon closer examination, it reveals a somewhat problematic attitude, which even the questioner himself often does not perceive.

First, the presumption is that the artistic treasures of the Vatican belong to the pope personally and that he is wallowing in the lap of luxury. Neither is true.

The occupant of the Chair of Peter is merely the custodian of the patrimony of the Church; as such, it is his responsibility to safeguard these works and ensure their availability for generations to come. So much good has come from these treasures; I myself have received a number of people into the Church as a result of their having beheld these works of art and having come to a realization that the Church occasioned these works by her promotion of the human spirit. On the second score, the papal apartments (which I have seen many times) are indeed beautiful but by no means luxurious, and I am sure that anyone who would want to live in those dank chambers in humid Roman springs and winters would get a slightly different view of papal splendor.

But the critical question really comes down to how much good such a papal action would achieve: Would countless millions of starving people truly benefit? Experts say that were the Church to divest herself of all her art and give the proceeds to the poor, each hungry person in the world would get less than two dollars. In other words nothing would have been wrought, except to engage in some empty tokenism, which is really insulting to the poor.

More than two decades ago, then-Bishop Fulton Sheen became the Bishop of Rochester, N.Y. In his genuine love and concern for the poor, he decided to sell one of their churches and give them the money. They were hurt and shocked that he would have done such a thing, presuming to think that they were more interested in temporal welfare than spiritual. The great bishop acquiesced to their will, understanding then that they needed a spot of beauty and transcendence in their otherwise mundane lives. Many of us need to learn that same lesson.

Fiftieth anniversary

Q. Can a couple celebrate their fiftieth wedding anniversary with a Mass if they are not married in the Church?

A. If you mean, can they schedule a special anniversary liturgy, complete with renewal of vows and priestly blessing, the answer is no, since the Church cannot publicly celebrate what she cannot publicly acknowledge. On the other hand, I would suggest arranging for a Mass to be offered "For the intentions of Mr. and Mrs. Jones," and then discreetly attend that Mass. Of course, you may want to take advantage of this occasion to see if there is anything you can do to regularize the marital situation; sometimes circumstances change over the years and give us new opportunities to set things right.

Help for priests

Q. I thought that you might be interested in knowing about a group especially dedicated to prayer for priests. The Lay Associates of the Priesthood pray and sacrifice for a particular priest or bishop whose first name is sent by the Handmaids of the Precious Blood (P.O. Box 68, Jemez Springs, NM 87025). Members receive a certificate of membership containing a daily prayer with the priest's first name. No membership dues are required. A weekly Mass is offered for the Lay Associates and their intentions. Those interested in joining should contact the Handmaids of the Precious Blood.

A. Thank you; we need all the prayers we can get.

Sacramentals

Q. In conversation with our new pastor, I used the word "sacramental" in referring to holy water. He chastised me and made it very clear that holy water is not a sacrament, which, of course, I knew. As I explained the difference between sacrament and sacramental, he said that he had never heard the word "sacramental" before. Has this word gone into disuse?

A. Not at all, and the new *Catechism* deals with this topic under that very title in paragraphs 1667-1679.

A prayerful season

Q. The following appeared in our church bulletin: "Sunday, November 28, will begin the Advent Season. That is a four-Sunday Season of prayerful preparation — without feasts, parties, or festivities — for the great celebration of the Birth of our Savior on this earth." Please comment on "without feasts, parties, or festivities." Thank you.

A. I think your pastor is to be applauded. He is absolutely correct and quite courageous to fly in the face of the secularization and commercialization of Advent and Christmas. I guess I resonate rather well to his plan of action because I have always maintained such a policy in parishes for which I have been responsible. If the Church cannot keep to her own calendar, how can we expect anyone else to do so?

A question of celibacy

Q. I have a number of priest-friends with whom I have developed friendships as I discerned a possible vocation to the priesthood. Before entering the major seminary three years ago (at the age of twenty-eight), celibacy was not so much an issue with me. In recent months, however, I have felt that perhaps my call is to the permanent diaconate instead, as I now seem to be rather begrudging in giving myself in a vow of celibacy (though I am in no way bitter toward the Church about this). If I discern that my vocation is to be married, may I invite these priests to my Wedding Mass? May any concelebrate? If so, how many?

A. Clerical celibacy is intended to be a sacrifice, as are marriage and parenthood. I think you need to develop a better sense of the charism of celibacy through prayer, study, and spiritual direction. Beyond that, the diaconate should not be viewed as a second-rate, stopping-off point for those who can't "hack the real thing."

The follow-up questions have me somewhat confused since I don't know why, should you leave the seminary, you would foresee a difficulty in inviting priest-friends to your wedding. After all, a man is free to choose another vocation until such time as he has committed himself to celibacy at his diaconate ordination (for priesthood candidates, that is). You would have given the priestly vocation a try, and no one can fault you for that. My concern is that you really understand what you are accepting or rejecting before making any major decisions.

Meatless Fridays

Q. I have lost patience with fallen-away Catholics who use the excuse of the Church absolving the duty of abstinence from meat on Fridays. I've explained that it was only a Church ruling, but they come back with the retort: "The Church told us it was a mortal sin to eat meat on Fridays. Does this mean that people who deliberately broke this rule went to hell? And what happened to those who did the day before the rule was changed?" Is this going to happen with other rules? This small change seems to have had a more widespread effect than was ever thought. Can you help explain this problem?

A. In some way this is related to an earlier question in this issue, but there is a special angle here which needs consideration.

First, the Church still maintains Friday as a day of abstinence from meat; the only difference is that the faithful are permitted to substitute an alternate penance if they so desire. As I have said and written until I'm blue in the face, it's amazing how people never seem to hear the second clause of that sentence! So, in point of fact, the law has not really changed. But, suppose it had? And it could.

It is crucial to understand why the Church has a particular law. What is she trying to accomplish by mandating or forbidding a specific activity? In the present case, the Church was underscoring the need for Christians to do penance for their sins, making explicit Our Lord's statement that when the Bridegroom would be taken away, the disciples would fast (cf. Mt 9:15). Therefore, the ecclesiastical law simply put some flesh on a divine precept to live lives of repentance (of which there are many examples throughout the Gospels).

If someone consciously and willfully disobeyed this norm, that person was putting himself above the Church and the will of Christ. The matter, then, was not that he ate a hot dog instead of a tuna sandwich; rather, it was that he felt comfortable in declaring his independence from the Church in her role as Mother and Teacher of the faithful, the role accorded to her by the Lord Himself: "He who hears you, hears me." "Faithful in small matters, faithful in greater affairs." "Whatsoever you shall bind on earth shall be bound in heaven." Thus, in reality, eating meat on Fridays was not really such a petty concern, to begin with.

Finally, what about people who disobeyed last week, died, and presumably went to hell for the offense when the law was about to change the following week? It's always easy to poke fun at situations like this by coming up with seemingly silly scenarios, but let's analyze it a bit. Consider this:

If there is a traffic light on the corner of Main and Tenth Streets, and I run the red light with full knowledge and consent and get a summons for it, would my guilt be mitigated in the eyes of the judge simply because the following week the traffic light was removed? Of course not. I broke the law when it was a law, well aware of the consequences of such action. Doesn't the analogy fit with ecclesiastical law as well?

Priest as godfather

Q. Is it permissible for a priest to act as a godfather and, at the same time, perform the rite of Baptism?

It happened a couple of months ago in my parish when a visiting priest baptized his niece's son, alleging that although it was not allowed in the past, it is permissible now.

I still have my doubts about it. Is there any canonical ruling prohibiting such a strange arrangement?

A. The contemporary Code of Canon Law eliminated the prohibition against having clerics serve as sponsors.

However, I cannot envision that the priest who would function as a sponsor would likewise administer the sacrament. I think that this is a serious confusion of roles, and he should have chosen one or the other.

Annulment price tag?

Q. Someone I worked with told me that when his sister got an annulment in New Jersey, she was asked to give part of the divorce settlement to the Church — about $10,000, according to him. This supposedly took place a few years ago. Not knowing anything about such procedures, I can't defend the Church. What do you have to say?

A. Some of these annulment-fee stories can get pretty wild, but I think this one takes the cake! First of all, the Church cannot touch a marriage until a civil divorce is already granted; therefore, it would be rather difficult to cash in on a divorce settlement after the fact. In my experience, most nullity cases come to the Church years after a divorce. Second, the fees for such cases are incredibly modest, usually somewhere between $500 and $1,000, which does not even begin to cover the cost of psychologists, secretaries, canon lawyers, etc. And in no instance may a tribunal make payment a condition for the granting of a decree of nullity; justice and fair play demand that people pay for the procedure if they can afford it, but lack of financial wherewithal cannot and does not block the attainment of one's rights in the Church.

Protestant summer camp

Q. We have a lovely daughter, a professional woman who has dedicated her life to her husband, four children, and service at her local parish. She sends all of her children to Catholic schools.

During the summer the whole family attends a summer camp completely under the direction of Protestants. She sees nothing wrong with this. Will you address our controversy?

A. If there is no Catholic camp available and there is no proselytism of Catholics on the part of the Protestants, I can find nothing problematic with the situation.

Adopt a priest

Q. Would you be kind enough to give some publicity to our organization, called Mission H.O.P.E., Inc. (Help Our Priests Evangelize), the purpose of which is to adopt a priest spiritually for one year through personal affirmation and encouragement of him? Interested persons may write for further information to: Box 1982; Scottsdale, AZ 85252. Thank you.

A. Thank you.

Protestant-Catholic union

Q. A year ago I married a Protestant man who reads his Bible daily. I have attended Protestant worship services, instead of Mass, so I could worship God with my husband. I have been told that this is wrong; could you please tell me the Church's position? I don't get as much out of their services as I do the Mass, but I didn't feel it was as big a sin as was implied.

A. To miss Mass deliberately on a Sunday or holy day of obligation is a mortal sin. While your motivation is good, the action (or non-action in this case) is wrong. Why not go with your husband to his church either before or after having attended Mass? Remember: an important part of your married vocation is to provide a good example for your non-Catholic spouse; your failure to live up to your own obligations does nothing for his growth in understanding and appreciation for the Catholic Faith.

Holy day obligations

Q. Is there a plausible reason to excuse Catholics from the obligation to attend Mass when a holy day falls on a Saturday or a Monday? I cannot understand why those two days should be any different from the other weekdays.

A. The rationale offered seems to be twofold. The first maintains that in rural areas which may be "priest-poor," it is an excessive burden on the clergy to have back-to-back liturgical celebrations (e.g., Friday vigil for feast, Saturday feast, Saturday vigil for Sunday, Sunday, and maybe even Sunday evening).

The second line of argument holds that the lay faithful "get confused" by the two concomitant obligations (e.g. Can I fulfill my holy day obligation by attending a Saturday vigil Mass and then go again on Sunday for the Sunday obligation?).

My own experience leads me to assert that these are far-fetched rationalizations to eliminate a healthy sense of duty which will eventually lead to the abolition of most, if not all, of the holy days.

As far as overworked clergy, I can only say that a diocesan bishop already had the authority to dispense the laity from a holy day obligation if he judged that the burden was excessive for anyone. So why a national policy on something that could have been handled locally?

Parish councils

Q. Does canon law require the establishment of a parish council or any other committee at the parish level?

A. The Code of Canon Law mandates the establishment and functioning of a finance council in each parish; a pastoral council is optional. Canon 537 reads: "In each parish there is to be a finance committee to help

the parish priest in the administration of the goods of the parish."
Canon 536 says: "If, after consulting the council of priests, the
diocesan bishop considers it opportune, a pastoral council is to be
established in each parish. In this council, which is presided over by
the parish priest, Christ's faithful, together with those who by virtue
of their office are engaged in pastoral care in the parish, give their
help in fostering pastoral action." It goes on to note that such a council
"has only a consultative vote."

Canon 295 of the Code of Canons of the Eastern Churches covers
the same territory.

Confirmation class

*Q. This is my second year teaching confirmation class in our parish. I
find that approximately half of the students are not practicing Catholics.
That is, neither they nor their parents attend Sunday Mass and most
have not received the Sacrament of Penance since their first confession.
I've spoken with other teachers, and the same situation exists in their
classes. I'm troubled by this and have talked to our pastor and
confirmation program coordinator and requested that they consider
confirming only students who are practicing the Faith. It seems to me
that at least we should make Mass attendance a mandatory part of the
confirmation program, in hopes of getting them active in the Church.
While sympathetic, their position seems to be that we're planting a seed.*

*My concern is not only for the students, but for the Church. If
there is no intent, either by the students or their parents, to practice
the Faith, what are we doing? It seems to reduce the sacraments to a
magic ritual.*

*I know that these are the types of Catholics who show up in the
polls as favoring contraception, abortion, women priests, divorce, etc.
For sure, confirming such people weakens the Church. I would
appreciate your thoughts.*

A. I could not agree with you more. If we cannot make any demands
and set standards for the reception of the Sacrament of Confirmation,
I don't know what kind of training or "seed-planting" we are doing
— shallow at best and counter-productive at worst. Most confirmation
preparation programs contain a Christian service component, and I
doubt that any CCD coordinator would consider having a youth
confirmed who had failed to complete that portion of the program —

and I would support such a decision. Why not see the necessity of making Sunday Mass attendance an integral part of one's living of the Catholic Faith? Indeed, Church law mandates the latter under pain of mortal sin.

Fatima question

Q. How are we supposed to discern the truth in the controversy over whether or not Russia has actually been consecrated according to the wishes of Our Lady of Fatima?

A. When private devotion (which is what the Fatima devotion is) becomes divisive and destructive of ecclesial unity, something is wrong. If someone is not willing to take the word of the Sovereign Pontiff and the only surviving seer (Sister Lucia) on this, then I think the whole situation has really gotten out of control.

Forty Hours

Q. May parishes still have the Forty Hours devotion? If it is permissible, why does it seem to have become almost extinct?

A. Current liturgical legislation is such that eucharistic devotions (like Forty Hours) should be more feasible (and therefore frequent) today than at any time in our recent past. Why these devotions seem to have fallen off the radar screen, I cannot say, except that some have an allergic reaction to them, seeing in them "pre-conciliar" forms of eucharistic piety (which, of course, is untrue), while yet others maintain that when they schedule such events, no one shows up for them. I suspect that a bit of truth can be found in both statements, which should provide clergy and laity alike with ample opportunity for an examination of conscience.

Wanted: a good parish

Q. We find ourselves in a difficult situation because we have changed parishes often. My husband and I have two small children and want only to attend a parish that teaches the Catholic Faith without alteration. It has becomes harder and harder to find a parish (in our area, at least) where the rules of the Church are obeyed. Our questions are these: Which offenses are the most serious and should not be tolerated at all? Obviously, changing the words of consecration cannot be overlooked, but what about other Mass prayers? We have always met with the priest before joining the parish — are there any specific questions that we should ask? And what happens when our search is exhausted, and we find no parish that meets all the criteria? Do we then go back to the parish with the least amount of abuses?

My husband is in the military and we move frequently; therefore, these searches are conducted over and over. Quite frankly, we are growing weary of it. Where are all the good priests? And how do we find one?

A. I can empathize with your desire to have the liturgy celebrated according to the approved rites of the Church. It is surely a sad commentary on the state of things that intelligent people of goodwill have such difficulty in finding what the Church's law asserts is their baptismal right. The problem is, as you know, not unique to you; so serious is the dilemma that Pope John Paul II himself used his *Dominicae Cenae* to apologize to the lay faithful for such aberrations and to demand that priests follow the liturgical laws of the Church.

I regret that I can do no more than to urge you to use prudent judgment in discerning what is tolerable and intolerable and to pray for the gift of fidelity for Christ's priests. And, yes, to go to a parish that has the least egregious violations.

Opus Dei

Q. So often I read of an "Opus Dei takeover" of the Church. I have generally dismissed it as emanating from left-wing malcontents. Now, however, I have come across a book titled Opus Dei: An Investigation into the Secret Society Struggling for Power within the Roman Catholic Church. *It is frightening, to say the least. What's your reaction to this book, if you have read it?*

A. The book has been on the market for some time now and, yes, I have read it. Even the title betrays the approach — tabloid journalism. Not long after its appearance, a thoughtful and careful refutation of it was done by a member of Opus Dei, entitled, *Opus Dei: An Open Book*. It is very well done, and even folks who are not fans of Opus Dei have admitted that it does much to dispel many of the myths attached to the movement. Alba House has also published *Opus Dei: Who? How? Why?* It is written by Giuseppe Romano and contains a foreword by Cardinal James Hickey of Washington. Finally, Scepter Press has recently released *Immersed in God*, which is an insight into the mind and heart of Opus Dei's founder, Monsignor José María Escrivá de Balaguer, as seen through his successor. It is both informative and edifying.

There are many movements in the Church; not all of them are for everyone. Indeed, the spirituality of the Catholic Church has often been compared to a big umbrella, under which there is a lot of room for a wide variety of approaches to God. In my experience, however, I have generally found that most of the more vocal and even vicious opponents of Opus Dei often use Opus Dei as code language for their real opposition to the program of the Pope himself. Given the Pope's popularity, they find it easier to attack an impersonal and frequently unknown institution, thus garnering little negative feedback for their assaults, which are largely unfair, unfounded, and beyond all proportion to truth and reality.

Religious update

Q. From time to time, you have called our attention to "good" communities of women Religious. Have any updates for us?
A. Yes, I do. The Sisters Minor of Mary Immaculate are a congregation of women in the Franciscan tradition and according to the spirituality of St. Maximilian Kolbe. They are completely faithful to the Magisterium, to prayer, and to religious identity. Their American headquarters are in Connecticut. They may be reached at 305 Washington Blvd, Stamford, CT 06902; phone, 203-323-4546.

Prayers for the dead

Q. My wife died two years ago after forty years of marriage. We considered ourselves to be good Catholics. We never missed Mass on Sundays and holy days of obligation without a good reason. We sent our nine children through Catholic high school. Since my wife's death, I try to have at least two or more Masses offered each month. How often and how long should I continue to have Masses offered? What happens to our prayers, Masses, and sacrifices once the person for whom they were being offered is in heaven?
A. After a number of years, I would continue to remember the deceased with Masses on certain key dates, for example, anniversary of death, birthday, and anniversary of marriage perhaps. If the person's soul is already freed from purgatory, the doctrine of the Communion of Saints informs us that the Lord will apply those prayers and merits to those who need them most.

Cautious convert

Q. I am finding that I am not alone on my journey to Catholicism. The Catholic Answer contains much information that is helpful as I grow more and more fond of this ancient, wondrous Church. But, please, I find that the Catholic Church has its problems, too. How can I discern which Catholic programs and organizations are genuine expressions of Catholicism? For instance, I have yet to attend Mass or even approach any Catholic clergy. I don't want to run into liberalism in what ought to be the stronghold of truth.

And, on a very practical level, my inquiries into the Faith have had the unexpected effect of getting my address onto the mailing lists of many fund-raising agencies. Which of these best deserve my contributions? I don't know what novenas are, or oblates, or intentions, but I am constantly being solicited to contribute to them. As a lifelong Protestant, I have some sense of how to separate sheep from goats in mail solicitations, but in the Catholic realm I am without a clue. A word of guidance would be greatly appreciated.

A. First of all, welcome to the pilgrimage of faith!

It is a sad but true fact of life in the Church today that although the Catholic Faith has not changed one iota, the presentation of it varies from person to person, with more than just an occasional idiosyncratic spin on the ball. It is important for you to become thoroughly informed about the Truth, and two or three basic works can give you that information and assurance. It goes without saying that you ought to have your own copy of the *Catechism of the Catholic Church*; read it in an organized manner. Although the *Catechism* is not easy reading, it is manageable; furthermore, there are a number of good aids to reading it (and a number of bad ones, too, so let the buyer beware). I have just produced one, entitled *A Tour of the Catechism*, published by Prow Books in Libertyville, Illinois (call 1-800-743-1177). You should also have the two-volume set of *Vatican Council II: Conciliar and Post Conciliar Documents* (Costello Publishing Company), available at most Catholic bookstores. Finally, Our Sunday Visitor's one-volume *Catholic Encyclopedia* would also be helpful (call 1-800-348-2440).

As far as negotiating the minefield of Catholic charities, good luck. Lifelong Catholics have difficulty, so don't feel bad. However, if you start reading good and reliable Catholic literature, you will start to see certain names pop up in the right environment, and when you are solicited by them, you will have some confidence about the organization in question. One final word: Do not feel compelled to give to any or all of those who approach you. Do be charitable, but do not be gullible.

Nomenclature

Q. Why do we address our priests as "Father" when we laity are addressed as "brothers and sisters"? To my recollection, our parish priest used to call us his "children," which seemed more compatible with our calling him "Father."

A. I agree that there is an anomaly in contemporary practice and, yes, I too remember our priests calling us their "sons and daughters." I suppose the change in nomenclature came about so as not to sound patronizing or condescending.

That having been said, priests and people have a twofold relationship. As fellow members of the Church, priests indeed relate to others as their brothers and sisters (a result of the Sacrament of Baptism); zeroing in on their unique identity bestowed through Holy Orders, they are fathers.

Painful moments

Q. Why does the Church allow bishops and priests who seem to delight in hurting people to continue to do so? Why is there no recourse for sheep who are hurt by their so-called shepherds? The only thing that gets any attention from the hierarchy is if a priest is accused of abusing altar boys or some such thing. There are lots of nonphysical ways to abuse people, and their effects usually last longer than the effects of physical abuse. I know that clergy are human, and I don't expect them to be perfect. But I do think we have the right to expect them to care for us. Isn't that what priesthood is all about? Does it seem right to you that men who enter the seminary desiring to become priests should come home so terribly hurt that they never laugh again? Or never go to church again? It seems that bishops don't have to explain or apologize for anything because they are the almighty hierarchy and, therefore, whatever they do must be good, because they say so.

A. Your pain is apparent and most unfortunate. We clergy are at times grossly insensitive, and among the most unhappy of situations are often programs of priestly formation. All of us have suffered at one time or another from unjust exercises of authority; the key through it all is to be able to distinguish the man from the office, to pray for the abusive authority figure's conversion, and to pray for oneself, not to become bitter and resentful. Admittedly, easier said than done, but nonetheless essential to one's own spiritual and psychological welfare.

Still secret?

Q. Has the Pope said, or even hinted, as to when he will reveal the "last secret of Fatima"? I understand that Sister Lucy, in 1950 or thereabout, communicated this in a letter to the then-reigning pope and instructed him not to reveal the secret until some future time. In view of the terrible state of moral decay throughout the world, it wouldn't surprise me if that time is imminent. Any information you may have about this would be appreciated.

A. I do not put much stock in extraordinary forms of private revelation. As Jesus indicated in His parable of the rich man and Lazarus, if the people had Moses and the prophets and did not heed them, why would they pay attention even if someone came back from the dead? I don't think that is a cynical assessment, but I do believe it is quite realistic.

Freebie

Q. A free leaflet "Bishop Sheen Prayers" is available by sending a stamped, self-addressed envelope to: Father Rawley Myers, 22 W. Kiowa, Colorado Springs, CO 80903. Thought your readers might be interested. Thank you for making the information available to them.

A. Thank you, Father.

St. Philip Neri

Q. Last year I heard an awful lot about St. Philip Neri and his Oratory. I know very little about either. Is there any good book that can bring me "up to speed" on these matters?

A. In connection with the fourth centenary of the death of Saint Philip Neri in 1995, Alba House released a new book, *Philip Neri: The Fire of Joy*. It was written by Father Paul Turks of the Aachen Oratory, who was, for two six-year terms, the Delegate of the Holy See for the Oratory, a position which entailed making visitations to all of the Oratories of the world. This gave him a unique understanding of how St. Philip's way of life continues to be relevant in our own day and age. The translator, Father Daniel Utrecht, has been a member of the Toronto Oratory since 1980.

Philip Neri (1515-1595) is one of the most lovable and popular of saints. Christian humanist, practical joker, and one of the Church's great contemplatives, he had such an impact on the degenerate Rome of his day that he quickly became a leading figure in the recovery of Catholic spirituality and culture that we associate with the Counter-Reformation. He has been described as "the Christian Socrates" for his gentle friendship with the young, and as the "Apostle of Rome" for his success in drawing multitudes of people from all strata of society to a living practice of their faith.

The religious congregation founded by St. Philip is known as the Oratory, and its communities have grown up in towns all around the world. It counts among its illustrious members John Henry Cardinal Newman and Frederick Faber, who saw in the Oratory a vehicle for bringing about a "second spring" for the Catholic Faith in England. *Philip Neri: The Fire of Joy* draws on the most recent scholarship to paint a vivid portrait of one of the most attractive and inspiring figures of Christianity.

Pastoral coordinator

Q. Would you please comment on the following article which appeared in our parish bulletin: What the Appointment of a Pastoral Coordinator Means for Parishioners. *"Since Sister X was installed at St. Y, her duties will be to coordinate religious education, sacramental programs, and liturgy planning; participate in planning the Rite of Christian Initiation of Adults and the Rite of Anointing during Mass; preside at the wake service and celebrate the Liturgy of the Word and final commendation according to the Rite of Funerals; preside at weekday Liturgies of the Word in accord with canon law and liturgical norms; occasionally preach when pastorally and canonically appropriate; coordinate the material assets of the parish, including, but not limited to buildings, finances, fund-raising, and budget preparation. Sister X will report regularly to the newly appointed non-resident pastor of St. Y, Father Z, on all facets of parish life."*

The names have been omitted, but could you please comment if this is the norm.

A. On the surface, it looks like all the bases have been covered. I can only say that I firmly believe that having non-ordained pastoral administrators is going to lead us down another blind alley within the decade. I am sure many of our readers saw many of the same television stories as I during Pope John Paul's 1995 American visit, which regaled us with details of such situations around the country. The inescapable conclusion each time has been tremendous confusion among the laity about the differences between the ordained priest and the non-ordained "minister" and, not infrequently, the expressed desire to see this person (male or female, but usually female) get ordained.

I don't think I'm being hard-hearted when I say that if people could travel thirty miles to church decades ago with less-than-efficient modes of transportation, I see no reason why the laity can't travel today, especially since most of them probably do so for work and school, anyway.

700 Club query

Q. For quite some time now I have been watching the 700 Club *on television. Recently I went to visit my sister in Virginia and while there I heard her pastor tell her that she shouldn't be watching the* 700 Club. *My perception is that since the Second Vatican Council, there has emerged in the Church the discipline of ecumenism where we respect the religion of our fellow Christians, rather than living in the pre-Vatican II days where there was a clash between different faiths. Is this pastor correct in asking his parishioners not to watch the* 700 Club, *or is he a bit conservative?*

A. I think much depends on the theological sophistication of viewers. If Catholics know their faith well and cannot be swayed by scriptural proof-texting, I see no difficulty. With the *700 Club*, much of the material concerns a Christian angle on socio-political affairs, and it is quite common for Fundamentalist Christians and Catholics to converge on those issues.

As far as ecumenism is concerned, I am always reminded of a comment of a former philosophy professor of mine: "It's good to be open-minded, but not so open-minded that your brains fall out." The Vatican II document on ecumenism was most careful in encouraging us to be open-minded, but not empty-headed.

New sect

Q. What do you think of the American Catholic Church, based on this "foundational" document? It reads: "We see ourselves as Catholic members of the Mystical Body of Christ, our bishops' apostolic succession coming through the old Catholic Church. The pope is the visible head of the Church, much the same as the monarch is head of the United Kingdom or Spain, and we recognize his authority when he speaks in union with all the bishops and the sensus fidelium — *beliefs of the faithful in general.*

"Our beliefs and practices are those of traditional Catholicism, as found in her creeds, declarations and Ecumenical Councils, the few basic exceptions being those in conflict with our founding principles, namely:

"1) the doctrine of Papal Infallibility; 2) our authority structure will allow for greater equality and a more democratic process in allowing the laity to take their rightful place in the government of the Church; 3) the discipline of celibacy; 4) admitting women to all ranks of the clergy; 5) a more inclusive policy, embracing and reconciling those excluded by the Church and society at large, we do not withhold the reception of sacraments from any qualified person who desires to receive them; 6) we recognize that marriage until death is the ideal toward marriage until which all should stride [sic], there are occasions that cause irreconcilable partings of the ways. Remarriage after divorce does not constitute a legitimate barrier to the reception of any sacraments; 7) we affirm the right of individuals to make morally conscionable decisions regarding prudent family planning; 8) although we do not condone abortion, we affirm a woman's right to control over her own body. This must be handled with the utmost sensitivity and compassion on a case-by-case basis.

"We do not intend to separate ourselves from the Mystical Body of Christ. In affirming the principles of loving compassion as Christ taught us, the American Catholic Church is being established to meet the needs of those who share these beliefs.

"While hoping that spiritual unity may one day be realized, we are building a Church which affirms the dignity and fundamental rights of all persons, and which recognizes the importance of adopting a more humanitarian pastoral approach, honoring both tradition and contemporary thought. With a sense of hopefulness we look toward the

future and embrace the challenges of the twenty-first century as we strive to uphold the essentials of our Catholic Faith and heritage."

Where does this sect come from? Is there a danger of their spreading?

A. They were established by a former Catholic priest in the Diocese of Syracuse. Of course, the group has no standing in the Church. The bad spelling, punctuation, and sentence structure of this "foundational" document provide a clue to the bad theology of the whole operation. The founders would do well not to reinvent the wheel; every goal they have set forth has been more than amply considered and handled by the Episcopal Church, which would undoubtedly welcome them and their entire agenda with open arms.

Mass stipends

Q. I have been a practicing Catholic for forty-four years, but I still have a problem accepting the practice of Mass stipends and stole fees. I believe that Mass stipends and stole fees smack of simony. It is said that the Mass stipends for the welfare of the celebrant and is not for the purchasing of a Mass. I reject that notion, however, because for me to have a Mass said, I must be up-front with my $10 or there will be no Mass said for me.

Why is it necessary to pay a priest to have a Mass said for someone when there is a built-in opportunity to pray for one's dead in the eucharistic prayer of the Mass? Some of my non-Catholic friends have asked me this very question; sadly. I don't have a satisfactory answer for them.

Based on the definitions given in the Funk and Wagnall's Standard College Dictionary of "simony," I believe that Masses sold at $10 apiece is an act comparable to the sale of indulgences. From the definition of "stipend" — "an allowance, salary, and the performance of a service for a fixed payment" — it is readily apparent that the proffering and the acceptance of money for Mass constitutes a sale. I think it is an act of degradation for priests to have to accept "tips" for doing their job.

My thoughts on stole fees follow the same pattern. I realize that probably in the early Church stipends were perhaps necessary for the support of the priests. And I can even accept supporting some of the mission priests through stipends; however, in today's affluent American churches, I believe it is an abuse and a scandal.

I have a serious problem reconciling myself to these practices. This is seriously affecting my spiritual life and my faith is being compromised. I would greatly appreciate your addressing these areas of concern.

A. Several items you raise need to be sorted out.

First, the definition of "stipend" or "simony" that we need to use is not that of Funk and Wagnall's but of the Church! Beyond that, the 1983 Code of Canon Law actually does shy away from using the word "stipend," and prefers "offering," precisely to avoid the semblance of trafficking in Masses, etc.

Second, one of the reasons for the mandatory weekly celebration of a *Missa pro populo* ("Mass for the people") is so that the parish priest would indeed remember the intentions of his flock, whether or not they have asked for such prayers or whether or not they can afford to make an offering.

Third, canon law is clear that a request for a Mass cannot be refused because of the size of the offering.

Fourth, I agree that priests should not have to depend on stipends or stole fees for survival, but the truth of the matter is that, put bluntly, Catholic people are generally quite cheap. Catholic giving is the lowest of any denomination in the country, and our clergy are the absolutely lowest paid. I should note, however, that if you can see some legitimacy to stipends for priests in mission lands, then you cannot really have a conscience problem with the practice in other circumstances, if you are to be thoroughly logical.

Fifth, whether or not the priest receives a stipend is, in many ways, immaterial. What is involved is that the faithful should be connected to the offering of the sacrifice (of the Mass, that is) by their own personal sacrifice. This is clear throughout the Old Testament priesthood and Temple sacrifices, especially in a passage like 2 Maccabees 12:39-46.

Sixth, in 1991, the Congregation for the Clergy came out with a decree on Mass stipends (*Mos iugiter obtinuit*), confirming the traditional practice, but also giving a whole theology and psychology of it. I strongly recommend it to you.

Catholic celebrations

Q. What should our children know about the real St. Nicholas? What kinds of meals can we prepare to celebrate Fat Tuesday as they did in ancient Christendom? How do Easter eggs fit into the Christian Paschal ritual? How should we instruct our children on the fun yet reverent celebration of All Hallows' Eve? Are there any books or resources on questions of this kind?

A. The Firefly Press offers a series of books that give Catholic families informative and entertaining instruction about these and many more traditions and practices of our Faith. It includes *Cooking for Christ* by Florence Berger, a classic that adds traditional recipes to the feasts and seasons of the Church calendar; and *The Easter Book*, by Francis X. Weiser. Father Weiser, S.J., was the spiritual director of Georg and Maria von Trapp, and has written three books, including this one, on the origins and development of Christian liturgical traditions. These books make a superb addition for the contemporary Catholic home.

Ordering information is as follows (all prices are postage paid): *The Year and Our Children*, by Mary Reed Newland, $14.95; *Cooking for Christ*, by Florence Berger, $15.95; *The Easter Book*, by Francis X. Weiser, S.J., $14.95. Send all orders to: The Firefly Press, P.O. Box 262302, San Diego, CA 92196; call or FAX (619) 549-3802; or e-mail to firefly-pr@aol.com. For credit card orders, call 1-800-205-8254.

Rosary mysteries

Q. This was sent to me concerning the Rosary: "While there is good reason to preserve the basic division of joyful, sorrowful, and glorious (and the traditionally recommended days for usage noted above), we are free to adapt these divisions or to choose other events from Christ's life and the Scriptures which more closely correspond to the liturgical season or to the events of our lives.

"For example, other mysteries for reflection might be: the Baptism of Jesus, the temptations in the desert, the calling of the disciples, the Sermon on the Mount, the Transfiguration, the Last Supper, Jesus on the cross entrusting his Mother and disciple John into each other's care, the disciples on the way to Emmaus."

What do you think about this? Is it not tradition that the Blessed Virgin Mary gave the fifteen mysteries to St. Dominic?

A. The Rosary already existed in its basic form long before the time of St. Dominic. What Our Lady did was recommend the use of the Rosary as a tool in the saint's battle against the Albigensian heretics.

I agree that there is merit in retaining the traditional structure of the Rosary, but there is certainly nothing wrong with using alternate mysteries. In fact, Pope Paul VI envisions just this in his document on Marian devotion, *Marialis Cultus*. Furthermore, the various chaplets which the faithful use do employ a number of other events from the life of Our Lord and the Blessed Mother — for example, the Franciscan Crown.

Godparent and sponsor duties

Q. What are the duties and rights of a godparent? In the baptismal ritual, the godparents are asked if they understand their duties. What are those duties?

A. Under the heading of Baptism, the Code of Canon Law gives specific attention to what the responsibilities of sponsors are, and likewise under Confirmation. Since Baptism and Confirmation are but two parts of the tripartite process of Christian initiation, we can apply what is said in one place to the other. The baptismal canon says: "In the case of an infant Baptism, the role is together with the parents to present the child for Baptism, and to help it to live a Christian life befitting the baptized and faithfully to fulfill the duties inherent in Baptism" (Canon 872). Canon 892 states the following: "The sponsor's function is to take care that the person confirmed behaves as a true witness of Christ and faithfully fulfills the duties inherent in this sacrament."

Baptized to evangelize

Q. Pope John Paul II has raised a question that disturbs me. He asked, and I'm paraphrasing, "Can we who believe be saved if we fail to evangelize?" I am disturbed because I arranged an appointment with our new pastor asking to work on the evangelization program, and he turned me down. He said that I wasn't educated enough. I have worked in another parish on their evangelization program. I have two associate degrees and have taken a course on evangelization at the seminary, but that didn't impress him at all. How can I evangelize without the cooperation of our pastor? Is he not putting my salvation in jeopardy? Can you identify when and where the Pope made his statement on evangelization and salvation?

A. I do not believe we can be saved without evangelizing since that is an essential component of living the Gospel message. Pope John Paul has spoken of this in numerous settings, for example, his encyclical

Redemptoris Missio (on the permanent validity of the Church's missionary mandate) and *Crossing the Threshold of Hope.*

Now, I do not know why your present parish priest does not want you involved in the evangelization program; it might be a good idea to ask him for the concrete criteria he has for such work. That said, participation in his program is by no means the only — or necessarily the most effective — manner of spreading the Gospel. The first and most important method is the witness of one's life and using the opportunities that God offers us in the normal course of our day-to-day existence at home, in the neighborhood, at work, at school.

One of the biggest post-conciliar fallacies is that if one is not officially deputed to perform a task, one has no role to play. All too often, such an attitude betrays a strong strain of clericalism. Appointment by the pastor does not commission a believer as an evangelist. Baptism did that!

Prayer ads

Q. Enclosed is a clipping from our local newspaper. The publication of the "prayers" after favors are granted seems to be commendable, but the increasing number of the same type of prayer and the acknowledgment by initials or first names only leaves me with an uncomfortable feeling. Is the impression this sort of advertisement gives one of superstition and "bargaining with God"? They seem almost akin to chain letters. I am skeptical about the authenticity of these ads and feel that they open up the Catholic Church to unnecessary criticism. What do you think?

A. I agree with you. Personal piety should never be worn on the sleeve, to start off, but it is particularly dangerous when it is displayed in an environment where it will almost assuredly be completely misunderstood. Your fears are well-founded, and I have often asked people to refrain from sending in such "testimonies," especially to secular newspapers.

Sacrilegious

Q. I was reading another Catholic periodical (normally reliable) and came across the following statement: "If you are not conscious of mortal sin, it is not only acceptable but pleasing to God to recite an Act of Contrition before every Communion. If you are in a state of mortal sin and are in some situation where you cannot get to confession but must go to Communion (school graduations, weddings and so on), sincerely reciting a perfect Act of Contrition will absolve the sin, but not the obligation to confess it later."

I am terribly confused. Nobody should receive Communion in a state of mortal sin without going to confession. Besides, are graduations and wedding circumstances when you MUST go to Communion?

A. I think the advice given was incorrect. As I read the reply, the first thought which came into my head was the very one you expressed in the last line of your inquiry: Who says these situations demand reception of Holy Communion? We know for sure that we may never receive the Eucharist unworthily because, as St. Paul instructed the Corinthians, to do so means eating the Lord's Body unto our condemnation (see 1 Cor 11:27-29). A concern for human respect is no justification for the sin of sacrilege, which is what receiving unworthily is properly called. The *Catechism* puts it most starkly: "Anyone conscious of a grave sin must receive the sacrament of Reconciliation before coming to Communion" (1385).

Masons

Q. My boyfriend is a member of the Masonic Lodge, and I am a Catholic. I would like to know if Catholics can join the Masonic Lodge or Eastern Star. If not, why not? Further, if they are not permitted to join such organizations, can they marry a Mason and raise their children Catholic as long as they practice their faith?

A. No Catholic may belong to any Masonic organization, as the Congregation for the Doctrine of the Faith stated most clearly more than a decade ago, because the Masons hold positions in opposition to Catholic teaching. (In the United States, the Masons seem to shy away from a religious identification.)

That having been said, a Catholic could marry a Mason (as he or she could an atheist), so long as there would be no danger to the practice of his or her own faith or to the raising of any children in the Faith.

No deal

Q. I have been told by a friend that Pope Leo XIII had a vision where Satan was talking to God and said that if given a specified amount of time, he could overthrow the Church. So God granted Satan this century to seduce and ensnare all of humanity. It appears that the devil has been successful, spreading his evils and a rejection of God. Would God do such a thing? Have you ever heard of this vision before? I would appreciate any information you can give me.

A. I believe I have heard rumblings of this kind in some strange, apocalyptic literature. I give no credence to it for any number of reasons. First, God doesn't make deals with anyone, the devil included. Second, God certainly would not wager the eternal salvation of those He loves, even if He were the betting type.

If you read the writings of people down through the centuries, you find a constant theme: The present age is evil; faith is gone from the earth; the devil is in control. The truth of the matter is that life and the Church go on, and we do have Christ's promise that His Church will last until the end of time. Now, that does not mean that the Church, in a particular time and place, will last until the Lord's Second Coming (therefore, the need for ongoing conversion and penance), but it does indicate that no power, earthly or demonic, will ever be able to "overthrow" Christ's Church as a whole.

No problem

Q. Is there any reason someone who had an abortion cannot enter religious life? The abortion occurred years ago, and the lady in question is very repentant.

A. No, I see no difficulty.

Faithful to the Magisterium

Q. Please inform your readers of a Prayer Network for Sisters faithful to the Magisterium of the Church: "All for Jesus through Mary." For further information, please contact: Sister Mary, P.O. Box 726, Maggie Valley, NC 28751.

A. I am all in favor of any association that will give some kind of support to women Religious who wish to remain faithful to the Holy Father and are all too often persecuted within their own religious communities for their fidelity.

I should also note the existence of the Council of Major Superiors of Women Religious, which has full canonical status with the Holy See. That organization can be contacted by writing to: Box 4467, Washington, DC 20017; or phone 301-559-6308.

Christmas Eve fast?

Q. Could you please clarify if Christmas Eve was ever a day of fast and abstinence? I am in my mid-seventies, and I seem to recall that it was, but my sister (younger by ten years) is adamant that was not so. Regrettably, this dispute has caused a rift between us, so the sooner you can settle it, the better it will be, since I sorely miss my sister's company.

A. Let's begin with the more important issue first. No theoretical discussion should ever have the effect of bringing about division between sisters. When that happens, we are face-to-face with misplaced priorities or even prideful self-assertion. Therefore, I would urge you — regardless of who "wins" this one — to set about the Christian and human work of reconciliation.

That having been said, I believe that Christmas Eve was observed, universally, as a day of fast and abstinence. However, I also know that many ethnic groups had a discipline, which differed from the universal norm, and with full ecclesiastical approbation. Some, for example, followed the fast until noon, while others did so until sundown. According to the best of my recollection, everyone maintained abstinence, but surely Eastern Europeans and Italians were given to huge banquets on Christmas Eve — of the completely piscine variety!

Artificial flowers

Q. In my church artificial flowers are used. Somewhere I read that nothing artificial is to be used on the altar. Can you tell me if I am correct, and, if so, where the directive can be found. Our sacristan says that she has never heard this.

A. While there is no strict law forbidding the use of artificial flowers, it seems they should be avoided. Just as the Church does not permit "canned" music for the liturgy or electric lights for real candles, the principle should be applied similarly in the present case, in my opinion. With all the lovely potted plants that are so readily available today, it appears quite unnecessary to resort to synthetic products.

Sanctuary lamp money

Q. Since the days of my childhood, the sanctuary lamp has always been a reminder to me of the Real Presence of Jesus in the tabernacle. I have recently heard of parishes where for $20 you can write the name of anyone you wish remembered and have it placed near the *sanctuary lamp, with parishioners or visitors being reminded to pray for your intention.*

To me, this simply means that Jesus must now share the respect due only to Him with anyone whose family has $20. I find this outrageous. Is this something new that the Church has initiated or just another way for certain pastors to put a few dollars in the bank?

A. If you find nothing wrong with Mass stipends (and I presume you don't because the Church doesn't), then what's the problem with memorializing a sanctuary lamp? It's the same principle as lighting any other vigil light, except that this one burns before Christ Himself, rather than an image of Him or one of the saints.

By the way, I must tell my parishioners that the offering in your parish is $20 because it's only $10 in mine!

Cardinals' titles

Q. Lately I have noticed a change in the way the media, both secular and Catholic, refer to cardinals. The title used to be placed after the Christian name and before the family name; now it is placed before the baptismal name. Was there any specific reason for the placement of the title between the two names, and when did that practice originate?

A. Either practice is now considered acceptable, and Roman documents use both.

The traditional order has a certain charm about it, provided one knows the significance. The word "cardinal" comes from the Latin word *cardo*, which means "hinge." Having the man's first name joined to his last by the title of "cardinal" produces the "hinge-effect," highlighting the cardinal's role as a "hinge" between the local church or ministry he performs and the Sovereign Pontiff.

Cathedral names

Q. I understand that most of the Anglican cathedrals in England pre-date the reign of Henry VIII, and so would have been Catholic. Most appear to bear the name of their town or city, rather than a patron saint's name. Was the use of a place name an English custom even before the time of Henry VIII, or did the Anglicans merely rename these cathedrals to rid themselves of "popish" taint and influence?

A. Throughout Europe, people referred to their cathedrals as "the cathedral of Orvieto" or "the cathedral of Florence," and England was no different in that regard.

All these churches do have patron saints as well, and their saints' feasts are usually celebrated with great solemnity, even to the extent of being civil holidays in many places up to the present moment.

By giving the city name, one simply notes that the cathedral church is the mother church of the diocese which bears that name.

Our Lady of Akita

Q. What do you know about Our Lady of Akita?
A. A video recently has come to my attention of Our Lady's apparitions to Sister Agnes in Akita. Japan in 1973. These apparitions have been approved by the Church.

The messages of Our Lady deal with the coming chastisement and how we should respond. For a copy, please contact: The Monks of Adoration, P.O. Box 546, Petersham, MA 01366: phone 508-724-8871. It is available in video or audio tape.

Pagan elements?

Q. One of my sisters is a conservative Protestant and has given me a book to read, entitled Babylon Mystery Religion, *by Ralph Woodrow. In it, he shows how these cults spread to the surrounding nations, were absorbed into the Roman Empire and then got their teachings taken into the Catholic Church. Could this be true? It's incredibly shocking to me.*
A. No serious scholar, Protestant or Catholic, would give even a nod to Woodrow's scurrilous work. It is a favorite sourcebook for inveterate anti-Catholics, such as those that work for Chick Publications. That having been said, we have never denied that certain elements of paganism were indeed taken into Christianity, albeit with a purified and Christian meaning assigned them.

For example, the use of incense was common not only in Judaism but in all the pagan religions; similarly, the Church took the Roman feast of the *Sol Invictus* (the Unconquered Sun) and transformed it into a celebration of the Lord's nativity.

And this has gone on for two millennia, which is why the Fathers of the Second Vatican Council could speak of other religions with respect, noting that they have elements of truth within them and, therefore, ought to be honored for those things, all the while preaching the Gospel of Jesus Christ and allowing it to purify in those religions what is in need of purification.

The pagan Roman poet Terence said: *"Nil humanum mihi alienum est"* ("Nothing human is foreign to me"), and this has always been the Church's approach as well. Put another way, should the Church deny belief in only one God just because Muslims hold to it, too? Does it not make more sense to rejoice in what we have in common and use that as the basis for the work of evangelization?

Finally, when people have truly heard and accepted the Gospel, should we not be open to their using cultural forms with which they are familiar, particularly if they enforce Christian teaching and do not contradict it in any way?

Distractions at Mass

Q. I feel like such a hypocrite, in that I force my teenagers to go to Mass but find my own mind wandering terribly when I'm there myself. Is this my own fault? Is this common, from your pastoral experience? Is there any help for this problem?

A. The French philosopher Blaise Pascal put it quite well when he reminded us that "the desire to pray is prayer." Now, that should not be taken as carte blanche to cave in to distractions during prayer and especially at Mass, but I think it does put things into perspective.

I have recently come across a fine book dealing with this situation in a manner which is theologically correct and pastorally sensitive: *If Your Mind Wanders at Mass*, written by Thomas Howard and published by Franciscan University Press in Steubenville, Ohio.

Holiday Masses

Q. At the end of the school year, the students are admonished "Do not take a vacation from God; don't skip Mass and use your time productively." I would like to carry this idea one step further and ask a question, although not related to children.

Why is it that on Memorial Day, Independence Day, Labor Day and other civil holidays, almost all churches seem to adopt an abbreviated Mass schedule, in most places only having one Mass? It upsets me that it is more difficult for people to get to Mass on their free day, but even more that the priests kick back and enjoy a day not ministering to the people! It would seem to me that anything else the priest does all day long pales in comparison to offering Mass. Can it be that the priest loses sight of the love and grace bestowed upon him by our Savior?

A. I suspect you're engaging in a bit of overkill. First of all, Labor Day and the like are not religious holidays and, therefore, there is no reason why a priest needs to have a Mass schedule as though they are. And an abbreviated daily schedule is not out of order in my estimation, either. Granted, not all priests work as hard as they should, but should you begrudge a priest a holiday that you yourself are enjoying? If there were two or three priests in a parish and no Mass at all on such days, that would be a different story, but your own letter indicates that is not the situation.

Hispanic resources

Q. I am newly ordained and have just been appointed to work in a predominantly Hispanic parish where there has been no serious apostolate or outreach to the Hispanics. Any suggestions for resources?

A. This past spring the Bishops' Committee on Hispanic Affairs produced a compendium of documents (Hispanic Ministry: Three Major Documents). Phone 1-800-235-8722.

Religious instruction

Q. My children's mother (a non-Catholic) and I are divorced; they live with her. Two years ago, I returned to the Catholic Church and am desirous of having my children instructed in the Faith. The parish priest has chosen not to help me because he fears some kind of disagreement with their mother. Is there anything I can do to provide them with the proper education in the Faith, or must they do without because of my mistake in marrying a non-Catholic woman who later divorced me?

A. If your wife has custody of the children, it would appear that she holds all the aces. The only thing I would suggest is a consistent appeal to her sense of decency, especially since (if you were married in the Church) she knew in advance of the expectation that all children born of the union would be raised Catholic. Another angle would revolve around child support. Perhaps the court can be persuaded to allow you to have a say in the religious upbringing of the children if you are paying the bills.

Papal speeches

Q. Can you please recommend a publication which does not edit the sermons of Pope John Paul II?

A. I'm not exactly sure of what you have in mind. If you desire the Holy Father's addresses (sermons, speeches, homilies, etc.) in their full form, you can obtain the vast majority of them from two principal sources: the weekly English edition of *l'Osservatore Romano* (Via del Pellegrino, 00120 Vatican City, Europe) and *The Pope Speaks* (Our Sunday Visitor, Inc., 200 Noll Plaza, Huntington, IN 46750).

Painful truth

Q. I am writing in reference to one of the questions in [a recent] edition of TCA. The question involved a priest who "left the active ministry and shortly thereafter was married in a Protestant Church. A number of priests in good standing were among the invited guests and attended the ceremony." You replied that ". . . the behavior of the clergy was reprehensible. They owe an apology to the entire diocese and the whole presbyterate for their act of defiance. . . ."

I was curious which act of defiance this might be referring to. Was it not abandoning a friend who has taken a wrong path, by your standards? Was it politely honoring an invitation to a friend's wedding, even if you don't agree with it? Was it acting with great charity, forgiveness, and kindness? If these are sins, then our Church needs more sinners.

I think that if the priests had refused to go to the wedding, it would have been rude, snobbish, hateful, and unforgiving. They didn't have to condone what the ex-priest did; they could have even made their opinion publicly known. There is no excuse for being rude or condemning the man. God is the only one with that privilege.

Also, the last time I checked the Bible, Jesus was dining and associating with lepers, prostitutes, and tax collectors. Does this make Jesus reprehensible? Our religion, which is, believe it or not a Christian religion, is based on Jesus. Being Christian means that we try to live and act as Christ did. Too many Catholics get caught up in protocol and forget that above all, we are supposed to act with great mercy and love.

What the ex-priest did might have been wrong, but for the priests to act any other way than what Jesus might have done — that would be truly reprehensible. As for the apology, I think that the priests do not owe it, rather it is owed to them.

A. First of all, let's set the record straight: What the former priest did was wrong; not might have been wrong. He backed out of a solemn commitment, made after eight years of prayerful reflection and many years of pastoral ministry.

Over and above that, he deliberately violated Church law, failing to petition for a decree of laicization. Further, he submitted to a rite in a Protestant denomination, which would have no effect in the eyes of God, thereby publicly committing himself to a union of fornication.

Finally, going back to his old parish to do this was a scandalous act, designed to call into question the authority of the Church to demand celibacy of her priests and to hold believers to a Gospel way of life regarding human sexuality.

Now, with all that in clear relief, can anyone still argue that priests should have participated?

Beyond that, their participation proceeded to violate other ecclesiastical norms: Their act of "concelebration" gave implicit approval to the validity of the Eucharist in an ecclesial community which we hold does not have valid Orders and, therefore, no valid Eucharist; their reception of the Eucharist was also a statement that full ecclesial communion already exists between that denomination and the Catholic Church — and that is not true.

All too often today, people have a very soft, Milquetoast image of Our Lord as a type of "I'm OK, you're OK" personality, but that flies in the face of the data of the New Testament. It is important to recall that the Jesus of love and compassion had some very harsh words for those who caused scandal ("better that a millstone be tied around their necks") and hypocrites who want to use religion to feel or look rather than be good (He called them "whitened sepulchres").

As you can see, I stand by my original evaluation; in fact, in retrospect, I think I'm even stronger than I was, to begin with.

Priest's wedding, inclusive language

Q. I do not recall the original question in [a recent] TCA on priests concelebrating another priest's invalid wedding, and I do not question your response. However, as I was reading [a recent] letter from "M. M., Pennsylvania," I found myself agreeing with the writer's opinion condoning the actions of the priests since they showed "charity, forgiveness, and kindness." But I assumed that the priests in question had merely attended the wedding as a sign of friendship.

Your response, however, referred to the priests as having "participated" and spoke of their "concelebration" and "reception of the Eucharist." (Why did you use a capital "E," if such is not a valid Eucharist?)

If the priests "participated" and "concelebrated" and "(received) of the (Protestant) Eucharist," then I totally agree with your response; what they did was wrong! But, if they just attended out of friendship, merely sat with the congregation, and did not received a Protestant Eucharist, would they be doing wrong?

I have another question: I am a member of a secular institute in permanent vows; while I do not have the same public witness as a priest, I certainly try never to do anything that would cause scandal of any sort or to go against the teachings of the Church. If I were ever put in the position of being invited to the same type of wedding we have been discussing or that of divorced Catholics marrying in a Protestant church, would I be wrong in attending (just by sitting in the congregation and not receiving) out of friendship? What about the wedding reception?

One last point: Without getting into the controversy over inclusive language in liturgical texts, please note that many women, myself included, find it offensive to be constantly referred to as male. I bring this up because of your answer [in a recent] TCA, entitled "Norm for Salvation." Christ did not die for all men, as you said. Christ died for all people, male and female. Wouldn't you find it offensive to have female words to describe everybody, even though you were told that you were really included in that language? Until that longed-for day when the male hierarchy can understand all this and changes the liturgical texts, it is very much appreciated when such language is not used in everyday speech, such as your answer in the latest TCA.

A. We really have two big issues here.

First, let's take care of the priest's wedding. Yes, the priests inattendance actually received and/or concelebrated the service. But my objection would be nearly as strong if they had merely sat in the congregation. Why? Because their presence can support and give credibility to a sinful action, namely, the priest's departure from the active ministry and his entrance into an illicit union. I tell parents that they should not attend the weddings of their children who do not abide by Church law for the very same reason —that their presence will appear to sanction an immoral act. To answer your personal question, I would never attend a friend's invalid wedding ceremony, or the reception following, for the basic reason that the reception is, literally, the icing on the cake.

As for capitalizing a Protestant Eucharist, this is done not to acknowledge its validity but as a common courtesy.

By the way, one does not abstain from receiving Communion at non-Catholic services only because the sacrament might be invalid but also because of the lack of ecclesial unity. Thus, while accepting the validity of an Eastern Orthodox Eucharist, we are not to receive Holy Communion from them, nor they from us (under normal circumstances).

As to the concern about so-called "inclusive language," please be advised that *The Catholic Answer* magazine shall always use standard English and not be cowed into bowdlerized, politically-correct usage which is designed to advance an agenda at odds with much Church teaching. As one observer has put it, "linguistic engineering always precedes social engineering." And that surely applies today. Interestingly enough, even *The New York Times* does not consistently cave in to your hang-ups, for yesterday's edition had a bold headline employing the word "mankind."

Finally, using your logic, were I a male living in any of the countries where the Romance languages are spoken, I should feel most alienated, for the word for "person" is feminine in grammatical gender and followed up by a feminine pronoun. Oddly enough, I have yet to see any of their men (males, that is) mounting the barricades or "manning" picket lines.

Three-quarters of the world has not heard the name of Jesus Christ, and fewer than 30 percent of Catholics who receive Holy Communion in this country every Sunday believe in Christ's Real Presence in the Eucharist. Let's get on with what should be the real business at hand.

Religious goods
Q. Would you kindly give publicity to our collection of rosaries, religious printed matter, etc. for the Church in Lithuania and Ukraine? All may

be sent directly to: Tom Wall; Ballinookera, Whitegate, Midleton; Co. Cork; Ireland.
A. Happy to do so, especially since they are the precise places of origin for my own family!

Angel Saints

Q. Why is it in the Ordo and in all Catholic literature that the three archangels (Michael, Gabriel, and Raphael) are called "saints" when, in fact, they were never human? Catholic doctrine teaches us that a saint is a human being who has died and is now in heaven. This is true of none of the archangels.

Could you offer an explanation?

A. The definition you give is a good general working definition for a saint, but other possibilities also exist. For instance, St. Paul (and the early Church, following his example) referred to all Christian believers as "saints." Furthermore, your understanding would obviously exclude a human being like Elijah (since the Scriptures tell us that he never died but was merely whisked away to heaven in a whirlwind). Simply put, the Church accords the title of "saint" to anyone who now enjoys the beatific vision.

It should be noted, by the way, that the *Catechism of the Catholic Church* specifically refers to the three archangels whose names we have as "saints" (335).

Funeral faux pas

Q. At a parishioner's funeral recently, the female Episcopal priest was invited to do the prayers of committal before Mass and to read the Gospel during the Mass. Some of the deceased's daughters attend the Episcopal church. It seemed a sensitive gesture, but confusing all the same. Was it proper to involve Protestant clergy in this way?

A. First of all, "the prayers of committal" follow the Mass; perhaps you are referring to either the service at the funeral home or the greeting of the body at the door of the church. Some participation of the priestess in those events would be possible, but always with the understanding that scandal will be avoided. No non-Catholic minister, however, may ever read the Gospel. Rules on preaching vary from diocese to diocese, but generally the delivery of a homily by a non-Catholic cleric requires the explicit permission of the bishop.

Catholic update

Q. It is very confusing to try to keep up with Church teaching by reading the accounts in most newspapers. Could you please identify some sources available to the Catholic laity that provide accurate information on current Church teaching?

A. Well, I think that's what we try to do here in *The Catholic Answer*! Having the *Catechism of the Catholic Church* and making a friend of it is the best guarantee of being thoroughly up-to-date in one's understanding of the Catholic Faith. For access to the constant flow of new documentation, general summaries can usually be found in the Catholic press; for complete texts, *l'Osservatore Romano* newspaper or *The Pope Speaks* magazine perform the service quite well.

Church concerts

Q. We recently had an orchestra perform a concert of American music in our church. It brought many outsiders to visit the church and was a beautiful concert. What is the official position about having concerts in church? While I enjoyed it, it made me somewhat uneasy. Please comment.

A. Historically, the Church has served as the patroness of the arts. In regard to music, one must realize that churches were generally the places where concerts were given until recent centuries, if for no other reason than the fact that concert halls did not exist.

Within the past few years, due to uneasiness on the part of many like yourself, the Holy See has offered guidelines on the matter which include the following points: (1) Only sacred music ought to be performed; (2) a spirit of prayer should permeate the event; and (3) no tickets may be sold, nor may the appearance of an admission price be given.

Catholic burial

Q. Can a non-Catholic be buried from the Catholic Church just because the individual raised several children who converted to Catholicism and did not interfere? When this request was granted by a young priest at our parish, I found it hard to accept. Could you please comment on this situation?

A. I don't see how what happened squares with church law: "In the prudent judgment of the local ordinary, ecclesiastical funeral rites can be granted to baptized members of some non-Catholic church or ecclesial community unless it is evidently contrary to their will and provided their own minister is unavailable" (Canon 1183.3).

Pastor's authority

Q. Should a couple — a nominal Catholic and a non-Catholic — getting married in the Protestant church be allowed the use of the Catholic parish hall for a reception following the wedding? They refused to be prepared for marriage by the priest and get the dispensation to have the wedding in the Lutheran church. They insulted the pastor by saying that the Catholic Church has never meant anything to them. The pastor refused the permission for the hall to be used as a result. Now the parish council and the hall committee have turned against the pastor. In your opinion, what should the course of action be in such a situation?

A. The parish priest is absolutely correct, and he needs to assert his pastoral authority over a parish council that obviously understands neither a Catholic theology of the sacraments nor the rightful and respective roles of clergy and laity. Committees such as you describe, and their reactions, stand as a warning of what can happen when people either usurp the responsibility of the pastor, or are allowed to do so.

It should be stressed that this is not simply a question about the exercise of power; rather, it is intimately related to a priest's ability to preach the Gospel. This type of lay trusteeism plagued the Church in this country for nearly a century; it continues to inhibit the pastoral work of many Protestant and Orthodox clergy. There is no excuse for such things to occur within the Catholic community because church law is quite clear about the lines of demarcation between a priest's authority and lay consultation and/or involvement.

Reverence gone awry

Q. Although I realize that the event described in the enclosed article is not exactly the same as the money-changers in the Temple, isn't it still a profanation of God's house to have even a "religious party" in a church?

A. For the benefit of our readers, let me summarize the content of the article: A parish CCD director staged a "welcome summer" event in the parish church, with the children encouraged to come as you would to any summer party, along with surf boards, beach balls, rods and reels, wet suits, etc. The tune of the day was "Summertime, sum-, sum-,

summertime." Everything got washed down with a few healthy scoops of ice cream.

The description, in and of itself seems to say enough, requiring no commentary. However, I would note that as bad as all the frivolity was in God's house, I found the prayer service to be particularly problematic, not unlike some ancient pagan rite to the sun.

I hope that when the bishop found the write-up in his diocesan paper, he took some action. With this kind of nonsense going on, is it any wonder that so many of our young people opt out of Catholicism and get into cults and fundamentalist sects which, for all their failings, at least maintain some sense of the sacred?

Meditation

Q. My question deals with meditation and how it applies to the Catholic Faith. I have seen a great many books offered in Catholic bookstores that instruct a person to read a certain passage out of the Bible and meditate on it. I'm confused about what this actually means. Does it mean just to think (reflect) about the passage, or does it mean "meditate" in a more technical sense which involves body posture, breathing techniques, etc.? It seems possible that one could be misled during meditation. Should a Catholic meditate? If so, what is a spiritually safe way of doing it? Could you recommend any books that outline the proper steps for meditation for Catholics?

A. Meditation is an integral part of spiritual living. It is important not to import notions to this process or activity that may have tainted the word in some way. And just because abuses are possible and/or have occurred, it does not mean that a particular activity is bad or should be avoided automatically.

What should be included in one's meditation, that is, thoughtful and prayerful reflection, depends in large measure on the individual; for some people or at some times, that will involve body posture and the like; for others, meditation is possible without the use of physical aids.

For a beginner, I would suggest placing oneself in the presence of God, preferably before the Blessed Sacrament; clearing the mind of distractions as much as possible; and then taking a passage of Scripture or some event from the life of Our Lord or other mystery of salvation. Begin to think about its meaning in itself and in reference to yourself.

That should stir up emotions of gratitude, love, devotion, etc. and lead to certain resolutions for one's own life in Christ.

All the great spiritual writers offer guidelines on how to meditate. Works by St. Ignatius Loyola, St. John of the Cross, St. Teresa of Ávila and St. Francis de Sales all come to mind immediately.

Last but not least, I would refer you to paragraphs 2705-2708 of the *Catechism of the Catholic Church*, along with the following section on contemplative prayer.

Holy day holidays?

Q. Is it proper for Catholic schools to hold school on holy days of obligation? Both the Catechism of the Catholic Church *and your own Catholic Encyclopedia maintain that holy days need to be maintained, as far as possible, as Sundays. What is your thinking on this?*

A. In an ideal world, I would agree that Catholic schools should be closed on holy days of obligation. As a former Catholic school administrator, however, I know that I often supported keeping schools open for one basic reason — to ensure that the students would at least get to Mass on such days. If that is the case, then I do believe that the day should be treated in a most special and spiritual manner, with no regular classes held. For example, an extended homeroom period dealing with the feast and its significance, perhaps with a video; student body Mass; games or recreational movie; lunch; early dismissal. This kind of a schedule actually has the advantage of teaching youngsters how to observe a holy day in a truly Catholic manner.

Devotions endorsed

Q. I know some get carried away in their devotions, but is it wrong for a priest to brand First Friday and Saturday devotions "superstitions"?

A. Granted, as you implicitly suggest, devotions can move into the realm of superstition, but that calls for good preaching and teaching, not their elimination. Furthermore, the very highest authorities in the Church have not merely tolerated these two particular devotions; they have enthusiastically endorsed and recommended them.

Positive press

Q. Why doesn't the Church counteract all the negative publicity gets from the secular media by offering inspiring stories of people who have found meaning and beauty in their lives as Catholics? Are there any such books, or am I just missing them?

A. There are such works available, although I certainly agree with your basic point and the urgency you exhibit. One book comes to mind immediately, having had the opportunity to review it in manuscript form: *Surprised by Truth: Eleven Converts Give the Biblical and Historical Reasons for Becoming Catholics* (Basilica Press, Box 85152-134, San Diego, CA 92186; $15.90). The title pretty much says it all, and I could not recommend it more highly, both for its spiritually uplifting nature and for the high caliber of theological wisdom it imparts in addition to which, it is a most enjoyable read.

Worship disturbed

Q. Some months ago my diocesan newspaper carried an article about a Protestant man who was sentenced to prison for four years because he illegally received a consecrated host while attending Mass. The incident occurred in Kefamenanu, Indonesia, in March 1994. This reaction of the Indonesian government seems absurd to me. Can a secular power make a law about such a thing as the reception of Holy Communion? Should not the Church intervene to secure his release even now? Please comment.

A. As I recall the incident, the government's involvement was justified because it was treated as a disturbance of religious worship and also potentially riot-causing. Even in the United States, we have laws that prohibit similar activities, although they seldom seem to be enforced on behalf of the Catholic Church!

Intercommunion query

Q. My wife and I are Catholic, but my family is Lutheran. We would like to know if we are allowed to receive Communion in the Lutheran church when we visit my mother. We were always under the impression that we couldn't, but when my father passed away some months ago, my mother expressed a strong desire that we receive Communion at his memorial service. She mentioned that a Catholic friend of hers frequently attends her Lutheran church and receives Communion.

When we expressed our reservations, my mother discussed the issue with her pastor, who agreed with her. He felt that if we were to attend the memorial service without receiving Communion it would demonstrate the "broken Body of Christ" and he would rather not have a Communion service at all.

Thoroughly confused, we consulted the priest at the parish we attend when visiting. He indicated that staying away would do more harm than good, and that it was permissible for us to receive, though the consecration of the elements was not valid, and a Lutheran service did not fulfill our Mass obligation.

I'm still not comfortable with this solution. What should be done on our next visit to my mother? Thank you for your help.

A. You were absolutely correct, and the clergy — Catholic and Lutheran alike — were wrong.

The Lutheran pastor is correct in asserting that your non-reception of the Eucharist "would demonstrate 'the broken Body of Christ,' " which is exactly what must happen. To pretend that full unity exists within the Church (the Lord's ecclesial Body) is to engage in self-deception at best.

If the Lutheran minister has any regard for personal conscience, he would never attempt to place you in the position of having to choose between an alleged form of Christian hospitality and the truth of your Faith. I would make it eminently clear to your mother that you will not receive Communion at the Lutheran service and, if she or the pastor find that offensive, you will simply not attend at all in the future.

Date of Christmas

Q. My sister, who was raised Catholic, has left the Faith for Judaism. On Christmas Eve at a family gathering, she was tearing down the Faith and the celebration of Christmas. Among other things, she said that December 25 could not have been the day of Christ's birth because it snows in Palestine at that time of year; therefore, the shepherds would not have been out in the fields. She went on to say that the day was connected to an Egyptian/pagan holiday in order to attract Christians.

I know what she says is nonsense; however, I am unable to "answer" her. Could you please explain the origin of the celebration of Christmas on December 25?

A. Liturgy does not reenact life; it represents life. Therefore, when we celebrate a particular feast, it does not necessarily mean that the date in question is the precise day on which that event occurred historically. And that is certainly true in regard to Christmas.

Scholars speculate that the selection of December 25 was aimed at replacing the pagan Roman winter festival dedicated to the *Sol Invictus* (the Unconquered Sun), if for no other reason than to give Christians the ability to celebrate the nativity of Christ with due solemnity and yet not arouse too much attention in a time when Christianity was still actively persecuted.

Furthermore, the Church has, from the very beginning, always sought to salvage from other cultures and religions whatever is possible, "baptizing" or purifying it, as it were, and then using it for the worship of the one true God.

The long and the short of it all, then, is that your sister's information is essentially on target. You, on the other hand, need not be defensive about the facts.

'Jesus' letter causes upset

Q. My second-grader, who attends a Catholic school, made his First Holy Communion last week. Among the items that he brought home was a letter which was penned and signed by the CCD director as "Jesus." This letter was brought to my attention by my husband, who is a non-Catholic. He was appalled that a person could so easily put words to paper and attribute them to Jesus. I have to say that I am repulsed that anyone teaching CCD would take such liberties. Are we overreacting to this gesture, or is the CCD director off the mark?

A. First of all, I am confused that your Catholic school student brought home a letter from the CCD coordinator, unless you mean the director of religious education who may also take care of all religious classes in the parish.

That aside, I think your reaction may be a bit excessive, but I am also somewhat uncomfortable with the procedure. I don't think we should presume to speak for Our Lord, even when the message is innocuous or even positive. That is also one of my gripes against some of the contemporary liturgical music we have of late: For the first time in history, we are hearing hymns that are not our words to God but supposedly God's words to us and mouthed by a cantor or an entire congregation.

Good intentions need to be balanced by prudence and humility.

A complex case

Q. I am writing to find out what is necessary for a lapsed Catholic to reenter the Church. I was baptized and received my First Holy Communion in the Catholic Church. Shortly thereafter, my family stopped attending Mass. As a married adult, I began attending the Episcopal Church with my wife and was confirmed by the Episcopal bishop in 1976. In February 1992, the rector of our Episcopal church decided to seek ordination as a Catholic priest. Approximately forty families left at the same time. Our local bishop approved the establishment of an Anglican Usage parish, and we are now waiting for Rome's approval for our priest's ordination.

I have been told that I would need to make a confession to a Catholic priest regarding my departure from the Catholic Church. When I make this confession, will it be necessary for me to include any sins confessed to an Episcopal priest? Would I be allowed to continue attending the Anglican Usage parish, or would I have to return to a Latin-rite parish? My wife of twenty-three years was previously married. Would it be necessary for her to get an annulment before I am allowed to participate in the sacraments of the Church?

I really want to do what is right. I am very confused, and no one seems to have the answer. Hopefully, you can be of some help in clarifying these issues.

A. Yours is a very complex case because so many variables are present. Let's take things one by one.

(1) Anyone desiring to return to full communion with the Catholic Church must make an integral confession of all sins committed since departure from the Church, including any sins confessed to invalidly ordained clergy (which is usually the case for Anglicans).

(2) That person must then make a Profession of Faith and be confirmed. Again, the Anglican confirmation would not be deemed valid since we do not accept the validity of the Anglican episcopacy.

(3) But these relatively simple procedures are complicated due to the previous marriage of your present wife. She would have to obtain an annulment, presuming she had contracted a valid marriage. But maybe it wasn't. For example, is she or her husband a Catholic? And if so, was she married in the Catholic Church? If one party was Catholic and the marriage was not celebrated in a Catholic ceremony recognized

by the Church, it was automatically invalid. On the other hand, if both parties were not Catholic, whatever ceremony they had was valid. As you can see, this is not easy to resolve in writing. The best thing to do is contact your parish priest. But your re-entry into the Catholic Church cannot proceed until the marital question is settled first.

(4) If everything goes well and your situation can be rectified, there is no reason why you cannot belong to the Anglican Usage parish when it is established; that is the purpose for which the Holy See erects these entities. By the way, the Anglican Usage is part of the Latin rite, as is the Ambrosian rite (used in the Archdiocese of Milan).

Doctrine

Sacramental confusion

Q. Thanks so much for your contribution to TCA! This magazine is a blessing from heaven for my family. I'm hoping you can clarify for me some of the terminology and theology that are currently being presented at my parish.

I have recently attended several sacramental meetings for parents. The presentations seem questionable to me. During the presentation for the Sacrament of Reconciliation, the religious coordinator made the statement that after the children have left the confessional they should proceed to the pew and say some prayers. "We used to call that penance," she said. "Reconciliation is a time of joy, not fear!"

A few months later at the eucharistic meeting, the coordinator began with a story about a woman receiving a bone marrow transplant. The story ended with her son looking lovingly at the transplant material and saying, "This is my body." The coordinator concluded by saying to the group, "This, my friends, is Eucharist!" The deacon then proceeded to explain the theology of the eucharistic meal. He stated that when we consume the Eucharist, we become Eucharist! All of this sounds a bit pantheistic to me, and I simply cannot accept these sayings. Concluding, the deacon said the most important part of the Mass was the dismissal.

Last, I would like to know the proper use of the word "ministry." Enclosed is a flyer we received from the religious education office. If everything and anything we do is a "ministry," then I feel the word is meaningless.

My mind is confused, and my heart is heavy. I feel isolated, lost, and out of touch. I cannot relate to this parish. One moment I feel confident that I know and understand my faith, but the next minute I feel like a foreigner. Please help with some explanations, if you can. I fear that my children will soon become very confused.

A. First, I made my first confession in the "bad old days," and I found the Sacrament of Penance to be "a time of joy, not fear."

Creating "bogeymen" about the Church's past, recent or remote, does nothing to advance the truth.

Second, the coordinator's comments on the Eucharist must be

judged by the Church's Magisterium. In the light of *Sacrosanctum Concilium* (the Constitution on the Sacred Liturgy), from the Second Vatican Council, and the *Catechism of the Catholic Church*, her grasp and presentation of Catholic doctrine are woefully inadequate. While there is a sense in which such statements can be made, given the context of her remarks, it would seem that she is attempting to downplay the unique and irreplaceable presence of the Lord in the Blessed Sacrament. The deacon's comment is a takeoff on the German proverb, "A man is what he eats." Again, there is a sense in which what he says is true, but it must be put forward in a very nuanced manner. So, it would be more accurate to say that in consuming the Eucharistic Lord, we are challenged to become Christ for others — or some such thing. In point of fact, many of us do not do so, and therein lie our sin and scandal to others.

Third, bizarre statements found in the handout from the silly magazine *Eucharistic Minister* must be dismissed out of hand by any right-thinking person. How is one to take seriously things like the following: "We hiked to a mountaintop in Vermont and drank in the beauty of the mountains and the surrounding lakes and shared a snack at the summit — and realized we celebrated Eucharist." Or, "As I gave (the poor people) bananas, the people grasped my hands and kissed them. . . . 'Eucharist' happened through a banana." This is both stupid and sacrilegious.

Fourth, all documents of the Magisterium — from Vatican II to the pope to the Roman Curia — have refused to ascribe the word "ministry" to the non-ordained. And when the word is used in that context, it is always by way of delegation, that is, "ministry" does not belong to the laity by right or as a normal reality. In his apostolic exhortation *Christifideles Laici* (The Christian Lay Faithful), Pope John Paul II warns against "an indiscriminate use" of the word, for the very reason that you give.

Christ's presence

Q. This is not so much a specific question, but more of a request for references addressing certain observations I have made in regard to the meaning of the Eucharist.

Recently, I have seen a lot in print about the three modes of Christ's presence: in the community, in the Word, and in the Eucharist. Of these three, the presence in the community is singled out as primary. This resonates nicely with a statement which friends of mine — on the liberal side of the fence — passed on to me from their pastor, that in order to have the Eucharist there needs to be community. Along with this emphasis on the community is the adoption of the Protestant notion of the Eucharist as a meal.

Even some of the hymns used by Catholic press companies have questionable lyrics, such as: "We become for each other the bread, the cup, the presence of Christ revealed. . . ." Aside from being a dumb song, I believe the above quoted wording to be quite impossible to reconcile with a Catholic understanding of the Eucharist. Please give some guidance.

A. Let's make some important distinctions here. First, on numerous occasions I have dealt with the question of the multiple forms of the Lord's presence in the eucharistic sacrifice and, each time, have stressed what the Second Vatican Council itself said, namely, that His presence in the eucharistic species is preeminent. That must be a given, or else one is not holding to authentic Catholic doctrine.

Next, the Eucharist as a meal is not a "Protestant" concept; the meal dimension is as integral to the Catholic theology of the Eucharist as is that of sacrifice. What is Protestant is having the meal push the sacrifice out of the picture; both must go together — as they do in the *Catechism of the Catholic Church.*

While the Church certainly envisions the offering of the eucharistic sacrifice in the presence of an assembly of worshipers, that is not an absolute. The Code of Canon Law, for example, says that a priest ought not celebrate Mass without a congregation, except for serious reason (cf. Canon 906). The possibility of the exception, however, highlights a critical aspect of Catholic teaching on both the Eucharist and the priesthood: A community of five hundred cannot confect the Eucharist without an ordained priest to preside; a lone priest can confect the Eucharist without a single lay person in attendance. Now, that possibility is not normative, but it is instructive. And anyone who cannot accept that truth falls from a Catholic understanding of both sacraments.

Finally, contemporary eucharistic hymns. Aside from a handful (e.g., "Gift of Finest Wheat"), I would throw them all into a garbage heap; most of them are sentimental nothings at best and heretical at worst. The one you cite is both.

Mary's pain — and joy

Q. Did Mary suffer the Passion in her heart as Jesus suffered physically?
A. I think any mother suffers emotionally what her child suffers either physically or psychologically. Add to that Our Lady's intimate union with her Divine Son and one can legitimately imagine the inexpressible sorrow that was hers as she witnessed the rejection, passion, and death of her own innocent Son, Jesus. But to balance the budget, let us not forget the equally inexpressible joy that must have been hers as she beheld Him gloriously risen three days later.

Modernism

Q. Could you please explain the heresy of Modernism? It has me stumped.
A. Modernism has been referred to as "the synthesis of all heresies" because, slowly but surely, it erodes belief in all the essential doctrines of the Faith by attacking the very foundations of faith in general and Catholicism in particular. It was an attempt on the part of some Catholic thinkers at the turn of this century to accommodate Catholic doctrine to modern ways of thought. Some of them went to such extremes that they called into question the divinity of Christ, the inerrancy of the Scriptures, the divine origin and authority of the Church, etc. Pope St. Pius X reacted with vigor and dispatch to squelch this unhealthy approach to doctrinal development with his 1907 documents *Lamentabili* and *Pascendi Dominici Gregis*. Many people have maintained that Modernism was never totally eradicated and has reared its head again in our own age. Looking at the writings of various dissident theologians, one is compelled to see strong linkages with previously condemned positions.

Mary's place

Q. I became Catholic last year, having come into full communion from the ranks of the Presbyterians, and it has been the best decision that I have ever made! I am, however, having a problem finding the proper place for Our Lady in my life. I believe that Christ should be the focus and center of the Christian life, and I find many Marian devotions rather alarming. On the back cover of [a recent] issue of Catholic World Report, *there is an ad for a Marian consecration conference. At the bottom of the page are these words from St. Louis de Montfort: "May the soul of Mary be in each of us to glorify the Lord. . . . When will souls breathe Mary as the body breathes air?" Shouldn't we be more concerned with having our souls breathe Jesus? I am proud to be a Catholic, I adore the Church and I know there is a place for the Blessed Mother in my life because there is a place for her in the Church. I want to be 100 percent Catholic, but on this issue I am still confused. Can you please clarify my misunderstandings?*

A. Believe it or not, your own letter provides the best example of the language of exuberance or love, which is not the most precise but surely not intended to be heretical. You state that you "*adore* the Church," by which I am sure you do not in any way intend that that verb be understood literally; after all, one adores only God. In the same way, some spiritual writers are given to excess, saying things that the cold, clinical language of theology would certainly avoid.

Much of Catholicism is caught, not taught. Marian *devotion*, being devotion, is something into which one grows — unlike Marian *doctrine*, which is taught in precise categories and to which one assents with Catholic Faith. In your position, I would not delve into works like those of St. Louis de Montfort or St. Alphonsus Liguori at the outset; they reflect a culture and an age that came at things in slightly different fashion from us. I would instead suggest that you make friends with two major contemporary works of the Church's Magisterium: Pope Paul VI's *Marialis Cultus* (for the right ordering and development of devotion to the Blessed Virgin Mary) and Pope John Paul II's encyclical *Redemptoris Mater* (on the role of Mary in the mystery of Christ and her active and exemplary presence in the life of the Church), both of which are eminently readable and available from the Daughters of St. Paul, St. Paul Books & Media, 50 St. Paul's Ave., Boston, MA 02130.

New Marian title?

Q. For many years, living in areas where churchgoers are overwhelmingly evangelicals, I have substituted the phrase "Mother of God the Son" for "Mother of God." No evangelical ever misunderstood this or has disagreed with it, whereas most of them insist that "Mother of God" implies that Mary is the mother of the Trinity and, therefore, eternal.

A priest-friend of mine insists that "Mother of God the Son" is a heretical expression (Nestorian) and "splits the divine nature." Liberal Protestants, in many cases, object to the expression "God the Son," although they generally accept the expression "Son of God." Would you care to comment?

A. Your priest-friend is really correct. Part of the difficulty concerns the English translation, which seeks to render the Greek *Theotokos* or the Latin *Deipara* (literally, "God-bearer"). However, "Mother of God" is entirely correct because Jesus was and is God; therefore, since Mary brought Him into the world, it is accurate to speak of her as His mother and, as your priest notes, it is not possible to split Christ's personality.

I think your observation about the objection of many Protestants to Jesus as "God the Son" is on target, which demonstrates how closely Mariology and Christology are joined. Many theologians, including a convert like John Henry Newman, saw how a weak Mariology had the effect of giving rise to a weak Christology. And so, far from avoiding the expression, it might be wise to continue to use it so as to be able to explain it and touch on other areas at the same time.

No 'Mother God'

Q. This past summer a visiting priest came to my sister's parish where he spoke on evolution and "Father God/Mother God." My sister wrote the pastor expressing her concern that the sermon did not accurately present the teaching of the Church. The pastor supported the views of the homilist. My sister and I are not knowledgeable enough to be able to cite sources of his errors. I enclose a copy of the pastor's letter; could you please comment?

A. Your pastor is incorrect in asserting that the Scriptures refer to God as both Mother and Father. While both Testaments ascribe certain characteristics traditionally seen as "feminine" to God (e.g., tenderness, mercy, etc.) or speak of Him as being "like a mother" (metaphorically speaking, then), nowhere can one find an example of any direct address to God as "Mother," while the contrary has literally hundreds of examples which could be brought forward. Simply because an individual mystic may have used that title for God (some even called Jesus "our Mother"!), that does not mean that this should be regarded as definitive for Christian spirituality, let alone doctrine. It is certainly true that God has no gender, being a pure Spirit, but it is equally true that when human beings begin to speak about God, they need personal images, which is why Jesus taught us to call God "our Father."

As far as "the words crossed out in the lectionary" referred to in your pastor's letter, your pastor is once more off base. He claims that these changes of his are merely what has already "been approved by Rome." That is patently false; Rome has approved no changes in any lectionary. Frankly, I would be more comfortable with a priest's saying to a parishioner that he had taken it upon himself to make these changes than to play footloose with the truth and treat the laity as simpletons who know no better. The second offense is probably worse than the first.

A gift of faith

Q. Is it possible for a baptized and confirmed Catholic not to have the gift of faith? Last year our thirty-four-year-old daughter startled us by asking: "What is this gift of faith you have always talked about? What is it like? Does it happen all at once?" We now realize that she never really believed in the Church, but only went through the motions to please us. She is an obvious casualty of the post-Vatican II breakdown of legitimate religious education. Is our daughter a member of the Church in an imperfect way or a fallen-away Catholic?

As a victim of Vatican II ecumenism, she is a two-time loser. She has been in an invalid marriage for over four years; her non-Catholic husband had been through a previous marriage and divorce. They went to a deacon for instructions to plan for a Catholic wedding. He told them her husband-to-be would have to apply for an annulment which would cost $600 and that he didn't think they could get one anyway! That was the end of the instructions; they married in a Protestant ceremony. We took part in the wedding with the hope of keeping avenues open for reconciliation of her marriage in the Church. We still have that hope, but we are bitterly upset and can't understand why they could have been validly married without an annulment prior to Vatican II but not after. I truly wish that the Council had never happened.

A. You have me thoroughly confused!

First, on the question of faith. You yourself said that it was a gift, so how can we hold someone responsible for not having it if she hasn't been given it or at least doesn't know that she has it? I would suggest the need to raise your daughter's consciousness about what happened to her in Baptism and Confirmation and invite her to claim the theological virtue of faith which was poured into her when she became a member of Christ's Body, His Church, at the time of her Baptism.

The power is lying dormant, in much the same way that electrical current can be available but does no good until a switch is turned on. Furthermore, I'm not so sure that your daughter is faithless; after all, she did approach you to ask about faith, and that doesn't sound closed to the movements of grace, does it?

Second, I don't know what you mean by "a victim of Vatican II ecumenism." Surely you know that even before the Council Catholics could obtain dispensations to marry non-Catholics.

Third, if the deacon operated as he did, he should be reprimanded, but the behavior of your daughter and her would-be spouse was also rather immature. Let me add that I think your participation in the wedding ceremony was problematic, in that it gave your daughter the impression that either you approved of her invalid marriage or didn't care. Communication is never helped by sending ambiguous signals.

Fourth, your puzzlement over "why they could have been validly married without an annulment prior to Vatican II but not after" has me puzzled, to say the least. If the man was previously married to a non-Catholic woman in a non-Catholic ceremony, that was an ostensibly valid union, both before and after the Council. If he married a Catholic woman in a non-Catholic ceremony, it was invalid, both before and after the Council. If he married a Catholic in a Catholic ceremony, it was valid, before and after. So, absent any further information, I don't know how to answer that point.

Fifth, I cannot agree that "I truly wish that the Council had never happened." I truly wish that a few people would begin to take the Council seriously enough to begin its full and proper implementation.

Temporal punishment

Q. What's meant by "temporal punishment"? If Christ paid for our sins on the cross, why do we go to purgatory for temporal punishment?

A. If a husband offends his wife, he asks her forgiveness, which she extends to him readily if she perceives him to be truly sorry for his offense. However, she does have hurt feelings, and he needs to convince her by his words and deeds that he is truly sorry; hence, a night out or a bouquet of roses to make the point. Although all analogies limp (especially when we try to compare heavenly and earthly realities), the example may help us understand what is involved with the concept of "temporal punishment" due to sin. While the guilt of sin is indeed removed through the Sacrament of Penance, the demands of divine justice must be met through sacrifices and prayer in this life or else be atoned for in the next.

This should not be seen as God's offering but partial forgiveness, let alone His being vengeful or vindictive; rather, it is God's way of taking seriously our human will and giving us the opportunity to demonstrate our sincere desire for forgiveness by giving signs of our desire to make up for our lack of love toward Him and our neighbor.

Kingly astrologers

Q. The Three Kings are said to have been astrologers and it was by observing and reading the stars that they learned of the birth of Christ. Why is it that today the laity is advised not to give any credence to the science of astrology, particularly in dealing with everyday problems? I would appreciate your comments on the subject.
A. The first matter to address is your according to astrology the status of "science," which it is not.

In biblical times, astronomy and astrology were blended together. Matthew's Gospel gives no indication that it was astrological information that brought the Magi. Admittedly, even the Church tacitly tolerated astrological involvement for centuries, but once the science of astronomy demonstrated clearly the inanity of much of astrology, the Church distanced herself from that pseudo-science. The biggest problem the Church has with astrology is that not infrequently its adherents put more credence in the stars than in God and His divine providence, thus making astrological prognostications into idols.

Contradiction?

Q. Does it not seem a contradiction to believe in a place of eternal punishment and to be "pro-life"? Surely, no one would want to bring others into existence when there was a chance that they might end by experiencing eternal torture.
A. Hell is our doing, not God's. In fact, hell is a sign of God's great respect for our dignity and freedom to choose our own form of happiness, both temporal and eternal. To be "pro-life" has nothing to do with the issue, logically speaking. The only connection I can see is that good Christians would always do everything in their power to see that neither they nor anyone else would go to hell. That is accomplished

by keeping the commandments oneself and by encouraging others to do the same, by word and example.

Purgatory and Protestants

Q. Since Protestants do not believe in purgatory, when they die, do they still go there? If so, knowing that other Protestants would not pray for them, how would they ever manage to get out of purgatory and enjoy the beatific vision? Please comment.

A. Just because I don't believe in a place doesn't mean I won't end up there. If I don't accept the existence of Mars but find myself on a space ship headed in that direction, I will still land there, regardless of my own personal wishing or believing otherwise. The same is true of places like purgatory or hell.

As far as Protestants and purgatory go, you seem to evince some confusion. The souls in purgatory are aided not only by the prayers and good works of their relatives and friends but by the entire Communion of Saints. In other words, the intercession of the saints in heaven and of the Church on earth benefits them each and every day. In the eucharistic prayer, the Church prays daily for *all* the departed — not just Catholics. Protestants, by virtue of their incorporation into Christ through Baptism, are members of the one Church of Christ, even if imperfectly so.

Lastly, it is important to recall that "getting out of purgatory" is not only possible but necessary; it is, by definition, a temporary state. St. Catherine of Genoa once made the point that a day in purgatory — in spite of the pain of separation from God experienced there — is happier than all of one's earthly life put together. Why? Because once in purgatory, we have absolute assurance of the beatific vision, sooner or later. Sometimes we tend to forget that and get too mired down in negative aspects of purgatory, whose whole purpose is positive — offering us the means of purification to bring about our final and permanent face-to-face encounter with Almighty God.

A valid Eucharist?

Q. Lutherans and Episcopalians speak of the "Real Presence" with respect to the Eucharist even though they do not accept transubstantiation. Is their Eucharist a valid sacrament?

A. To have a valid Eucharist requires a valid priesthood. The general, objective judgment of the Church is that both ecclesial communities to which you refer lack apostolic succession. In certain situations, through accidents of history, particular Lutheran or Anglican communities have been found to possess a link to apostolic succession, thus providing valid orders. Beyond that, isolated Lutheran or Anglican clergymen have obtained valid orders by being ordained and/or consecrated by Eastern Orthodox bishops. It is important to note, however, that apostolic succession involves more than just having hands imposed by someone who himself stands in the line of succession; it calls for succession in true doctrine as well.

Here is just one more angle to consider also: Simply because a community does not have a valid Eucharist should not lead one to suppose that they have no life of grace at all. They do have valid Baptisms and are thus members of the Body of Christ. They have the presence of the Holy Spirit in varying degrees and thus have their reading of God's holy Word guided and graced in some measure. Our hope and prayer is that the Lord will use whatever means of grace they have at their disposal to come to a knowledge and acceptance of the full truth, which is found in communion with Peter's successor in the Apostolic See of Rome.

'Comfortable' dissent

Q. During the visit of the Holy Father to Denver for World Youth Day, many priests and nuns who advocate a married clergy, women priests, etc., managed to make their views heard through media coverage. How do these heretics retain the status granted to them as clergy and Religious? Don't Holy Orders and the profession of vows require obedience to the pope and bishops?

A. That such people are able to get media attention is no surprise since their agendas are generally quite compatible. That such people remain in the Church is also no real surprise since it is rather comfortable to be able to dissent from official teaching and yet maintain a salary, a roof over one's head, etc.

These two situations are not new to Church history, in all reality, except that media as such did not exist, but movers and shakers of public opinion did. The new development is an apparent decision on the part of the Church up until the present not to force these types of individuals to "fish or cut bait." While we have to be careful not to summarily dismiss folks from either the Church or religious life (and especially to follow correct canonical procedures), it seems to me that there comes a time when the confusion they sow is so overwhelming that it is almost impossible to teach authentic Catholic doctrine or morality because of their counter-positions being presented and advanced. Granted, Our Lord's parable of the wheat and the chaff calls for patience with the errant, but there is also ultimate accountability. I think Pope John Paul II's natural inclination is toward great forbearance, but even he seems to have reached the end of his rope with dissenters, as can be seen in the final paragraphs of his encyclical *Veritatis Splendor*, in which he calls on bishops to ensure the integrity of the Catholic moral vision and, if necessary, remove from individuals or institutions the name of "Catholic" for failure to represent accurate teaching.

I should hasten to add that neither the Pope nor I are calling for gestapo tactics but simply that people who wish to be considered Catholic begin to think and act like Catholics and deal honestly with those committed to their pastoral care. This is no more or less than what the secular sphere would speak of as "truth in advertising."

Union with God

Q. I've enclosed an article that appeared in our archdiocesan newspaper on the subject of the Eucharist. Are the thoughts expressed in "Without touch, God is monologue" sound eucharistic theology, especially the author's comparison of the Eucharist with sexual intercourse?

A. I read the article in question very carefully and find nothing problematic about it. In point of fact, the author takes most seriously Catholic teaching on the Real Presence.

I suspect your reaction may be based on a kind of squeamishness related to the sexual imagery. The metaphor is powerful and evocative, to me; but it is probably spoiled because of the perversity of so much sexual activity in our day and age. The sexual expression of love within marriage, however, is good, beautiful, and holy — indeed, the most profound form of interpersonal communication available to man on earth. And that is why St. Paul uses the marital image to describe the relationship between Christ and His Church. Perhaps if we can purify our notions and re-Christianize them, then we can see the deep significance of God's great love for us, a love so great that He allows His Sacred Body to enter ours, so that — as in marriage — the two become one flesh.

'Jesus, pray for us'?

Q. *When I was in school, we were always taught to say, "Jesus, have mercy on us." Now I notice that in various prayers they're saying, "Jesus, pray for us." Since Jesus is God, isn't this an incorrect invocation?*

A. The Letter to the Hebrews (7:25) does say that Jesus lives to make intercession for us, which is His priestly role. St. Thomas Aquinas notes that Jesus exercises His priesthood in and through His sacred humanity. When we ask Him to "have mercy on us," we are adverting to His divinity. Liturgically, the Church always addresses Christ in this latter manner. Popular piety at times and certain mystics have occasionally stressed the former. It is important to recall at all times, however, that Jesus' humanity and divinity are inseparable and need always be taken into account, if not explicitly at least implicitly.

Why intercommunion is not allowed

Q. *I am a Lutheran married to a Catholic, and our three children have been raised in the Catholic Faith. We are all devout in our respective religions and try to bridge the gap as much as possible without doing anything against either faith. We concentrate mostly on our fundamental beliefs that are the same. However, having chosen to raise my children Catholic, I work to teach them the Catholic Faith; that is why I subscribe to* The Catholic Answer. *At the same time, I am personally very dedicated to my Lutheran faith. The answer you gave to a question in [a recent] issue of TCA regarding inter-communion disturbed me.*

I wonder how you could say that the Body of Christ was broken by someone taking communion outside the Catholic Church. After all, our Lord has risen fully intact. Is not the Body of Christ a unified Church? This would seem related to the true meaning of "catholic," that is, "universal." When St. Paul speaks about the members of the body, he reminds us that no one part is greater than another.

The Evangelical Lutheran Church in America does believe that the bread and wine change into the Body and Blood of Christ. How can the Catholic Church then refuse communion to people who share this belief? Surely such a recognition can be a small step toward oneness, instead of insisting on the "broken" Body of Christ. I think you have missed the opportunity.

A. First, a matter of terminology. You refer to Catholicism and Lutheranism as "respective religions;" this is incorrect. The Lutheran confession is part of the Christian religion, as is Catholicism. "Religion" signifies a different creed, but that is not the case between us, thank God.

I didn't say that a Catholic who receives the Eucharist outside the Catholic Church breaks the Body of Christ; I said that because the Body of Christ (the Church) is sadly broken by disunity, it is wrong to receive the Eucharist from one of the "separated brethren."

In the Catholic view of things, receiving the Eucharist is a sign of unity already present, not a promise of a unity for which we wait and pray. Other Christian communities do not have the same idea about eucharistic and ecclesial communion coinciding, but we do — and we must be faithful to that vision.

I also happen to believe that it is likewise the correct understanding; after all, are any of the Protestant denominations that have engaged in intercommunion for decades now any closer, organically, than they were at the outset? I don't think so. Simply put, sloppy ecumenism does nothing — long-range — for the overall goal of a reunited Christian family.

Catholic salvation: Faith that works

Q. I have read that the Masons teach or stress salvation by good deeds and self-improvement only. I know many Protestants who are Masons and yet believe in salvation by grace (faith) alone. What is the official Catholic teaching on salvation?

A. Just what Masons believe is often hard to determine, especially in this country, where they have tended to play down their doctrinal positions.

Catholics, too, believe in "salvation by grace (faith)," properly understood. The grace of Christ moves the heart and mind of a person to faith, which launches him on his pilgrimage and sustains him throughout the process, which is lifelong. God's grace presents an individual with the gift of faith; if accepted, that person is then incorporated into Christ through Baptism (which frees one from original sin and inserts him into the Lord's paschal mystery) as well as into Christ's mystical Body, His Church.

Having become a Christian, the believer must then live like one, and that is where good works find their place. It has been said that one is not reborn by good works but to good works. Because one has received the gift of new life in Christ, he must give evidence of a lively faith by living a godly life, especially by attending to the needs of the poor and the oppressed (cf. Mt 25:31-46).

This style of life is not an attempt to curry favor with God or rack up "brownie points" to "earn" salvation; rather, it is a response of love and a powerful witness to the grace of election. For a devout Christian, there can never be any opposition between faith and works, for the first necessarily leads to the second. The Epistle of James has given classical expression to this insight: "What good is it to profess faith without practicing it? Such faith has no power to save one, has it? . . . faith without works is as dead as a body without breath" (Jas 2:14, 26).

It is critical to highlight the fact that grace is present throughout the working out of one's salvation: It is grace that first moves us to accept God's offer of salvation; it is grace that supports a loving response, renewed daily; it is grace which guarantees fruitfulness and final perseverance. Which is to say that man depends totally on Christ for his salvation which, also by divine will, engages the cooperation and participation of the human person, or, as St. Augustine put it so well: "The God Who created us without our participation has not willed to save us without our participation."

Feminist information

Q. In our diocese, we are assaulted by radical feminists who are aided and abetted by many clergy in their take-over of diocesan and parochial positions. I would like to stop engaging in skirmishes to hold them off and get to the root of the problem, which is feminism itself. Do you know of any good books on this topic, whereby I can educate myself and then give some bite-size portions to many of our priests who, in my opinion, are not bad men but largely misinformed, uninformed or terrified of these bullying women?

A. The situation you describe is not at all unique, unfortunately. I also agree with your solution, which is to obtain correct information and then to disseminate it widely.

The best book I've seen lately on all this is by Father Francis Martin, *The Feminist Question: Feminist Theology in the Light of Christian Tradition*, published by Eerdmans, Grand Rapids, Michigan. At nearly five hundred pages, $30, and heavy-duty theology, it is certainly not for the faint-hearted, but I think it provides a superb analysis of feminism, good and bad forms alike.

Donna Steichen's earlier work, *Ungodly Rage: The Hidden Face of Catholic Feminism* (Ignatius Press), is also most worthwhile in this regard.

Buddhist philosophy

Q. A friend of mine says that there is nothing wrong with engaging in Buddhist forms of meditation; in fact, that there is no conflict between Buddhism and Catholicism. I find this hard to believe.

A. There are elements of truth in all religions — a point made by the Fathers of the Second Vatican Council, to be sure, but also made by the early Church Fathers, who referred to this phenomenon as *logoi spermatikoi*, that is, "seeds of the Word." In other words, what is good and true in various religious systems can and often does serve as a preparation for the preaching and reception of the Gospel of Jesus Christ Who, however, is the only Way, Truth, and Life.

Beyond that basic point of concurrence, however, there are inherent dangers in many of these philosophical and theological traditions. The Congregation for the Doctrine of the Faith issued a similar warning a few years back — even while acknowledging what is of value in such traditions. Buddhism, by the way, is not really a religion but a philosophy.

Thomas Case, who has written for TCA, has recently published a book on his own dalliances with various spiritualities before his conversion to Catholicism. In that work *(Moonie, Buddhist, Catholic: A Spiritual Odyssey*, available for $12.95 from White Horse Press, 6723 Betts Avenue, Cincinnati, OH 45239; phone 513-522-8615), he describes his own sadness at having gone to a priest for a serious discussion about entering the Church, only to have the priest launch into a lecture on the glories of Buddhism. Mr. Case writes the following: "I realized in a flash that I could entertain this priest for hours about my Buddhist adventures (a story with the real thing, a real Tibetan Lama), and he would be attentive and excited. I despaired. Was the Church so vacated of spiritual substance that the best and the brightest had to go elsewhere? I was trying to step up to the higher mysticism of the Church, while this priest and his clientele were co-opting a religious expression I had left behind in Boulder. I felt like I was light-years ahead of the priest in experience. I was polite; I said nothing about my Buddhist past."

I think that pretty well summarizes the situation.

Supplementary text

Q. I'm in a dilemma as a religion teacher. Our diocesan education office has insisted that we use a text book which is good in the various methods it employs, especially regarding activities, but is watery when it comes to the content of the Faith. The director wants this text used, to the exclusion of supplementary material. She thinks this will present a more uniform approach to the Faith. There are other good texts (known to me personally) which could give more solid teaching to the children. As a teacher within the program, am I bound to obey her directive?

A. If the required text contains no heresy, I would use it, yes. But I think the diocesan director of religious education certainly exceeds her authority in banning *supplementary* material. In almost every course, good teachers supplement even excellent texts with enrichment aids.

Papal authority

Q. I was not fortunate in being born into the Catholic Faith; however, I converted when I was a teenager. My cousin is a member of the Greek Orthodox Church and has raised some disturbing questions, for which I did not have ready answers. Would you please give some direction on the following points my cousin brought up: (1) There was no pope in the Roman Catholic Church for the first 700 to 800 years. (2) The first Church that Christ established was the Greek Orthodox in Constantinople. I am convinced that my cousin is wrong on both accounts; please help.

A. Yes, she is, and no Orthodox theologian would ever hold to her theories — let alone any secular historian.

What most Orthodox theologians would argue is not that popes did not exist in Rome for the first several centuries but that they did not have the authority or jurisdiction of later periods. Some would also argue that the primacy of Peter within the apostolic college was not transferred or transferable to any of Peter's successors in the See of Rome. On that point, one can have an intelligent discussion, and the two Churches are indeed involved in serious theological dialogue on that front.

That Christ established the Church of Constantinople would come as a surprise even for Patriarch Bartholomew, the current bishop of that see!

A sense of faith

Q. In my reading I came across the term sensus fidelium. *The Catholic* Woman *by Jeanne Pieper says that this is a long-held teaching in the Church. I would like to know if this is true and if you could explain the teaching more thoroughly.*

A. The *Catechism of the Catholic Church* explains the expression thus: "All the faithful share in understanding and handing on revealed truth. They have received the anointing of the Holy Spirit, who instructs them [cf. 1 *Jn* 2:20, 27] and guides them into all truth"[cf. *Jn* 16:13] (91). Then quoting *Lumen Gentium* (The Vatican II Dogmatic Constitution on the Church), the text continues: "The whole body of the faithful . . . cannot err in matters of belief. This characteristic is shown in the supernatural appreciation of faith (*sensus fidei*) on the part of the whole people, when, 'from the bishops to the last of the faithful,' they manifest a universal consent in matters of faith and morals" [*LG* 12; cf. St. Augustine *De praed. sanct.* 14, 27: PL 44, 980] (92). And last but not least, it concludes with this: "By this appreciation of the faith, aroused and sustained by the Spirit of truth, the People of God, guided by the sacred teaching authority (*Magisterium*), . . . receives the faith, once for all delivered to the saints. . . . The People unfailingly adheres to this faith, penetrates it more deeply with right judgment, and applies it more fully in daily life" [*LG* 12; cf. *Jude* 3] (93).

Some people have misapplied this notion to argue that when some of Christ's lay faithful disagree with Church teaching that they can act on that feeling of theirs because they have the Spirit as well as the hierarchy. As can be seen from the text cited above, no justification for such a position can be found.

Celestial ordering?

Q. A visiting priest during his homily at Mass recently indicated that there would be a "pecking order" in heaven, depending on the type of life one had lived here on earth. Is this official Catholic teaching? And if so, where in the Scriptures is this view substantiated?

A. There is no official teaching of the Church on this, but many theologians from Aquinas to the present day have argued for what your homilist said. They maintain that, in a sense, God takes us where we are and puts us where we would be happiest. The *Catechism of the Catholic Church* has a fine discussion on the life of heaven (1023-

1029) but maintains a discrete silence on the point you raise. Very often people bring forth John 14:2 as the scriptural basis for a theory like the one you heard: "In my Father's house there are many dwelling places."

Side effect?

Q. Why do some priests consecrate hosts for the faithful every time they celebrate Mass? It seems that one of the side effects of this is that many no longer believe in the Real Presence after Mass and Communion.

A. Throughout this entire century, but especially from Pope Pius XII onwards, the Roman pontiffs and the appropriate Roman dicasteries have not only encouraged but even mandated that hosts be consecrated in such a way that the faithful may receive as Holy Communion altar breads consecrated within the context of the celebration which they attend. The purpose for the reservation of the Blessed Sacrament is, first of all, as Communion for the sick, and then for adoration; it is not the intention of the Church, however, that a priest consecrate a month's supply of hosts and then keep going to the tabernacle for regular use at Masses. Now, common sense also comes into play, too; if hosts remain after a Mass, they naturally must be reserved and, sooner or later, used — even at another Mass.

The Church's thought on all this is to make sure the connection is clear between this particular offering of the eucharistic sacrifice and the sharing of the fruits of that celebration with those present. By the way, this is one of the strongest arguments against "priestless Eucharists," in which pre-consecrated hosts are distributed; it is an argument of necessity, because such services lack the visible linkage between priesthood and Eucharist and also between sacrifice and communion.

Useless resentment

Q. We were taught that Baptism is administered to take away original sin. Period. Now I have learned that the Catholic Church — and other denominations, I presume — baptize to make the person a member of a certain denomination. If I was baptized to take away original sin, I am thankful for that, but I resent being made a member of a certain denomination without my knowledge or consent. Can my Baptism be declared null because I was not fully informed and did not give consent?

A. While Baptism does indeed remove original sin from the soul, it does more than that. It does something positive as well, namely, incorporating one into the Body of Christ, which is His Church. In point of fact, Baptism does not make a person a denominational member; it makes one a Christian and, by that very fact, a member of the one Church founded by Jesus Christ — even if only in an imperfect manner. That is why when a non-Catholic Christian "converts," we say that he is being "received into full communion" with the Catholic Church; prior to that, he was not in "full" communion but was in a relationship with the Catholic Church which was — depending upon the denomination — deep (Eastern Orthodox, for example) or less so (Methodist, Presbyterian, etc.).

The Catholic Church is not a denomination; it is the one true Church. If you resent having been baptized into that fullness of truth and life, you have a problem with Baptism in general and not just the aspect you identify. One cannot undo one's Baptism because, as St. Paul teaches, God's gifts and His call are "irrevocable" (Rom 11:29). Furthermore, one should see that membership in Christ's Church comes not through personal choice but through divine election, just as is the case for one who is born into a Jewish family. One becomes a member of the Chosen People simply by virtue of having a Jewish mother, with no more personal choice involved than was the case in deciding on whether or not to be born.

In short, you should be rejoicing that God's love was lavished upon you in making you a part of His holy Church, rather than spending your time in useless resentment.

Eucharist and unity

Q. If the Catholic Church in America were to split from the Church of Rome, would attending an American Catholic Church service and receiving the Eucharist be valid?

A. First of all, I don't see any such development on the horizon, if for no other reason than the fact that so many of the folks that are disposed in that direction know that they are doing far better financially and in terms of prestige by staying within the Church, instead of by forming a fledgling institution which would have no status, let alone monetary backing.

Presuming that validly ordained priests joined such a community, their Eucharists would be valid. Attendance at such a Mass, however, would be a schismatic act since it would be encouraging the split and using the Eucharist (the sacrament of unity) to advance disunity and even heresy. This is the exact same judgment to which one would have to come in reference to Masses celebrated by priests of the late Archbishop Marcel Lefebvre.

Anything that aids and abets the destruction of unity in the Church is sinful, and using the Eucharist to "seal" such moves is blasphemous.

Son in hell?

Q. I was reading Father Van Hove's article, "Prayers for the Dead" in [a recent] issue of The Catholic Answer. *As I understand, death does not sever the relationship between the living and the dead. If this is the case, how can a mother be happy in heaven if her son is in hell? As Father Van Hove says, "Divine love overcomes everything, even death. Bonds of love uniting us creatures, living and dead, and the Lord Who is resurrected, are celebrated both on All Saints' Day and All Souls' Day." So if the bonds between the living and the dead are not severed, surely the bonds between two dead souls cannot be severed; therefore, surely a mother could not simply forget her son. Please comment.*

A. There are many mysteries associated with death, but the one you point to is frequently raised by people who fear that a loved one may have died in the state of mortal sin. "How could I ever be happy in heaven knowing that my son is in hell?" And, of course, having perfect knowledge in heaven, the mother would know and not merely suspect this.

Theologians like St. Thomas Aquinas have tried to deal with this apparent dilemma by informing us that our love for God in heaven will be so intense and the power of the beatific vision so overwhelming, that no earthly relationship or sorrow connected to it could ever diminish the experience of life, love, and joy given to the blessed in heaven. I find that to be a reasonable and satisfying explanation.

At the same time, we must admit that all our attitudes and expectations of the afterlife are, necessarily, conditioned by life here below; it is essential to recall, however, that life in the hereafter is so qualitatively different that it might be fair to say that what we do not know about it is far greater than what we do know.

What is sure, though, is that a gracious and loving God would never permit us to be eternally weighed down by a sadness which would detract from our eternal bliss, and so, it is probably best to leave it in His fatherly hands.

What's essential?

Q. My father claims that the Church changes its mind on teachings for its own sake. He cites changes in the Mass and says they have removed some saints, especially St. Christopher. Has the Church changed any beliefs or doctrines? Do we still believe in St. Christopher?

A. First of all, we don't "believe in St. Christopher" or any other saint: we only believe in the Triune God.

It is important to distinguish between essentials and non-essentials in the Catholic Faith. Matters of discipline or non-substantive liturgical matters have changed dozens of times over the Church's two-thousand-year history. What cannot change — and has never changed — is the substance of Catholic doctrine. Now, that does not mean that our understanding of doctrine is static; on the contrary, being faithful to the truth of the Faith sometimes requires us to present the truth in a form that is more in keeping with contemporary needs and linguistic changes.

Furthermore, the Church, under the guidance of the Holy Spirit and with the assistance of faithful theologians, comes to a deeper appreciation of certain teachings as time goes on; this process is referred to as the development of doctrine. It is similar in some ways to a wife slowly but surely getting to know her husband better with each passing year; presumably, her insights into his personality and identity are far more finely tuned on their fiftieth anniversary than they are on their fifth. Why? Not because she has come up with a new image for her husband, but because their faithful and loving union gives her access to aspects of the relationship which only time and much devotion can offer. It is much the same with the Church as she strives to know and understand her Spouse, Jesus Christ, Who promised that His Holy Spirit would guide her "to all truth" (Jn 16:13).

As far as particular saints are concerned, the Church never said these individuals never existed or "de-canonized" them; all the Church did was rework the liturgical calendar and remove several who had become rather obscure and whose stories were more heavily shrouded in legend than in verifiable fact.

Birth of the Church

Q. In Cardinal Ratzinger's book of daily meditations he writes: "Mary didn't hesitate to stand under the Cross; she was present when the Church came into being." During the Paschal supper on the night before He died, Christ instituted the sacraments of the Holy Eucharist and Holy Orders, which presuppose a valid Baptism, to which Confirmation was organically joined originally. And, since there's no dogma of apostolic preservation from personal sin, we'd also expect an absolution of some kind. Does this imply that the sacraments antedated the founding or the institution or the coming into being of the Church? Does this mean that the apostles were ordained to the service of — and Peter the head of — a nonexistent Church? Can you please help clarify this issue?

A. We have to be very careful when we use later theological language and transfer it to an earlier epoch. And that is surely the case when we start talking about the apostles and the sacraments. After all, our concepts about the sacraments took centuries to refine; it would be most unrealistic to assume that the apostles had some kind of intuitive knowledge of all this from the start.

First, when we speak of Our Lord's institution of sacraments during His earthly life and ministry, we do so in a most nuanced manner. When we point to John chapter two as a foundation for the Sacrament of Matrimony, we do not mean that the couple in question entered into what today we would call a sacramental union. We would say, however, that Our Lord's presence and activity at Cana indicate His esteem for the natural state of marriage and that St. Paul's reflections on the spousal union and how it ties in with Christ's relationship to His Church provide us with the basis for our understanding that Christ "raised marriage to the dignity of a sacrament."

Second, I think it quite correct to say that from the first moment of the incarnation, the Church came into existence. Why? Following the ecclesiology of *Lumen Gentium* (The Dogmatic Constitution on the Church), one could say that Jesus is the primordial Sacrament, that is, the sign of the Father's love for man. The Church, in her turn, embodies Christ's salvific mission, so that she becomes a sacrament of Him.

Third, the seven rites which we classify as sacraments are extensions of the saving presence and ministry of the Lord Himself. In other words, once Almighty God "decided" that He wished to communicate with the human race by means of signs, starting with His own Son as

God-made-Man, the whole sacramental structure of salvation was implicit and just "waiting" to be worked out.

Finally, taking Cardinal Ratzinger's line, I would say that Our Lady was indeed present "when the Church came into being." She was there at three different moments: at the Annunciation, when the Word became flesh thus inaugurating a mode of salvation involving earthly realties; at the foot of the cross, when blood and water (symbolizing Baptism and Eucharist) flowed from the Savior's wounded side; and on Pentecost, when the "gestation" period of the Church had come to full term with the Church's "birth" from the Holy Spirit and her subsequent mission to the world.

The Bread of Life

Q. Our parish priest does not like the memorial acclamation, "When we eat this bread and drink this cup . . ." because it incorrectly refers to the consecrated species as "bread" when in reality it is the Body of Christ, I tend to agree with him. Is this another attempt to introduce erroneous teaching through faulty translations?

A. I understand your priest's concern and empathize; I also see it as a translation problem, but this time I don't perceive a malicious intent. The acclamation, as you know, is a direct citation from St. Paul's First Epistle to the Corinthians (11:26); as such, it obviously cannot be heretical. The difficulty comes in attempting to translate the Greek word *artos*, which can mean "bread" or "loaf," etc. Most Romance languages, for example, use a similar word that can carry a variety of meanings; English does not possess one such word. When we say that we eat "this bread," we really mean "this loaf," which admits of a significance beyond that of simple or natural bread. At the same time, we must also recall that Our Lord referred to Himself as "the Bread of Life." Given the abysmal lack of eucharistic faith today, this all merely points up the need for constant, ongoing catechesis to reinforce the very basics of our Catholic Faith — from the pulpit, in the classroom, through personal study and, most especially, by a devout and reverent celebration of the eucharistic sacrifice.

Yes, confession is necessary

Q. My husband is a non-Catholic. He attends Mass with me regularly and was supportive of a Catholic education for our six children, who are now grown. I have long prayed that he might be given the grace to embrace the true Faith. He has a problem with the words in the Creed, "I confess one Baptism for the remission of sins." He does not see confession to a priest as necessary; he says one Baptism is enough. We have been through the scriptural reference in the Gospel of St. John. Can you provide any additional information?

A. No creed is a complete statement of faith, and is never intended to be such. One must always rely on the Church that produced the creed to provide background, context, etc. In reality, the Fathers of the Church often referred to the Sacrament of Penance as a "second Baptism." Furthermore, even Martin Luther regarded Penance as a true sacrament, precisely because he was convinced by the scriptural texts and the witness of the early Church.

Regular readers will recall that TCA had a series on the sacraments; Penance was covered in the July/August 1993 issue, to which I would refer you and him for a detailed discussion covering the scriptural, doctrinal, and patristic bases for this sacrament.

Purgatory and Revelation

Q. After a Karl Keating seminar and a "Catholic Answers" tract, I still can't understand the teaching on purgatory. Scripture says "we are appointed once to die and then the judgment" and also that when we die we are "absent from the body and present with the Lord." Does God say that He is with us in purgatory? If Jesus is our Savior, why do the souls in purgatory have to depend on the prayers and sacrifices of the living? Purgatory seems like a very flimsy safety net to me. Is it only taught as a part of Tradition, or is there also a scriptural basis to it?

A. The doctrine of purgatory is poorly understood by many, which is why the November/December 1994 issue of TCA had two articles dealing with it. This is especially appropriate during November, the month traditionally designated as that of the poor souls in purgatory. So let me refer you to those pieces for the main point, but your last sentence is more troubling because it demonstrates a crypto-fundamentalism.

For a truly Catholic understanding of divine revelation, I would suggest a careful reading of Vatican II's *Dei Verbum*, the Dogmatic Constitution on Divine Revelation. The following passages are worthy of thoughtful reflection and analysis: "Sacred Tradition and Sacred Scripture, then, are bound closely together, and communicate one with the other. For both of them, flowing out from the same divine well-spring, come together in some fashion to form one thing, and move towards the same goal. Sacred Scripture is the speech of God as it is put down in writing under the breath of the Holy Spirit. And Tradition transmits in its entirety the Word of God which has been entrusted to the apostles by Christ the Lord and the Holy Spirit. It transmits it to the successors of the apostles so that, enlightened by the Spirit of truth, they may faithfully preserve, expound and spread it abroad by their preaching. Thus it comes about that the Church does not draw her certainty about all revealed truths from the Holy Scriptures alone. Hence, both Scripture and Tradition must be accepted and honored with equal feelings of devotion and reverence" (no. 9). Furthermore, "the task of giving an authentic interpretation of the Word of God, whether in its written form or in the form of Tradition, has been entrusted to the living teaching office of the Church alone" (no. 10). And finally, "it is clear, therefore, that, in the supremely wise arrangement of God, Sacred Tradition, Sacred Scripture and the Magisterium of the Church are so connected and associated that one of them cannot stand without the others. Working together, each in its own way under the action of the one Holy Spirit, they all contribute effectively to the salvation of souls" (no. 10).

Degrees of unity

Q. The following notice appeared on the door at the entrance of a monastery chapel: "The Roman Catholic and Orthodox churches see the reception of the Eucharist as a sign of the unity that exists with their communions. In faithfulness to their ancient truth, we cannot extend the invitation to receive the Sacrament to our brothers and sisters of other churches and faiths. Nonetheless, we earnestly invite all to join with us in Christ's prayer for the unity of His followers."

I do not see where there is unity between the Orthodox and Roman Catholic Churches, as is implied in the notice. Also, there is some contradiction here if one reads the guidelines for receiving Communion published in the missalettes and issued by the National Conference of Catholic Bishops. Finally, are there some guidelines to be followed if one receives the sacraments between the two Faiths?

A. Let me start by saying that I think that if you have copied the notice accurately, there is an internal contradiction. I suspect that the writer meant the following: "The Catholic and Orthodox Churches regard the reception of Holy Communion as a sign of full unity and, because that unity is not full between our Churches, it is inappropriate to engage in eucharistic sharing." That is certainly the position of both our communities.

Now, on to your observations. Ecclesial unity admits of degrees. For example, the extent of doctrinal agreement between a Catholic and a Baptist is considerable, in terms of the basics of Christian faith: Trinity, divinity of Christ, virginal conception of Jesus, the Lord's bodily resurrection and future return in glory, etc. With the Orthodox, however, we add an entire dimension of theological consensus on the very things that most Protestants, for instance, see as incredibly problematic— the nature of Tradition, the sacramental system, apostolic succession, devotion to the saints — indeed, the only serious sticking point is the matter of papal primacy and infallibility. Most importantly of all, we hold that because they possess valid Orders, they likewise celebrate valid sacraments. Hence, it is quite correct to assert that while our unity is not full, it is substantial.

As far as reception of each other's sacraments, I have treated this on several previous occasions.

A summary statement would be the following: In emergency situations, both Churches permit members of the sister church to receive the sacraments from a priest of the other communion. The Catholic position would actually allow for an even broader extension of this, but the Orthodox Church does not; therefore, out of respect for their discipline, we hold the line where they do.

To rise again

Q. In the Apostles' Creed we say: "on the third day He rose again from the dead" and in St. Mark's Gospel it says, "and on the third day he will rise again" (Mk 10:34). What is the significance of the word "again" in both of these citations? It seems to imply that He had risen before. Please comment.

A. The problem is one of translating correctly the Latin *resurgere*, which can mean "to rise again" or simply "to rise." This difficulty is not new, as even a cursory look at old missals and prayer books will demonstrate; both translations appear to have been used interchangeably over the centuries.

Deification

Q. A question came up at a prayer meeting that none of us understood, and we hope you can explain it. One person had read a statement that God became man so that man might become God. Also, St. Basil is said to have made the following statement: "We attain what is beyond our most sublime aspirations — we become God." Can you clarify these statements please?

A. I am not familiar with the precise formulation of St. Basil, which you cite, but the thought is certainly very common in patristic literature. St. Augustine, for example, says "God became man that men might become gods." Furthermore, in the rite for the mingling of the water and wine, the priest prays, "May we come to share in the divinity of Christ Who humbled Himself to share in our humanity." This process, technically known as "deification" or "theosis," has its scriptural roots in a passage like 2 Peter 1:4, where we read that God has called us to "become partakers of the divine nature."

Now, this should not be understood in any kind of Mormon or New Age sense, whereby we become God's equals or become a part of the Divinity in the way in which the Persons of the Blessed Trinity are. It is important to recall that in and through Baptism (and the other sacraments, too), we become "sons in the Son." Jesus is the Son of God from all eternity by nature; you and I enter into a relationship of filiation with the Father through grace. In other words, our relationship to the Father is qualitatively different from that of Jesus' — and always will be. With all those necessary caveats in place, however, it is truly astonishing to realize the great dignity that is ours as God's adopted children and heirs to eternal life. This doctrinal truth, of course, is the source for our resolve to lead truly moral lives, which point was consistently driven home by St. Paul and reaffirmed by Pope John Paul II in *Veritatis Splendor.*

The Pope on hell

Q. Some time back I heard Father Andrew Greeley react to the Pope's book, Crossing the Threshold of Hope. *He said that the Pope is not as "conservative" as some might think and gave, as an example of the Holy Father's supposed "liberalism," his apparent willingness to leave open the question of the existence of hell. Both my wife and I then read the appropriate pages (178-187) and found ourselves somewhat mystified that perhaps Greeley had gotten it right for once: The Pope does really sound "soft" on hell. What's your reading of this?*

A. It's truly amazing how different people can read the same text and come up with incredibly divergent understandings! Of course, the old Latin philosophical adage said, "*Quodquod recipitur in modo recipientis recipitur*" (Whatever is received is received according to the mind of the receiver); in short, we tend to interpret reality through our own particular lenses or prism.

I have read the Pope's comments on the afterlife rather carefully and all I find is traditional Catholic teaching. For example, on page 183, he says that "preachers, catechists, teachers . . . no longer have the courage to preach the threat of hell. And perhaps even those who listen to them have stopped being afraid of hell." I think that is clearly the case. Two pages later, the Pope writes that "the problem of hell has always disturbed great thinkers in the Church," which is true. He immediately goes on to note that the Church has always rejected any teaching in this regard which would, in effect, do away with hell because divine revelation would not permit such and because human dignity and responsibility seem to demand its existence. Once that is said, he then makes the point that the Church "has never made any pronouncement" on who has or ever will be consigned to hell — and once more he is right and "traditional." So, where does one find either "softness" or elimination of the teaching?

St. Peter's faith

Q. In paragraph 424 of the Catechism of the Catholic Church, *it is stated that "On the rock of this faith confessed by St. Peter, Christ built His Church." The confession of faith by St. Peter is found in the Gospel: "You are the Christ, the Son of the living God." It has been my understanding that Christ established His Church on St. Peter himself, rather than on his faith. Building His Church on St. Peter would affirm Peter as the "founding father" or pope of the Catholic Church.*

Please clarify whether Christ built His Church on Peter's faith or on Peter himself.

A. Peter was chosen by Our Lord precisely because there was in him a unity between his person and his faith; they were inseparable. If we read commentaries of various Fathers of the Church on the Petrine primacy, we discover patristic authors who use both expressions. Vatican

II's *Lumen Gentium* (Dogmatic Constitution on the Church) speaks of the Church "which the Lord founded upon the apostles and built upon blessed Peter their leader" (no. 19).

Regardless of how the matter is phrased, the incontrovertible witness of the New Testament is that Peter exercised a primacy within the apostolic college held by no other member of that body. A good analysis of all this is offered in Father Raymond Brown's book, *Peter in the New Testament* (Paulist Press).

By the way, the pope is not head of the Roman Catholic Church alone; he is head of the whole Catholic Church. As bishop of the Diocese of Rome (the Roman Church), he is the visible head of the entire Church, with all her particular churches and rites. That is why I rather studiously avoid the use of the expression "Roman Catholic," and why we published Kenneth Whitehead's article on this topic in the May/June 1995 issue of TCA.

Creed variations

Q. I've noticed that the wording of the Apostles' Creed seems to contain two versions. One says, "He descended to the dead," while the other says, "He descended into hell."

Are both versions correct? Is the difference significant? Please explain.

A. These are equivalent terms. The hell being referred to is not, of course, the hell of the damned but the abode of the dead: *Sheol* (Hebrew) or *Hades* (Greek). The *Catechism of the Catholic Church* uses them interchangeably. Thus we read: "By the expression 'He descended into hell,' the Apostles' Creed confesses that Jesus did really die and through his death for us conquered death and the devil 'who has the power of death' (*Heb* 2:14)" (636).

Norm for salvation

Q. Does the Church hold that people who do not follow Jesus and do not qualify as being ignorant of His teachings (e.g., Jews, Muslims, etc.) absolutely cannot go to heaven?

A Baptist friend of mine says that if you are aware of Jesus' teaching and still don't follow Him, remaining a Jew or Muslim, you can never get to heaven. And if you can get to heaven by staying in your original faith, then what's the point of Jesus' coming, he asks.

A. The norm for salvation is explicit membership in the Catholic Church, however, the Church teaches that those who either have not heard the Gospel or are not convinced of its truth can be saved by living a good life and in ways known only to God.

So, your Baptist friend is right — up to a point. Simply being aware of someone's teachings does not constitute conviction that the teachings are correct. For instance, I am reasonably well informed of the doctrines of Islam, but I do not "buy" them; they move me neither emotionally nor intellectually. Besides that, I find the behavior of all too many Muslims to be problematic — and to be so precisely in conformity with traditional Islamic beliefs.

Applying all this to Christianity, one can say that just because a Jew or Muslim knows about Catholic theology, there is no guarantee that the Faith has been properly and convincingly presented. Furthermore, it is not inconceivable that what he has seen of the Catholic faithful has become a stumbling block to his acceptance of Christ. Therefore, his culpability is diminished or totally negated.

What is the purpose of Christ's coming, if salvation is available otherwise? Simply put, the Incarnation of the Son of God graced our world in a definitive manner, such that nothing else can ever happen here which remains untouched by His presence. In this way, one can say that anyone who is ever saved is saved by Christ Himself because God (in His Christ) pitched His tent among us, died for all men, and has given us the promise of everlasting life in and through Him.

In the case of a deliberate and conscious decision to refuse membership in Christ's Church, the Second Vatican Council says the following: "Hence they could not be saved who, knowing that the Catholic Church was founded as necessary by God through Christ, would refuse either to enter it or to remain in it" (*Lumen Gentium*), [Dogmatic Constitution on the Church], no. 14).

Virgin birth

Q. At a religious information class conducted by our priest, the subject of the birth of Christ was discussed. He said that the Blessed Virgin Mary did not actually give birth to the Christ Child — He merely appeared in her arms. His reasoning was that if Mary had actually given birth, she would no longer be a virgin. Can you please explain the Church's teaching on Mary's perpetual virginity?

A. While popular piety and certain spiritual writers have spoken in language similar to that of your pastor, the Church's teaching authority has been very careful about expressing itself in that way. The reason is that even the verb you used ("appeared") has the seeds of heresy.

In the early Church, a group called Docetists came on the scene, declaring that the Son of God merely "appeared" or "seemed" (Greek, *dokeo*, to appear) to have a human body and, subsequently, only "appeared" to suffer on the cross, etc. In other words, when the humanity of Christ is questioned, it invalidates the entire mystery of the Incarnation and the work of redemption in one fell swoop.

One should then be equally skittish about simplistic theological explanations of complex doctrines. While it is essential to maintain the belief in Our Lady's virginity before, during, and after the birth of Jesus, officially the Church keeps a respectful and even holy silence about what was entailed in the act of birth. Surely, one should stand in awe of this mystery and not probe into it in a prurient or invasive manner.

I am not comfortable, however, with the proposal of your pastor because of the potential to rip the guts out of the reality of the birth of the Word-made-flesh.

Purgatory question

Q. I was taught that the souls in purgatory cannot see or communicate with God until they enter heaven after their time of purification. Now I have heard some people talking about praying to the souls in purgatory, so that they might pray for us. Can the souls in purgatory pray for us? Please help clarify this issue.

A. I was always taught that the poor souls in purgatory can and do pray for us in the Church on earth. And this makes perfect sense when we think of the Church as "the Communion of Saints," whereby all are concerned about the salvation of all and involved in effecting that in one way or another. In other words, while our usual focus on those in purgatory is their need of our prayers (which is true), it would be unseemly for them to be but passive recipients of our intercessory efforts. Indeed, the very rationale for the state of purgation is the active engagement of the poor souls in their own purification, which is a sign of their desire to pass through this process into the full experience of the beatific vision.

The *Catechism of the Catholic Church* puts it thus: "Our prayer for them is capable not only of helping them, but also of making their intercession for us effective" (958).

Marian feasts

Q. Could you please explain the difference between the feasts of the Annunciation and the Immaculate Conception? I find this confusing.

A. The Immaculate Conception, celebrated on December 8, commemorates that doctrine whereby Our Lady was preserved from all stain of original sin from the very first moment of her conception in the womb of her mother, St. Anne. The Annunciation, observed on March 25, honors the event of the Incarnation as Mary heard the angel's message, agreed to be the Mother of the Messiah, and conceived Him in her womb by the Holy Spirit.

The point of confusion is that when some people hear "immaculate conception," they tend to equate that with "virginal conception," which is something entirely different. Mary was immaculately conceived, yes, but not virginally conceived. Our Lord, on the other hand, was virginally conceived (no human father) and likewise immaculately conceived (that is, no transmission of original sin occurred). The privilege of Mary's immaculate conception was hers in view of her divine maternity; in other words, so that she could be the worthy bearer of the sinless Son of God, God redeemed her in advance of the rest of the human race by virtue of the salvation her own Son would bring.

Church documents

Q. I have noticed various types of documents from the Vatican, the pope and his predecessors. Could you please distinguish among them and give the reason why there are different terms applied to these documents? Are some infallible? How would one know a document's status or weight? My list follows: professions of faith, ecumenical councils, synods, letters from pontiffs and replies, papal bulls, constitutions, encyclicals, apostolic exhortations or letters, and declarations. I am sure there are others.

A. There are indeed varying degrees of ecclesiastical teaching, conveyed, first of all, by the type of document used.

Professions of faith are, by their very nature, solemn documents, enshrining solemn teaching. Conciliar or synodal documents can carry different weights; at Vatican II, for example, the order of importance ran as follows: dogmatic constitution; constitution; decree; declaration. Similarly, with papal teaching, the texts would generally fall into the following order: bulls; constitutions; encyclicals; exhortations; letters/ replies. The degree of seriousness is usually apparent from the style and content of the text, and the degree of assent to the teaching should then reach a commensurate level.

Communion of Saints

Q. I came to the Faith nine years ago from a Baptist family and been trying to explain to my parents the Communion of Saints and why we can, as opposed to Baptist theology, ask the saints to pray for us. I showed them Luke 16:19-31, the parable of the Rich Man and Lazarus. That made no impact at all. Dad, with whom I was speaking at the time, said, "All that tells me is that it doesn't work!" Can you offer any advice as to how I might explain the Communion of Saints to them with scriptural backing? They also think that asking the saints to pray for us obscures Christ's one mediatorship.

A. In my experience, I have found that the basic problem for most non-Catholics is that they possess a faulty notion of life after death — that is, they conceive of it in terms not unlike those of the pagan Greeks and Romans, as some type of shadowy existence which is not quite real. Death for Christians, however, is life to God.

Surely, all Christians would see no difficulty in being asked to pray for someone else's intentions. If we can do that, with all our sins, why not the saints in glory, unless, of course, we don't believe that they are truly alive? I think that's the point that needs to be driven home: the reality of one's interim state until the General Judgment and, equally, the importance of a sense of Christian solidarity, which is not nullified by death. The *Catechism* deals with all this very well in paragraphs 988-1019 and 946-975.

Heresy-less

Q. "Were a pope to teach heresy, the College of Cardinals would have to convene to deal with the crisis and elect a successor." Is this statement accurate? Is it even possible that a pope can err in teaching faith and morals, as implied in the premise? If the pope can teach heresy, requiring correction from some higher authority, may we conclude that an error was made in the 1870 pronouncement of the First Vatican Council on papal infallibility?

A. The charism of infallibility, conferred on the Church by her Lord and exercised under certain conditions by the Sovereign Pontiff, is the very guarantee that such an eventuality is not possible. Try as hard as some opponents of the papacy do to find exceptions to this in history, they are unable to do so. Even the most sinful popes have never taught heresy — granted, they may not have taught the truth in all its fullness and splendor, but they did not teach falsehood. And, remember, infallibility is a "negative" guarantee, not a positive — that is, it is the assurance that a pope or council will always be preserved from teaching heresy.

By the way, according to Catholic doctrine, no body in the Church (including the College of Cardinals) is above the pope.

Purgatorial time

Q. *I asked our parish priest to say a Mass for each of three friends that have recently passed away. He said he would be glad to do so, and I received a notice from the rectory that it would be a year before the Masses could be said. Is the length of time in purgatory the same as here on earth? If someone has been gone for forty years, is it possible that he could still be in purgatory? If not, are our prayers utilized for other poor souls?*

A. First off, purgatory (like heaven and hell) exists outside time, which is why the Scriptures speak of a day being like a thousand years and a thousand years like a day (2 Pt 3:8). Purgatory can "last" as long as an individual needs it to be purified to live in the presence of Love. And, yes, works of expiation not "needed" by someone do not get "wasted" due to our doctrine of the Communion of Saints; in other words, we are all able to share in each other's merits.

A mystery so great

Q. *Whatever happened to the "Mystical Body of Christ," which is no longer mentioned in the Catholic Church, having been replaced by the jargon of "the faith community"? The understanding of the Church as the Mystical Body of Christ and the Bride of Christ figured prominently in the writings of Pope Pius XII. Why are the writings of this great pope so much ignored by contemporary Catholic leadership?*

As for me, I wonder about this "renewal," which is dumbing down and protestantizing the Catholic Church in the United States.

A. *Lumen Gentium* (Dogmatic Constitution on the Church), promulgated at the Second Vatican Council, was quite clear in stressing the fact that the mystery of the Church was so great and profound that no one image could capture her full reality. Hence the Council Fathers assembled a wide array of metaphors, ranging from "People of God" to "Body of Christ," the point being that all of these are mutually reinforcing, and by no means should any be perceived as mutually exclusive. The *Catechism of the Catholic Church* takes the very same tack (770-801).

God is love

Q. Does God love the devil?

A. Believe it or not, this is a most profound and not easily answered question. God hates sin and evil, but He does not hate anyone — including the fallen angels. Now, the situation with them was different than the case is with us. Why? Because angels are pure spirits, they are not affected by passions and have perfect intellects, so that they see and understand the truth of things instantly. Therefore, one sin from them was sufficient for their damnation. And ever since, they have been the enemies of God — by their own choosing.

God, however, is love. Therefore, He loves all and their refusal to love in return causes Him to be sad — if we might speak about God in human language. The devil and his angels, on the other hand, make a "career" out of hatred for God and of trying to lure people away from God. As a fifteen-year-old, the great poet W.H. Auden wrote "Pardon":

> They brought her to the place where Christ stood by
> A woman taken in adultery:
> 'We must stone her, Moses said,
> Such as these were better dead.'
> Christ made no answer, with His hand
> He drew strange figures in the sand
> What He wrote then we cannot tell
> But teeth were gnashed that day in Hell.

You see, what the young poet was trying to say is that God is always ready to forgive, and that makes the fallen angels furious — because they fear that someone might respond to God's love by repenting and loving Him in return.

Viewing a tragedy

Q. We have a problem in our family. My brother and his wife filed for divorce last April after twenty-eight years of marriage. In regard to the children, my sister-in-law did not provide time for their fifteen-year-old son to spend with his father. To make it more impossible, she allowed him to get a job and to begin running with older boys (seventeen, eighteen, and nineteen). In November, my nephew was killed in a high-speed auto accident with some of these "older" friends. Now my sister-in-law says it was God's will for their son to have died at a young age like that. Personally, I think it was negligence on her part, for allowing him to go out and party with an older crowd. How should I look at this tragedy?
A. Regardless of who is to blame, and I suspect multiple causes were involved, why engage in finger-pointing? Undoubtedly, your sister-in-law feels badly enough about this without your adding fuel to the fire.

A Christian approach to such a tragedy seeks to find meaning in suffering and death, which must always be viewed in terms of an unfailing belief in divine providence and in view of our uniting all our crosses to the Lord's own paschal mystery. In that light, we echo the Savior's words from the cross, "Father, forgive them, for they know not what they do" (Lk 23:34).

Infallibility

Q. Enclosed is a clipping from an article by our bishop in our diocesan newspaper that seems to identify three ways of exercising infallibility. The third, which is supported by an undocumented quotation, does not seem on track to me; after reading the entire paragraph, which follows, please comment:

"The Church is given the charism of infallibility exercised by the Pope in certain rare circumstances; by the bishops throughout the world when together with the Pope they concur on a single viewpoint on a matter of faith and morals; and by 'the body of the faithful, who as a whole cannot err in matters of belief when from the bishops down to the last member of the laity it shows universal agreement on matters of faith and morals.'"
A. I don't know what your bishop means by "concur[ring] on a single

viewpoint." The overall categories he lists find their origin in the Second Vatican Council's *Lumen Gentium* (the Dogmatic Constitution on the Church), which identifies the charism as being exercised by the Sovereign Pontiff under certain circumstances ("rarity" is not part of the doctrinal statement); by the bishops in ecumenical council; and by the body of the faithful, which quotation is given above in accurate form.

Your highlighting suggests your particular discomfort with the last of these three modes. Let's take a careful look at all this.

Paragraph twenty-five of *Lumen Gentium* makes it clear that the pope can teach infallibly not only under the rubric of *ex cathedra* pronouncements but, far more commonly, through his ordinary magisterium, which is to say, his daily teaching and preaching of the Catholic Faith, which corresponds to the deposit of faith taught in all places and at all times throughout the history of the Church. We are there taught that religious assent must be given to such forms of teaching — even absent the pope's invoking of the extraordinary mode.

Bishops, as members of the college of bishops and united to their head, the pope, engage in the collegial exercise of the charism of infallibility. Again, the precise quotation is, as follows: "The college of bishops exercises power over the universal Church in a solemn manner in an ecumenical council." Further, the college of bishops, acting in union with the pope, has "supreme and full authority over the universal Church; but this power cannot be exercised without the agreement of the Roman Pontiff' (emphasis added, *Lumen Gentium*, no. 22).

Now, on to the third, which in your bishop's column is also a citation from *Lumen Gentium*. We cannot read into that text a kind of egalitarian or "democratic" principle that might be construed as a type of public-opinion-poll approach to the formation and/or transmission of Catholic doctrine. Indeed, this passage presumes that the faithful have been properly instructed in "matters of faith and morals." It would be ludicrous to imagine that we should suppose that people who had never been presented with the Catholic truth on, say, the Blessed Trinity, would be able to enunciate that doctrine, let alone hold it as a definitive element of the doctrine of the faith.

For an excellent and honest presentation on this third dimension of Catholic teaching, I would most heartily recommend Cardinal John Henry Newman's famous work, *On Consulting the Faithful in Matters of Doctrine.* Any analysis that seeks to reduce this category to a show of hands is mischievous and not in keeping with the way in which the Church has always and in all places understood this.

No mistake

Q. An article in the January/February 1996 issue of The Catholic Answer, *"What Makes Us Distinctively Catholic," had a mistake in it. On page thirty-six, Father Michael Parise says: "This divine revelation is found in the Sacred Tradition of the Church, some of which was recorded as the Sacred Scriptures, the Old and the New Testaments." He is saying that Sacred Tradition includes Sacred Scripture. I have always been taught that they are two distinct parts of divine revelation. In the* St. Joseph Catholic Manual, *it says that tradition is "the handing down of revealed truth through channels other than the Bible. Tradition may be found in the writings of the Fathers, the Doctors, and the great theologians; in the teachings of the popes and the General Councils; in the Creeds; in the Acts of the Martyrs; in local books; and in the inscriptions, paintings, sculpture, and medals that have come down to us from the earliest days of the Church."*

Will you have the humility and honesty to admit that your magazine made a mistake and, further, will you include this letter in your column so that everyone can be informed?

A. Why be so "catty" in pointing out an alleged error? In our nine-year history, we have gladly corrected mistakes on several occasions. Here, I don't think Father Parise is guilty of an error as much as an imprecision.

In speaking of "some of [Tradition]" being "recorded as the Sacred Scriptures," Father Parise was simply reminding us that Tradition preceded Scripture in chronological terms. In other words, the truths about Christ, His Gospel, and His Church existed in the oral tradition before any of it was committed to writing. In *Dei Verbum* (the Dogmatic Constitution on Divine Revelation), the Fathers of the Second Vatican Council noted, "Tradition transmits in its entirety the Word of God which has been entrusted to the apostles by Christ the Lord and the Holy Spirit" (no. 9). And, further, "Sacred Tradition and sacred Scripture make up a single sacred deposit of the Word of God" (no. 10). The *Catechism* reminds us that the Gospel was handed on in two ways: orally . . . (and) in writing (76). The process of Gospel formation is described carefully in the Catechism in number 126, which was undoubtedly in our author's mind as he penned his reflections.

Deaconess question

Q. The secular press has had a field day recently with the report from the Canon Law Society of America that ordaining women as deacons in the Church would be in keeping with Catholic theology and past practice. Their statement stressed that "women have been ordained permanent deacons in the past, and it would be possible for the Church to determine to do so again." If diaconate — whether transitional or permanent — is a part of the Sacrament of Holy Orders, how can it be administered to a woman?

I know of cases in which men who were ordained as permanent deacons were later ordained as priests. The issue at present seems to me to be admittance to the diaconate, period. Their theological approach to the sacrament seems strange to me; is their historical recollection also off-base? Please help me to sort out this confusion.

A. Those who wish to advocate the ordination of women deacons often rely on historical evidence — including no less than a citation from the Council of Chalcedon — that needs further clarification. The following should be noted in that regard:

(1) The editor of the standard English translation of the documents of the ecumenical councils does not speak of "imposition of hands" but merely "ordination" — even though the Latin and Greek of the Chalcedon decree admittedly do so. Why? Precisely because there is no evidence to suggest that such "imposition of hands" was in fact ever done for women. Simply because the canon of a council mentions something does not necessarily mean that it was ever implemented. For example, the Council of Trent allowed for the restoration of the permanent diaconate in the Latin rite, but we all know that did not happen until a similar call came from the Second Vatican Council. In our own time, we know that Vatican II's *Sacrosanctum Concilium* (Constitution on the Sacred Liturgy), in numerous places, mandated the continued use of Latin and Gregorian Chant in the Roman rite [cf. nos. 36, 54, 116], yet the exact opposite has happened in reality.

(2) Even the report of the Canon Law Society of America on deaconesses acknowledges that the case for a true "ordination" of them is historically unverifiable.

(3) The Chalcedon citation likewise refers the reader to the Council of Nicaea's comments on this subject and has this to say: "We refer to deaconesses . . . for they do not receive any imposition of hands, so that they are in all respects to be numbered among the laity" (Canon 19).

(4) On the very matter of imposition of hands, however, it must be observed that, in and of itself, the action does not signal participation in major orders. To this day, the Byzantine rite uses this ancient gesture in ordaining to the subdiaconate (which it has retained, unlike the Latin rite in which it was generally suppressed), and in no way is it understood to admit the man to major orders. The same understanding prevailed in the pre-conciliar ritual of the Roman rite.

(5) The word "order" in the early Church had not received the specificity which it later attained. Thus, we read of the existence of "orders" of widows, virgins, catechumens, etc.

(6) Finally, I should note that there exists a theological debate as to whether or not even the diaconate participates in the Sacrament of Holy Orders, absent any clear doctrinal commitment from any magisterial source. For this reason, a commission of the Holy See has been established to deal with this very question in an organized manner for the first time in history.

Crucial distinctions

Q. I found your answer, titled "Norm for Salvation," in [a recent] issue of TCA confusing. Following your argument, it seems that everybody is saved. Does salvation come from Jesus Christ, the Church, or being good? This answer brings to mind government officials who would like to keep everyone happy.

Also, could you please explain why your answer in that same edition "Sharpshooter!" does not contradict the teaching found in Veritatis Splendor *which teaches that it is never right to perform an evil act to bring about a good effect.*

A. Please do not take offense at my comments, however, it seems to me that you have a desire not for simple answers but simplistic ones, and the difference is critical.

As one should understand, the question of attaining salvation is not something which can be handled in one hundred words or less; indeed, it is a matter of eternal consequences, therefore, it should surprise no one that an answer must deal with many aspects of a complex topic.

Having re-read my response, I am comfortable that I accurately reflected the constant Tradition of the Church. And no, I'm not a politician trying "to keep everyone happy." At the same time, it is important to recall that we Catholics are not Fundamentalists with quick slogans which can have the effect of dismissing entire groups of people or evading intricate side issues, simply to provide what will look like a black-and-white answer. The Catholic approach to theology has always engaged the intellect; when that happens, careful distinctions are required. I hope that does not come across as "fudging" because it's not.

For our third visit to the sharpshooter, let me refer you once more to the *Catechism of the Catholic Church*, paragraph 2263, which I cited already. If it helps at all, try to realize that the sharpshooter's action is good in itself and in intent: To save the life of the innocent; an unintended side-effect will be to harm and maybe even to kill the assailant. Once more, we find ourselves making crucial distinctions.

Purgatory and hell

Q. In the January/February 1994 issue of TCA when discussing purgatory (page 28), you stated that ". . . St. Catherine of Genoa once made the point that — in spite of the pain of separation from God experienced there — purgatory is happier than all of one's earthly life put together."

In my early Catholic education (more than fifty years ago), I was taught that the pain and suffering of hell and purgatory were the same, except that suffering in purgatory was temporary. If this is correct, and if you can be happy in spite of separation from God, can one be happy in hell? Please comment on this.

A. To be perfectly honest, no one knows exactly what the pains of hell or purgatory or the joys of heaven are really like — for the simple reason that they are experiences beyond what we can grasp this side of eternity; therefore, we always speak in analogous terms.

With those parameters set, however, I think you would agree that the pain one would suffer would be considerably different were it clear that it would, in fact, be temporary rather than everlasting. On the second matter, whatever we know or do not know about hell, we can say with certitude that, by its very definition, hell is the total absence of happiness.

Resurrected Christ

Q. I had often wondered when we receive the Eucharist is this the same Jesus Who walked with and taught the appostles, or the resurrected Christ? In a previous edition of The Catholic Answer *you said that we receive the resurrected Jesus.*

Further reflection on this point gives rise to another question: At the Last Supper, Jesus gave the apostles His Body and Blood to eat and drink. If He had not yet died and risen from the dead, how could this have been His resurrected Body and Blood?

A. The glorified Christ appeared, during His earthly life and ministry, to Peter, James, and John on Mount Tabor during the Transfiguration. What, for us, is a contradiction in terms is not necessarily so for the God-Man. So, yes, I still maintain that the presence of Christ in the Holy Eucharist is that of His risen Body, which is physical but also more than physical.

At the same time, it is good to recall that there is no disjunction between the earthly Jesus and the risen Christ; He is the same Person, in different form.

Resource sought

Q. For some time I have been unsuccessful in search of one reference book that lists, in summary form: a) all the Church councils; b) principal papal documents (encyclicals, bulls, etc.); and c) the heresies and "isms" which have plagued the Church. Certainly the data I seek is available, but only (so it would seem) in a disjointed fashion. Do you know of a concise summation which places not only the data, but also cross-references to the source documents which provide in-depth information, should anyone be inclined to research further?

A. To the best of my knowledge, all the information which interests you exists only, in your words, "in a disjointed fashion." If any reader has some better insights, please let us know.

Evolution query

Q. I have read Teilhard de Chardin's De Christo *and his work* The Heart of the Matter *on evolution and did not receive a satisfactory answer to my question. How does the Church reconcile the account of creation found in Genesis with the appearance on earth of the dinosaurs? I cannot believe that man evolved from such lizards. When*

I taught Origin of the Species *by Darwin, I taught that Christians could believe in evolution to the point where God infused a human soul in man; however, even this goes against my personal belief in the direct creation by God. What is the teaching of the Church on this matter?*

A. At least as far back as the time of St. Augustine, the Catholic Church has refused to get sucked into a futile debate about this question. In his *"De Genesi ad Litteram Opus Imperfectum,"* the great and saintly theologian stressed the importance of realizing that God's Word is not given to us as a science book but in order to teach us powerful truths that save.

In the midst of the Galileo controversy, Cardinal Baronius reminded all who would listen that the Scriptures "do not tell us how the heavens go, but how to go to heaven."

That trajectory has been followed right into modern times, including the teachings of Pope Pius XII in his encyclical *Humani Generis* and in the Second Vatican Council's discussion on inspiration and inerrancy in *Dei Verbum* (Dogmatic Constitution on Divine Revelation). The *Catechism of the Catholic Church* likewise speaks of the creation narratives of Genesis as using symbolic language (362).

On your specific point, Catholic teaching insists on two things: first, God is the Creator of all that is, having set the entire process in motion by His omnipotence and love. Second, however that process unfolded, the same God directly intervened when a creature emerged whom He deemed worthy of a soul "made in the image and likeness of God." And, as the *Catechism* states, that continues in each subsequent human creation: "The doctrine of faith affirms that the spiritual and immortal soul is created immediately by God" (382).

Eco-theology

Q. Please read the enclosed article, "God Is One with Us and All Creation," which recently appeared in our diocesan newspaper. I sense that there are grave doctrinal errors in this "eco-theology." Would you please comment?

A. Every heresy has some value and/or truth, which is why people get taken in by it. The latest theological gimmick seems to be "eco-theology." In its purest form, eco-theology reminds us that man is the steward of God's creation, not its abuser — a point made by Pope John Paul II on many occasions. Simply put, we need to revere creation because it, like us, comes from the Creator God.

Beyond that, as Catholics, we have an incarnational appreciation for all things; that is, we believe that created things and beings can put us in touch with the living God. Hence, our sacraments employ created realities like bread, wine, water, and oil, which then become vehicles or signs of deeper realities and become means of grace or divine life. All this, I trust, you will recognize as traditional Catholic sacramentology. The author of the article you sent, however, goes way off-base. Her Christology is Arian ("God becomes a creature in Christ"); her theology is pantheistic or at least panentheistic, which is to say that she so identifies God with His creation that the two become indistinguishable. Positions just like this led to the dismissal of Matthew Fox from the Dominican order.

In my experience, the average person espousing theories of this type is generally rather naïve and theologically confused more than malicious and overtly heretical; this is not said to excuse but to underscore the necessity of being careful about one's theological expressions and of remaining enlightened by the Church's Magisterium.

Scripture

Contradiction?

Q. I have a question regarding Dei Verbum *(Dogmatic Constitution on Divine Revelation) and the* New American Bible. Dei Verbum *says that the Gospels were written by the apostles and men associated with them — thus, by eyewitnesses and disciples of eyewitnesses. The apostles would necessarily be Matthew and John. The writers of the introductions to Matthew and John in the NAB say it is "untenable" that Matthew wrote the Gospel attributed to him, and they express doubt that the Gospel of John was written by John the Apostle.*

Dei Verbum *is a dogmatic constitution and has authority. How, then, can we be obliged to accept a Bible that contradicts it?*

A. Are *Dei Verbum* and the introductions in the *New American Bible* in conflict? I don't think so.

Your summary of the NAB material in no way contradicts the statements found in either *Dei Verbum* or *Sancta Mater Ecclesia* (the 1964 Instruction on the Historical Truth of the Gospels), which speaks of either "apostles or apostolic men." The relevant passage from *Dei Verbum* says that the Gospels are of "apostolic origin" and that the apostles "and others of the apostolic age handed on to us in writing the same message they had preached" (no. 18).

Admittedly, at times biblical commentators can be a bit dogmatic in their assertions and actually go beyond that for which they have good evidence, but it is also important to remember that whether or not St. Matthew wrote the Gospel which bears his name is immaterial as far as the book's inspiration, inerrancy, and canonicity. That is, whoever the sacred author was, we believe that he was directed in his writing by God's Holy Spirit, which thus guarantees the truthfulness of all contained therein which pertains to our salvation, which is why a particular book was incorporated into the canon of the Bible.

Many biblical exegetes are beginning to rethink some of their skepticism about questions of authorship, having learned that what they took for certitudes often lacks the depth and persuasiveness they once ascribed to them. When all is said and done, any honest scholar would be hard-pressed to demonstrate in an unequivocal manner that any given book was not written by the person whose name has been attached to it in Christian tradition.

My position, then, would come down to this: The sum of biblical interpretation neither rises nor sets on the question of authorship; that being so, why make such a production of it in either direction?

Informality is 'in'

Q. There is something — it might seem trivial — about the New Revised New Testament of the New American Bible *that bothers me. Why do the translators no longer capitalize "holy" in reference to the Holy Spirit?*
A. For the past several years, there has been a tendency to downplay capitalization across the board, not just in religious spheres. In its most benign form, then, this trend is simply part of a cultural phenomenon that favors informality. There are times, however, when it can cause some serious misunderstanding, and I think the case you cite is one of them. It seems to me that one's proper title needs to be capitalized, *in toto.*

Moses' last name?

Q. At a recent Bible study meeting someone raised the question as to why most, if not all, of the biblical personalities have only a single name (e.g. Adam, Eve, Moses, Joshua, etc.), but Jesus has two names. I could not answer the question; can you offer some explanation?
A. In the ancient world, with villages and towns being smaller, it was not necessary for people to have a surname; besides, a person's occupation served as his "second name," which is what also began to happen in the Anglo-Saxon world, thus explaining names like Mason or Carpenter. Children were also known as being of their father, as in "of John" or "of Peter;" this, too, came into English with patronymics like Johnson or Peterson. However, Our Lord did not have two names in our sense of a first and second (or family) name; his "second" name of Christ was a title, meaning the Anointed One.

RSV or grail

Q. Can I as a priest properly fulfill the daily obligation of praying the Divine Office if, in private recitation, I use the psalmody from the Revised Standard Version *(RSV) of the Bible instead of the less poetic Grail Psalter contained in the breviary? Unfortunately, I was never taught Latin in the seminary, so for the time being, praying the Office in Latin is out of the question. I know priests who use the English translation of the Office approved for the dioceses of England, Ireland, Australia, etc. Is this allowable for priests in the U.S.? What are the chances of there ever being a better English translation of the Office available in this country?*

A. I see no reason why you cannot use the RSV Psalms, as long as this is for private recitation. The same would hold true, in my opinion, for the British breviary. I know, however, that a big hoopla was created over this about twenty years ago, with some folks at the liturgy office in Washington going so far as to declare that clergy could not fulfill their obligation, except with the American breviary, but that is patent nonsense. I can appreciate the need to have one breviary for the country (as bad as the translation is) for purposes of public celebration, but to impose such a restriction for private use has no legitimate purpose or goal.

I think we will have a long wait for the revision of the English Divine Office, especially since the battle hasn't even been well engaged for the Order of Mass and the propers.

Skip the fanfare

Q. Would you please explain what Our Lord meant in Matthew 6:6 — "But when you pray, go to your room, close the door and pray to your Father in secret. And your Father Who sees in secret will repay you"?

A. Jesus was warning us against performing religious acts to win the approval of men. On the contrary, when we pray or fast or give alms, we should do these good deeds in a manner that seeks to attract as little fanfare as possible. In so doing, we have Our Lord's assurance that our reward in heaven will be much greater since our motivation will be purer.

This injunction of Christ, however, should not be understood as condemning public prayer or liturgy, for He himself clearly participated in the worship services of synagogue and Temple alike.

Douay and RSV

Q. I have just received my copy of the Catechism of the Catholic Church *and have a question. Why did they use the* Revised Standard Version *of the Bible and not* the Douay-Rheims *version? Was that the idea of the National Conference of Catholic Bishops? I understood that this catechism was the pope's idea, and I thought he would use a Catholic version of the Bible.* The Douay-Rheims *is the English version of the Catholic Bible. Why do we have four or five versions of the Bible? To my way of thinking, there should be only one approved version of the Bible.*

A. The *Douay-Rheims* version of the Bible was a product of the sixteenth century, the work of the professors of the English seminary-in-exile in France after the Reformation hit. It was a translation of the Latin Vulgate of St. Jerome and not in direct contact with the original texts in Hebrew and Greek, although the translators referred to the original languages for refinement and precision. At any rate, the *Douay* Bible was not an ideal translation, even though it performed a valuable service for many centuries. In *Divino Afflante Spiritu*, Pope Pius XII directed that all future vernacular translations of the Sacred Scriptures be done from Hebrew and Greek — to ensure as close as possible a careful correspondence between the original and the vernacular.

The French took up that challenge and came out with the *Jerusalem Bible*; unfortunately, English-speakers took a shortcut with that text and went from French to English — hence, no significant improvement over going from Latin to English and perhaps even worse. Eventually, American biblical scholars put their nose to the grindstone and, after twenty-five years of work, came up with the *New American Bible*, which had been preceded by the Confraternity Edition as a kind of interim text. The *New American Bible* is relatively accurate, but quite short on poetic qualities and is not really suited to liturgical proclamation. Finally, we discover the *Revised Standard Version*, which, as you say, was originally a Protestant translation, but it is one which is most accurate and very beautiful. Under the ecumenical impulse, Catholic and Orthodox scholars collaborated with Protestants in producing a text acceptable to all three Christian communities. A Catholic edition of the RSV was issued, complete with explanatory notes; this is my preferred translation of the Scriptures in English.

Regrettably, a revision of the RSV was done recently, and it caved in to feminist ideologues; therefore, it is not as accurate as the earlier version, and I would not recommend it (that version was generally found unacceptable to the translators of the *Catechism* as well).

As you can see, translation can be a tricky business, calling for true discernment. Facile labels don't work. Just because something is predominantly the work of Protestants or Catholics is not an automatic indicator of its value. The test is its accuracy and felicity of expression and, on those counts, the original RSV wins, hands down, in my judgment.

Scripture scholarship

Q. Please comment on Father Raymond Brown, S.S., and especially on his book The Death of the Messiah. *I have read conflicting opinions on both.*

A. I have great respect for Father Brown's scholarship and his fidelity to Church teaching. I have not always agreed with what I consider to be an overly-heavy reliance of his on the historical-critical method of biblical exegesis (which, in my judgment and in that of the Magisterium, has value but also hazards). But I think he has also begun to change in that regard. At a lecture this winter, I asked Father Brown for his reaction to the recent document of the Pontifical Biblical Commission, "The Interpretation of the Bible in the Church" (available from the Daughters of St. Paul). He was extremely positive toward it and indicated his agreement that the historical-critical method cannot and should not be the sole method of interpretation.

I read *The Death of the Messiah* during Lent and found it very good and helpful. Now, that is not to say that it is for the average parishioner, but it is certainly within the parameters of Catholic biblical interpretation and in accord with all Catholic doctrine.

Bible and tradition

Q. I understand that Catholic teaching requires the acceptance of both Scripture and Tradition, but which verses in the Bible actually deny that the Scriptures were intended to be the sole rule of faith?

A. From the very beginning, the Church has never operated as though the Scriptures were an all-sufficient guide to faith. Of course, the Church existed for at least thirty years before the first Gospel was written, so that fact in itself demonstrates the fallacy of a *sola Scriptura* posture. Beyond that, in his Second Epistle to the Thessalonians, St. Paul exhorts the community there to "hold fast to the traditions you received from us, either by our word or by letter" (2:15). While not enumerating them in his letter, Paul nonetheless advises the Church at Thessalonica to "hold fast to the traditions" it had received from Silvanus, Timothy, and himself.

Even the Protestant Reformers like Luther, Calvin, and Zwingli relied on ecclesiastical Tradition; *sola Scriptura* in the absolute sense is really a novelty of nineteenth-century Fundamentalists, who are separated from their theological forbears in the Reformation by light-years, in terms of mentality, emphases, and doctrine.

Scripture in context

Q. In reading an article in Our Sunday Visitor, *I recently ran across the following which has raised many questions in my mind: "God commanded them, 'Be fertile and multiply' " (Gn 1:28). If God commanded in this way, then isn't celibacy against God's law? How can Jesus then advocate celibacy to His disciples? Furthermore, this same command seems to have been given to the animals that are incapable of receiving a precept. Is the error in the translation or in the thinking?*

A. The first rule of biblical interpretation is to see the passage in context. In this instance, we realize that Almighty God is speaking at the dawn of creation when, in truth, the world does call for the various species to increase and multiply. Jesus, on the other hand, saw His mission specifically as one of ushering in "the end times" — the eschatological, or final, age, which brings the kingdom of God in all its fullness, a time which Our Lord tells us will involve those who neither "marry nor are given in marriage" (Lk 20:34-35).

In Catholic theology, both marriage and celibacy are signs of the Kingdom, but in different ways. Marriage (with sexual relations) is a sign of Christ's love for His Church right now; celibacy (without sexual relations) is a sign of the future and absolute union of Christ and His Church, or God and His People, when God will be all in all. These two ways of life, then, are not in contradiction to each other.

A final point to recall, in regard to the animals, is that Genesis 1-11 is written in poetic fashion and needs to be read in that light — that is, not taken literally. The inner truth of it all, however, is that animals (and rocks and trees and stars) do indeed "obey" God by acting according to their God-given nature — by being good animals, rocks, stars, etc. Their "goodness" corresponds precisely to their actions being in conformity with the divine will, and in this manner even animals have a lesson to teach humans.

A puzzling parable

Q. Our family has several questions about the parable in Luke's Gospel (16:19-31) of the rich man and the beggar. Since the rich man is said to be in a torment from which there is no escape after he died and was buried, it seems to us that he is in hell. At the same time, he has concern for his brothers. We are of the opinion that hell is full of hate and any love is impossible. How can the rich man have any concern or love for his brothers? Would this concern indicate in any way that he might be in purgatory, although this would seem to conflict with verse twenty-six? Is there any reason as to why Abraham refers to him as "my child" in verse twenty-five? An official explanation of this parable certainly would be helpful.

A. The story to which you allude is a parable; as such, it cannot be pushed too far for exact parallels to real situations. So, you are correct in expressing some confusion over precise elements: No release equals hell; but concern for others cannot equal hell.

Abraham refers to the rich man as "my child" because Abraham is the father of the Hebrew people; simply because a child has sinned, he does not lose his identity as one's child (that is as true in the supernatural order as it is in the natural).

By and large, the Church refrains from giving "official explanations" of Scripture passages, contrary to the impression some Fundamentalists have of our approach to the Bible. In point of fact, the Church has defined fewer than a dozen pericopes (Scripture passages) in her entire history. Usually, such definitions are not positive statements as to the exact meaning of a biblical text as much as they are designed to set boundaries. For example, at the Council of Trent, the Church condemned any interpretation of John 20:22-23 that *excluded* a connection with the Sacrament of Penance. The Church's mind on all this, then, is to allow us to search the Scriptures and seek out meaning ourselves, using the best information available at any given time in history. In other words, the Church is not prone to make infallible declarations unnecessarily. Catholics are to read the Word of God in the community of the Church, in the context of our whole tradition of faith, in the light of what scholarship (history, archaeology, linguistics, etc.) reveals.

The final point for some of our fundamentalist friends, brought out in this passage. Notice, the rich man calls upon Abraham as "father" twice (Lk 16:24, 27), and Jesus does not condemn the use of the title — even though it is applied to someone other than God. Apparently, Our Lord did not have the same trouble with the title that some of these folks do today.

'Apocryphal' books

Q. I have several questions about the apocryphal books of the Bible. When were the books accepted as inspired by the Catholic Church? If the books were accepted as inspired prior to the Reformation, why did the Protestants not accept them? My reading of the Books of Maccabees leads me to believe that the Jewish feast of Hanukkah has its foundation in these books. If so, why do the Jews not accept these books? I would be thankful for any other information that you might have about these books and why the Catholic Church alone recognizes them.

A. Let's start at the back and work forward.

The Catholic Church is not alone in recognizing these books. All of Eastern Christianity does too — as did all of Christendom prior to the Reformation.

The so-called apocryphal books of the Bible reflect the story of Israel's own division. The Jews were dispersed from the Holy Land on numerous occasions. Gradually, two different but related forms of Judaism began to emerge. Part of that was reflected in the development of the Septuagint text of the Hebrew Bible — that is, the Greek translation of the Word of God for the use of Jews living outside Palestine. The biblical text they used was longer than the one then in use within Israel (the Hebrew canon), by seven books. As things worked out, that longer canon (because it was already in Greek) was the one employed by the early Christians as well. Therefore, if you can read Greek, you will discover in the Greek New Testament that the citations of Old Testament passages (the Hebrew Bible) are direct quotes from the Septuagint text. So, it is clear that the primitive Church considered the longer canon to be inspired; that intuition was taken account of by several early councils as well.

Why, then, did Martin Luther revert to the Hebrew canon of the Bible? For reasons of expediency or necessity. You'll recall that part of his initial difficulty with the Catholic Church revolved around the existence of purgatory and his insistence that this doctrine be proved by direct reference to Sacred Scripture. When the Church brought forth Maccabees as a citation, he came to the decision to discount the canonical status of those texts. Coincidentally, he realized that the two Books of Maccabees were part of the longer Greek canon, which he then rejected in favor of the Hebrew, or shorter, canon.

Many — if not most — Protestant Bibles today include what we call "deuterocanonical" (what they call "apocryphal") books, albeit at the end of the Bible. Finally, simply because Jews do not consider Maccabees to be canonical does not mean that they do not regard those texts as holy or valuable. In point of fact, they do, and yes, the Feast of Hanukkah does have its origins in that source.

Pilate's skepticism

Q. Could you please explain exactly what Jesus meant in His exchange with Pilate about "truth" (Jn 18:38). Pilate's reply, "What is truth?" puzzles me.

A. It seems to me that Pilate was simply reflecting a school of thought at that time which earned for its adherents the name of "skeptics" because they doubted the existence of absolute truth or at least its attainability by mortal men. It was also a fine way to get himself off the hook, he thought.

Of course, Pilate has millions of spiritual progeny today among those who either question or deny the existence of moral absolutes, or who try to sidestep the personal application of such truths to their own lives by engaging in frivolous philosophical discussions designed not to learn the meaning of truth but to divert attention from their own unwillingness to be guided by it. Pope John Paul II's *Veritatis Splendor* ("The Splendor of Truth") is a long, detailed and carefully reasoned reply to any would-be modern Pilates.

Distracting

Q. Why is the name "Jesus Christ" sometimes used in reverse, "Christ Jesus"? It seems backwards to me and I find it distracting.

A. Some clarifications are in order. Our Lord's "first" name, to use modern terminology, was "Jesus" — a very common Jewish name (which was really "Joshua," meaning "God saves"), but in this instance, it was true to a preeminent degree in His very Person. His "second" name is not a family name but a title from the Greek *Christos*, meaning the "Anointed One," itself a translation of the Hebrew *Messiah*. In many languages today, it is normal practice to refer to Him (in French, for example) as *Jesus le Christ*, or "Jesus the Messiah." The inversion of the names, then, would not matter. And St. Paul himself frequently does this too (cf. Rom 8:1; 1 Cor 1:30; Gal 3:28).

'Jesus' as a given name

Q. What is the mind of the Church on the naming of baby boys "Jesus"? I note that this usually occurs within the Spanish culture.

A. Since I was born on Christmas Day, many Hispanic friends have pointed out to me that had I been born into that culture I would surely have been called "Jesus." I do not know of any other ethnic group that maintains the practice of naming boys "Jesus," but there is certainly nothing wrong with it. In point of fact, we are all called "Christians," which means "little Christs," so why not "Jesus"?

Sometimes people have the impression that Our Lord was the only Person in history to bear the name "Jesus" (Joshua, in Hebrew), but it was as common in His time as is "Joe" or "Tom" today.

Translation trouble?

Q. In Luke 2:5, we read that Mary was Joseph's "espoused" wife; some translations say "betrothed." This sounds as though they're only engaged, but then how is Mary called his "wife"? Is this a question of translation, or is there more here that I don't understand?

A. Dictionaries inform us that "espoused" and "betrothed" are synonymous. Ancient Jewish practice had it that when a couple was betrothed, they were considered married in every sense of the word (property and inheritance rights, for example), except for the right to engage in marital relations, which required the sealing of the engagement with the marriage ceremony. In fact, the breaking of a betrothal required a divorce decree.

Although the Scriptures never tell us when or where the marriage between Our Lady and St. Joseph took place, it is obvious that they did eventually get married, in light of the angel's directive to "not be afraid to take Mary your wife into your home" (Mt 1:20). That twelve years later they still appear together is further evidence of this intuition. Yet again, Christian tradition from time immemorial speaks of Mary and Joseph as spouses (in the Roman canon, for example).

Forbidden fruit

Q. What is the "forbidden fruit" that is spoken about in the Book of Genesis?

A. Given the fact that the first several chapters of Genesis are Hebrew poetry, involved with symbolic language, it is not possible to determine exactly what the "forbidden fruit" was. Down the centuries, however, theologians have always identified the sin of our first parents as a two-fold act against God: disobedience and pride, which sought autonomy from God. Seen in this light, we can realize how this is truly the original sin and, as such, the prototype of every subsequent sin in history.

The Book of Job

Q. Why did the Lord God give Satan the power to do with Job as he willed?

A. As in the previous question, it is important to discover the precise literary form of the biblical book in question. Just as we can see the early chapters of Genesis fit the poetic genre, so too we can classify the Book of Job as a drama, designed to teach some powerful truths about God and the human condition. Therefore, we have no way of knowing whether anyone by the name of Job ever existed, let alone that the biblical account is biographical. Commentators, Jewish and Christian alike, have always seen in the Book of Job an essay on the mystery of human suffering, an essay we might add, which has a less-than-satisfactory answer at the play's end. Of course, as Christians, we would assert that human suffering becomes comprehensible, tolerable, and even meritorious only in the light of Christ's cross.

So, as to your precise question, I do not think we can conclude that the Lord God gave Satan any such power over Job or over any other human being before or since. The sacred author merely used this as part of a literary device to heighten interest and move the story along, even as he sought to deal with the problem of evil and suffering from a religious perspective.

Morning Star

Q. In [a recent] issue of TCA you write that "it is true the New Testament speaks of Jesus as the Morning Star. . . . " I cannot find this and would appreciate it if you could give me the citation.

A. Look up 2 Peter 1:19.

Text is sacred

Q. In many Hawaiian parishes it is the custom to sing an "Our Father" written by local people. The text is as follows: "Our Father, Who art in heaven, hallowed be Thy name. Thy kingdom come, Thy will be done, on earth as it is in heaven. Please give to us all that we need, Lord, and forgive us all our sins, as we forgive those who harm us. And lead us not away from you. For thine is the kingdom and the power and the glory forever. Amen. Amen. Amen." The liturgical director of the diocese says it is permissible to use this version. It concerns me, though, when people begin tampering with such a sacred text. Could you please comment?

A. I would be concerned as well. Besides which, the doxology to the Lord's Prayer in the location where you note it obviates the possibility of the priest's recitation of the embolism prayer ("Deliver us, Lord") and/or the congregational response to it. While sung texts may differ slightly from the standard texts (for purposes of a musical nature), the changes cannot be substantive; in the present case, I find theological problems in addition to the liturgical ones I already mentioned.

Jesus is God!

Q. I have read and been told that Jesus is not God. As far as I know, that teaching appears only twice in the New Testament: in the prologue of St. John's Gospel and the appearance to doubting Thomas after the resurrection. I am going to be teaching the Bible to teenagers and need some help. Could you please clarify this matter?

A. Well, if the New Testament says it at least twice, which it does, isn't that enough? In point of fact, however, the Scriptures say it in innumerable ways and on dozens of occasions. Look through the Book of Revelation and see how Jesus is repeatedly accorded the worship due the Father. Realize that every time that Jesus is called Lord, that is a statement of belief in His divinity, for Lord is English for the Greek *Kyrios*, which in turn, translates the Hebrew *Yahweh*. Hence, when St. Paul sings in Philippians (2:11) that "Jesus Christ is Lord," he is saying "Jesus Christ is God."

Lord's Prayer query

Q. At the parish I attend we sing the common Protestant version of the Lord's Prayer which concludes with, "For thine is the kingdom . . ." instead of separating it as it appears in the missal. Is this a legitimate option?

A. No, it is not — because it destroys the flow of the prayers that follow. Besides which, the Church deliberately does not use that ending for the Lord's Prayer because it is not scriptural. The doxology is beautiful and ancient (Eastern actually, not Protestant in origin), but not the text we find in St. Matthew's Gospel. Therefore, in the revision of the Mass, it was included in a tangential sort of way by being tacked onto the "Deliver us" as a congregational acclamation.

Genesis question

Q. I am writing in response to your answer in [a recent] issue of TCA on "Mother-God." I agree with you that the Scriptures never refer to God as mother, but I do see God as a male/female being in Genesis (1:26-27; 5:1-2;). I admit that I don't understand fully what these passages mean; however, it seems to me that "man" is mankind. Since the first beings created by Him were male and female — and Scripture says He created them in His likeness — can I assume that God is both male and female? I realize that it is a rather absurd question; however, nobody that I've ever asked has been able to give an explanation. I hope and pray that you can and will.

A. God transcends sexuality and, in fact, all human categories. Maleness or femaleness is a necessary aspect of the definition of human identity, but definition means limitation, which cannot exist in God. God is a spiritual Being; sexuality is an essential component of physical beings but does not exist in one who is purely spiritual (like God or the angels).

For a detailed analysis of the early chapters of Genesis dealing with human origins and especially on sexuality, I would refer you to the collection of Wednesday audience talks given by Pope John Paul II several years ago and published by the Daughters of St. Paul under the title of *Original Unity of Man and Woman: Catechesis on the Book of Genesis.*

Off-target analysis

Q. Please peruse the attached excerpt from Liturgical Press. From my reading, John Pilch has a different idea about the Old Testament than the Catechism of the Catholic Church.

Could you please comment on the correct understanding of the Old Testament vis-à-vis the New Testament, especially as it relates to Paul's Epistle to the Romans? This letter appears to be a stumbling block to many.

A. For the benefit of readers, Dr. Plich says that the Law is "no longer normative or obligatory. Instead, Torah became a guiding story, a Sacred Scripture that tells how we all got to the present, but it no longer has any binding rules for the future." As his authority for this position, he cites Romans 3:20.

I think it fair to say that Pilch has "out-Luthered" Luther here. First, it is critical to distinguish between "the Law," understood as the totality of material which had to be observed by a devout Jew in St. Paul's time, from "the Law," understood as the Ten Commandments and other moral prescripts. Paul would hold that dietary laws and the like are no longer binding on believers in Jesus Christ, but he never taught that the moral code was abrogated.

Furthermore, the issue raised in Romans (and Galatians before it) has to do with how one is saved; Paul does not say that the Law is useless — indeed, he teaches that it is holy. Since the coming of Christ, however, the Law is subsumed into a Person, Who bears within Himself the total plan of God for man's salvation: He teaches it and lives it. And more, He provides the grace to live according to His example.

Admittedly, this is a very complicated matter in the Pauline writings, not given over to facile treatment.

The commentaries in the *Jerome Biblical Commentary* and in the *Navarre Bible* for the Epistles to the Galatians and Romans are most helpful. Suffice it to say, however, that Pilch's analysis is off-target.

Bible translations

Q. May one still use Challoner's revision of the Douay Bible*? The* New American Bible *and, to a lesser degree, the* Jerusalem Bible *seem to many of us to be stylistically inferior.*
A. For personal reading of the Bible, any text of Scripture is possible, but let me put in my oar on behalf of the *Revised Standard Version* (Catholic edition, 1996, recently reissued by Scepter Press).

Names of the Magi

Q. Where in the Bible can we find the names of Kasper, Melchior, and Baltazar? These are the names we used in blessing homes in the period after Christmas and prior to Epiphany.
A. The story of the Magi is found in Matthew's infancy narrative, but you will find there neither the number three nor the names of the Magi

(usually rendered Caspar, Melchior, Balthasar). Those pieces of information come from pious legends that sprung up quite early in the history of the Church. The judgment that there were three Magi is generally rooted in the number of gifts offered to the Christ Child, according to St. Matthew (gold, frankincense, and myrrh); the presumption seems to be that there couldn't have been more since no one would have arrived empty-handed!

Scripture explained

Q. The commandments tell us to honor our father and mother — and Jesus upheld this (Mt 15:4). It seems, however, that He contradicts His own teaching in Luke 14:26 when He says: "If any man come to me and hate not his father and mother . . . he cannot be my disciple." Could you please explain the meaning of the Scriptures in this regard?

A. The verb "hate" in Hebrew/Aramaic (Our Lord's daily language) does not always carry the full weight of the English. In this context, it merely means "to love less." In other words, Our Lord is saying that no earthly love — even one so good and holy as that of parents — can ever stand in the way of the first and most necessary love: the love of God.

Jesus Seminar

Q. In the November/December 1994 issue of The Catholic Answer *there was a question on the new book by Father Raymond Brown called* The Death of the Messiah. *I have a question about other scholars doing research on the life of Jesus and the Bible. Concerning the work of Dominic Crossan of DePaul University in Chicago and the "Jesus Seminar" that he leads, is there any official Church position regarding this group's writings and what they are saying?*

I do not at all like their theories because I feel that they do not really understand the essence and personality of Jesus. Only through historical research on the time in which Jesus lived are they hoping to arrive at some consensus on an historical Jesus. Could you please comment on the modern day search for an historical Jesus, and most especially on the writings of Dominic Crossan and the Jesus Seminar?

A. As I have indicated in previous columns, no mainstream Scripture scholar — Protestant, Catholic, or Orthodox — takes the Jesus Seminar seriously; it is born of a naïve reliance on the historical-critical method, as well as a heavy dose of arrogance. I do not deny the legitimacy of a desire to "get behind" some of the New Testament images of Jesus, but that must be done in the context of faith, first of all.

Second, we must accept that the "Christ of faith" presented to us in the Gospels is precisely the Person to Whom we pledge our life and love — and that He is in true and direct continuity with the so-called "historical Jesus" Who walked this earth two thousand years ago. Anything less does violence to the whole notion of revelation, inerrancy, and inspiration; it suggests that the Christ of faith is the figment of someone's imagination at best and a phantom at worst.

As an incarnational religion (that is, one that takes historical reality and circumstances seriously), Christianity insists that the "Jesus event" be real; otherwise, not only is it not worth believing in, it is a fraud to be eschewed.

Inclusive Psalms?

Q. I understand that nobody has the right to change the approved texts during the Mass. But please comment on some of the various arrangements of the Psalms put to music in use today.

We know that various members of the hierarchy have realized in their joint meetings that even they do not have the right to change the Psalm wording when they pray the Office together. Yet, we take almost for granted the singing of "poetic" versions of the psalms when set to music. And being that this already seems acceptable, our liturgist then argues that there is nothing to prevent inclusive language as a further poetic rendition of the Psalms — whether recited or sung.

I'm rather perplexed as I understand the changing of the text to fit the music, but fail to see how I can then object to other changes in the text. Please comment.

A. An old Latin proverb informs us that "abuse does not take away use." What do I mean? Just because a legitimate principle can be abused does not nullify the value or acceptability of the norm. For example, did you ever think that the existence of marriage makes possible the sin of adultery? After all, if a marriage bond did not exist, no one could be accused of having sexual relations with a married person (the definition of the sin of the adultery)!

So, I believe it is good and probably necessary to give musicians the leeway to adapt texts when art demands it. But poetic license is not carte blanche; it is certainly not a dispensation to advance ideology. And one thing we would have to say, with all candor and objectivity, is that these inclusive language changes have no poetry in them whatsoever; in truth, they literally hit people over the head with their tedious point of view.

In this, there is no substitute for having the mind of the Church, which never seeks to find loopholes to justify a preconceived course of action.

Jesus Seminar

Q. I have read an article reporting on a group of so-called biblical scholars who claim that Jesus probably didn't say 80 percent of the things that any of the evangelists record in their Gospels. This group calls itself the Jesus Seminar. Have you ever heard of these scholars? Is there any truth to their report?

A. It is the height of arrogance to make claims such as theirs, fully expecting people to take them seriously. It seems to me that a non-believer would find it easier to accept most of what the Gospels tell us Jesus said than to buy the poppycock of the Jesus Seminar. In truth, no serious exegete — Protestant, Catholic, or Orthodox — takes them seriously, which point was recently made in a *New York Times* article on this group.

Images of Christ

Q. A non-Catholic friend claims there are no citations in the Bible which permit or condone images of Christ to be displayed as we do in our churches. Can you direct me to some biblical authority for our practice?

A. First, we Catholics do not look upon the Bible as a big dictionary we consult for every move. Beyond that, our view of Scripture is not that we need a scriptural mandate for everything we do; all we require is that there be no biblical prohibition.

The only scriptural text to which Fundamentalists point is in the Old Testament, wherein the Decalogue forbids the fashioning of graven images. But even that law was not absolute, for the ancient Hebrews are likewise directed by the same God to make images of the cherubim to adorn the ark of the covenant, and Moses is told to make a bronze serpent on whom the children of Israel are to gaze.

Finally, Christian theology — from the earliest days — has held that while attempts to "image" God under the Old Covenant were not allowed and deemed blasphemous, this is not the case under the New Covenant since God has appeared in the mystery of the Incarnation of His divine Son, something highlighted in paragraph 2132 of the *Catechism of the Catholic Church.*

Grail Psalms

Q. What is your opinion of the Grail Psalms? Are they faithful translations or biased?

A. The latest edition of the Grail Psalms has been seriously infected with feminist ideology and should be studiously avoided.

Inclusive language

Q. Regarding the on-going controversy over so-called "inclusive language," why couldn't the publishers of Catholic Bibles produce two versions of the same Bible — one traditional and the other in inclusive language? Let the free market decide which is more popular with the Bible-reading public.

A. There is a kind of attraction to what you propose, at least from a pragmatic, American, free-market mentality, but there are also two problems that I see.

The first is that truly inclusive-language editions of the Sacred Scriptures are not real translations but paraphrases at best; doctrinally, then, the Church cannot allow these works to masquerade as the real thing — which explains why the Congregation for the Doctrine of the Faith indicated that the *New Revised Standard Version* could not be used for either catechesis or liturgy.

The second side, however, is also hard and fast: The proponents of inclusive language know that they have no grassroots support for their movement; they can only prevail by autocratic and bureaucratic sleight-of-hand, cajoling publishers into an all-or-nothing approach. Contrary to what they say, they know in their heart of hearts that the person in the pew has no interest in their nonsense and that, yes, given a genuine choice, will follow the traditional translations.The publishing success of the reissued (traditional) RSV verifies your instinct.

Twelve Apostles

Q. Did Jesus choose twelve apostles to represent the twelve tribes of Israel? If so, who are they, and what is their significance?

A. The twelve tribes of Israel find their ancestry in the sons of Jacob/ Israel, first discussed in Genesis Thirty-five. The names of these men were: Reuben, Simeon, Levi, Judah, Issachar, Zebulun, Gad, Asher, Dan, Naphtali, Joseph, and Benjamin.

Throughout salvation history, "the twelve tribes" have always symbolized the fullness of the People of God. No surprise, therefore, that Jesus would use this image in His formation of the new People of God, reconciled to the Father through His passion, death, and resurrection.

It should not be supposed that each apostle came from a different tribe, but that together — collectively — they embodied the whole People of God.

Bad Thief's name

Q. J.M. inquires in [a recent] issue of The Catholic Answer *as to the name of the Bad Thief who was crucified with Christ. An uncanonical Christian work (possibly of the fourth century), which is commonly referred to as the Gospel of Nicodemus, gives the thief's name as Gestas (chapter seven, verse three).*

A. Thank you — and the other sixty or seventy writers who sent the same information. It is clear that *The Catholic Answer* readers know their Catholic trivia.

A pricey Bible

Q. There seem to be so many Bibles on the market these days. Lately, I have seen an advertisement for the Schocken Bible, *which claims to be a critically acclaimed translation that brings the reader closer to the authentic voice of the Bible than has ever been possible before. Could you tell me what you know of this translation, please? It is to be published in volumes and could make the reading of God's Word quite an expensive proposition.*

A. Volume I takes in "The Books of Moses" or Pentateuch (Torah), the first five books of the Bible — and that is the only volume to appear thus far. The translator is Dr. Everett Fox, and I am intrigued by his product since he has a rather novel approach, in which he rather successfully attempts to capture the rhythm and poetry of the original Hebrew text. This is not to say that it is a perfect translation, but none is. Obviously not intended for a general audience, the work is a pricey $50 and available from Schocken Books in New York City.

Unforgivable sin?

Q. The Bible says the only unforgivable sin is against the Holy Spirit. What kind of sin is this? Why is it unforgivable?

A. For centuries, theologians have debated the exact nature of this sin "against the Holy Spirit" (Mt 12:32; Mk 3:29; Lk 12:10) with most coming to the conclusion that it is the sin of despair. You will recall that on Easter night, the Risen Lord conferred the gift of the Holy Spirit on the apostles, precisely for the forgiveness of sins; hence the Spirit and forgiveness are inextricably linked to one another in the intention of Christ.

If a person is unwilling to ask for forgiveness or refuses to believe that God's mercy is greater than his sin or sinfulness, then we find ourselves before the rejection of the Holy Spirit. It is unforgivable for the simple reason that the sinner does not ask to be forgiven.

St. James

Q. When I was growing up in the 1950s, we were told in Catholic school that the apostle St. James the Less was the person referred to in the Gospels as the brother of Jesus, along with Joseph, Simon, and Jude or Judas. We were also told that he was the author of the Epistle of James, as well as the first bishop of Jerusalem.

In more recent times, it seems that the apostle is not considered to be the author of the epistle or the first bishop of Jerusalem. If the apostle's feast is celebrated on May 3, along with St. Philip, on what day does the Church celebrate the other James, the Bishop of Jerusalem?

A. Many details about the lives of the apostles and others from the apostolic era are lost in the mists of history.

Post-Enlightenment biblical criticism has all too often operated from a "hermeneutic of suspicion" regarding authorship and the like, offering no more evidence against apostolic authors than the Tradition could offer in favor of it. Ironically, we are not infrequently supposed to accord more weight to the former than to the latter. I see no reason to believe twentieth-century skeptics more than Eusebius of Caesarea, who names James as the first bishop of Jerusalem. All this having been said, we should recall that the Christian Faith does not rise or fall on the basis of the identity of the first bishop of Jerusalem, nor does the biblical inspiration and canonicity of a biblical book rise or fall on knowing the name of the human author. *Our Sunday Visitor's Encyclopedia of*

Catholic History has a good write-up on St. James and on the authorship of the epistle that bears that name.

No NRSV allowed

Q. All of the lectors in my parish recently received a memo from the priest-moderator stating: "This year we will be using the New Revised Standard Version *[text] for our liturgies. Please be aware of this when you prepare your readings at home." I thought the NRSV was the version of Scripture in the Canadian Lectionary that was withdrawn from usage by the Congregation for the Doctrine of the Faith. Could you please clarify this issue?*

A. You are correct. Your priest has no right to use that Lectionary or version of Sacred Scripture. The diocesan liturgical commission and/or bishop should be informed, so as to bring the practice to a grinding halt.

Morality

Legal and ethical?

Q. Is it ethical and in harmony with the Church's teaching to take steps to protect a couple's assets (in advance) so that possible confinement of a spouse to a nursing home will not result in the other spouse's being reduced to a near state of poverty? It is my understanding that Social Security and pension benefits would automatically go to the nursing home, in addition to most of the couple's assets which have been accumulated over the years. Some say it is legal *to take this action, but is it* honest?

A. All too often we are faced with possible actions today that are the source of a moral dilemma for good people. As you describe the process, I would consider it not only legal but ethical. Other examples come to mind as well. For instance, priests are routinely asked to witness clandestine marriages for senior citizens who, were the union publicly celebrated and registered, would lose half of what little income they presently have. Many clergy judge the tax policy so unjust that they deem the couple's desire to be moral and their own activity as well.

Parents making out tuition payments to the parish church instead of the school (so as to qualify for a tax write-off) is another example. All too frequently, welfare mothers are actively encouraged by flawed policies not to marry, lest they lose significant benefits for themselves and their children. A government that operated from a holistic moral view would not put people into such situations, and that is the primary question to be addressed, in my judgment.

Sci-fi quest

Q. I'm an aspiring writer working on a Christian science-fiction novel. The story is "pro-life" in that it involves the rescue of more than one hundred embryos from a testing lab. The hero intends to implant these embryos in volunteer women to allow them to grow and have normal lives. The hero's ship is stranded on a space station run by an order of nuns; actually, a convent in space. When he realizes that he cannot repair his ship and make it to the planet where the volunteers are waiting, one of the nuns suggests that he implant the embryos in the sisters.

Given the Church's stand on things such as in vitro fertilization and other high-tech means of achieving pregnancy, would the local bishop be able to give the nuns permission to do this? If this implantation does not take place, the embryos will die.

I understand this is a strange question, but I do not want to write anything that would show members of the Church acting in violation of Church standards. Please comment.

A. I agree that it's a strange question and at the risk of seeming to rain on your parade, I would suggest that you abandon your plot for the novel! That having been said, no bishop or any other human authority can give permission to engage in a direct violation of God's law. *Donum Vitae*, the latest Vatican pronouncement on artificial insemination, sums it up in this manner: "Furthermore, the artificial fertilization of a woman who is unmarried or a widow, whoever the donor may be, cannot be morally justified." I would strongly recommend reading the entire document for an in-depth discussion of a very complex moral issue, which can rarely become the stuff of novels without serious loss of precision and nuance.

Conscience explained

Q. Please explain to me why now it's being taught that you can listen to the Church's teachings, examine, pray, and study an issue, and (then) make your own decision on whether to accept the Church's teaching or not! Is this something from Vatican II? What is wrong with blind obedience? Is it true that ultimately the practice of the people becomes the practice of the Church?

A. The Church has never advocated blind obedience because that would be to eschew the gifts of intelligence and free will with which Almighty God endows every human being. What we are to do is inform our conscience by taking in the truth that comes to us from the Sacred Scriptures and the Tradition of the Church, as well as the contemporary Magisterium; that is then integrated through personal prayer and reflection. The entire process prepares us to make practical judgments about the moral good or evil of particular actions when the time comes. All too many people of late equate conscience with personal opinion, but that is a false equation. Personal opinion has nothing to do with conscience formation, except that at times our private opinions need to be changed by the truths of faith.

Some say that they are comfortable in acting in contradiction to authentic Church teaching because they have a "clear conscience." I would respectfully disagree and suggest that they can do so not because of a clear conscience but due to having an unformed or misinformed one or, even worse, a dead conscience.

The Fathers of the Second Vatican Council faced such a theory head-on when they declared that "the faithful, for their part, are obliged to submit to their bishops' decision, made in the name of Christ, in matters of faith and morals, and to adhere to it with a ready and respectful allegiance of mind. This loyal submission of the will and intellect must be given, in a special way, to the authentic teaching authority of the Roman Pontiff, even when he does not speak *ex cathedra*" (*Lumen Gentium,* no. 25).

As far as "the practice of the people" becoming "the practice of the Church" is concerned, two observations are in order: (1) The Church is not a democracy, and so doctrine is not formed on the basis of the latest Gallup Poll. Church teaching is something revealed and received, not made from whole cloth according to the whims and fancies of a particular time or place. (2) Reality proves the assertion false as well. For example, although the vast majority of married Catholics in the United States have ignored Catholic teaching on artificial contraception for the past thirty years, not only has the teaching not changed, but it has been repeatedly restated, each time with greater force and urgency. We also have seen the same procedure in reference to the ordination of women; *Ordinatio Sacerdotalis* put forth the constant teaching in the clearest and most absolute of terms, despite more than twenty years of agitation for a change.

Sterilization query

Q. At a recent RCIA meeting at our parish, our pastor stated that he felt it was all right for a couple to have a sterilization if they had several children, the man was at a low-paying job, and the woman could not work. Is this in agreement with Church teaching?

A. No, it is not. The Magisterium has consistently taught that direct, non-therapeutic sterilization is to be repudiated. In his encyclical *Humanae Vitae* ("On Human Life"), Pope Paul VI wrote: "Equally to be excluded, as the teaching authority of the Church has frequently declared, is direct sterilization, whether perpetual or temporary, whether of the man or of the woman" (no. 14). Documents of the present pontiff and of the Congregation for the Doctrine of the Faith have reinforced that position forcefully and with regularity over the past twenty-five years.

A natural aid

Q. Is it permissible according to Catholic moral teaching to use a naturally produced hormone in an intramuscular injection to stimulate the release of an ovum from an ovary and then, after careful monitoring to know that the ovum has been released, to use another hormone that affects the uterus, so that the egg has a better chance of taking hold and growing?

A. If you are accurately describing the procedure and I am understanding you correctly, I can see nothing wrong with it since it merely appears to be aiding, in a natural way, to remedy a physical disability that makes pregnancy difficult, if not impossible.

An American classic

Q. Our son is a freshman at a Catholic high school. In his English class, he was required to read Of Mice and Men. *Throughout the book, the dialogue uses God's name in vain. As parents, we were thoroughly displeased that a Catholic school would have the students read such a book. The principal insisted that the book was good literature and added that there was an alternate reading list if parents objected to certain books, but this would be too hard on the child. It is our opinion that the school is in some sense promoting the use of God's name in vain. What is your opinion on this matter? Should we fight to have this book removed from the school reading list? It seems to us that it is wrong even to read the book.*

A. Thirty years ago, when I was a freshman in a Catholic high school, we had to read the same work — and I suspect that it was on reading lists long before that. Why? Not because Catholic educators want to encourage obscenity but because this happens to be a classic of American literature — in spite of the profanity.

I think it is quite possible to explain to teenagers that taking God's name in vain is a sin, all the while acknowledging the regrettable fact that some people commit that sin and that literature often reflects real-life situations. Pushing things like this to their logical (or illogical) conclusions, one would end up banning most of Shakespeare and the Bible because they recount immoral acts. In all cases, there is no substitute for common sense and prudence, a combination which knows instinctively when bad language and improper behavior are being advocated and when they are simply being presented at face value.

Seal of Confession

Q. Our grandson is attending CCD classes taught by our new pastor. Last evening, the class was told that there is one case in which the seal of confession can be broken, namely, in the case of child abuse.

While this is a very serious matter, I was always taught the seal of confession is absolutely inviolable, even if the priest is threatened with being put to death.

I am very concerned about this matter and I would be grateful to hear what the Church teaches.

A. The priest is absolutely wrong. Under no circumstances may the seal of confession be broken (cf. Canon 983); the penalty for violation of the sacramental seal is an automatic excommunication (cf. Canon 1388).

Superstition

Q. Inquiries were made as to the ecclesiastical approval of a devotion that has been promoted in our area. It consists of praying two thousand Hail Marys, with a promise that three petitions I announced at the start of the devotion will be granted. Is there any theological reason to accept this devotion? Can we accept this devotion because its promoter is a priest?

A. This is the type of "devotion" which gives a bad name to all genuine devotions, causing real stumbling blocks to those outside the Church who may be truly open to the Church. Superstition is superstition and ought to be called by its proper name.

Social reparation

Q. Regarding justice to Indians, whose land was taken from them by force and maltreatment, how does one do justice to their descendants as far as buying, selling, and renting land? Isn't land taken by force, deceit or broken treaties to be considered stolen property? Land is only one matter; slavery is another. What does the Church teach about making reparation for this kind of injustice?

A. Making reparations is a very delicate topic, and one which demands a good amount of common sense and prudence. To the extent that one can repair historical damage, that ought to be done. However, to whom and how? Most of these historical abuses occurred generations and even centuries ago. Land, in particular, has changed hands dozens of times since the original injustice. Certainly, it would be equally unjust to take the same land away from its current owners as a means of trying to undo the first sin.

If I were the heir of a person who had appropriated land or possessions unjustly, I think I would have a moral obligation to restore it to its rightful owner or his immediate descendant. Clearly, that is not possible with regard to either American Indians or Blacks. Similarly, it would be wrong to hold responsible young Germans today for what some of their ancestors did during the Nazi Holocaust. The best we can usually do under such circumstances is to learn a lesson from history and resolve never to repeat the errors in our own time and place. And that, it seems to me, would actually be the best way to honor the memory of the injured parties and to make worthwhile reparation.

Internal forum

Q. If your confessor is also your spiritual director, can he instigate or openly ask you about matters discussed in a sacramental confession during a private spiritual direction meeting which is also in the internal forum?

A. Permit me to set a context for readers who may not understand all the issues involved. When we speak of the internal forum, we refer to conversation that takes place under the guarantee of confidentiality. Both spiritual direction and sacramental confession partake of the internal forum. It is part of the seal of confession that a priest cannot initiate any conversation outside the Sacrament of Penance with a penitent about anything mentioned during a confession. Since both activities are in the internal forum, the questioner raises an interesting and important point.

I cannot find any conclusive answer to the inquiry, but I would reason through it thus: The most absolute and binding form of confidentiality is connected with the Sacrament of Penance; while other forms of communication admit of exceptions, that does not. Furthermore, since persons other than priests can serve as spiritual directors and only priests can be confessors, it would seem to me that a priest should go the extra mile in safeguarding the integrity of the sacramental seal and not give even the impression that the seal might be infringed.

If any canonist or moralist differs with me on this, I would be happy to receive that input and share it with our readers.

Infertility guidance

Q. My husband and I are having some problems conceiving a second child and are going to a clinic for infertility treatment. How far can we take this process according to the Church? There are some things I don't agree with, like the harvesting of eggs and in vitro fertilization outside the womb. I don't see a problem with insemination using my husband's sperm; however, I have been told this is absolutely forbidden by the Church. I don't understand why this would be so. Before we take this procedure too far, I want to know what the rules and guidelines are.

A. You need to get hold of *Donum Vitae*, the document on this subject from the Congregation for the Doctrine of the Faith. In short, the Church opposes techniques that separate the unitive and procreative aspects of the marital act. The Church condemns artificial contraception because it seeks to advance the unitive element at the expense of the procreative; the Church similarly condemns forms of artificial conception which advance the procreative at the expense of the unitive. For a thumbnail sketch of this teaching, see paragraphs 2373-2379 of the *Catechism of the Catholic Church*.

Donum Vitae explains the Church's skittishness about various procedures designed to promote fertility apart from normal sexual intercourse in this way: This type of act "entrusts the life and identity of the embryo into the power of doctors and biologists and establishes the domination of technology over the origin and destiny of the human person. Such a relationship of domination is in itself contrary to the dignity and equality that must be common to parents and children" (no. II, 5). Pope John Paul II also provides sensitive, pastoral guidance to childless couples in his document on the family, *Familiaris Consortio.*

Homosexual "marriages"

Q. I have been shocked by the claims made in John Boswell's book Same-Sex Unions in Premodern Europe *that gay marriage was practiced and sanctioned by the Church in Europe until the sixteenth century. Boswell is regarded by some as a pre-eminent historian and so the publication of this book will help to advance the cause of homosexual marriages, without a doubt. Since I am not an historian or a theologian, could you please comment on the claims made by Boswell? Was there a same-sex marriage ceremony dating from the earliest Christian liturgical sources which was only banned in the fourteenth century because of a misinterpretation and, if so, how did [and does] this reflect the constant teaching of the Church regarding sexuality? We need a learned rebuttal to this attack.*

A. Boswell was a bright man who generally had good control of his sources, but he is also widely regarded in the academic community as being a purveyor of advocacy literature. What I mean is that he takes bits and pieces of historical data and puts them together in such a way as to make assertions that the data do not truly justify. He did this in his first work on homosexuality several years ago and now again. Even objective, secular reviewers have been forced to remark about this tendency of his. It is surely a weakness of a researcher that he would allow pre-conceived notions to guide his research and, most especially, to make him form conclusions which are at best quite iffy and at worst absolutely untenable.

In terms of this specific issue of "gay marriage ceremonies," I should note that I have read Boswell's book and remain singularly unimpressed by it all. In point of fact, the bulk of the work was already published by the Vatican Archives years ago; therefore, one can intuit that the material could hardly be damaging to traditional Catholic moral principles and tradition. All that the author is able to demonstrate — without imposing a very skewed interpretation on things — is that the Early Church took over from Greco-Roman pagan culture the practice of men adopting other men to signify a particular bond between them and giving the "adoptee" rights in regard to the estate of the "adopter." In none of the literature is there ever so much of a hint that these ceremonies countenanced sexual expression within the relationship; although there are elements in common between the rites for male-female unions and the same-sex unions, there are also significant differences.

One final point is also critical to appreciate: In the Middle Ages, it was not unusual for even heterosexual unions to be lived as totally celibate, non-genital relationships (whether or not we would approve of that today is another matter entirely), but we should surely not project our own contemporary preoccupation with sex onto another age, let alone insist that what some people today might do was in fact done ten centuries ago.

Mass and sinners

Q. According to Canon 916 of the present Code, "a person who is conscious of grave sin is not to celebrate Mass. . . . I knew we couldn't receive Communion, but we aren't even supposed to celebrate (attend) Mass in a state of mortal sin?

A. That portion of the canon is referring to a priest. I guess your confusion stems from your supposition that the law is envisioning everyone as a "celebrant" of the liturgy, which is not the case here and is not so in Catholic eucharistic theology.

The celebrant of the eucharistic sacrifice is an ordained priest who functions *in persona Christi capitis* ("in the person of Christ the Head"); in that capacity, he represents the community of the faithful in a unique and irreplaceable manner. All others in the liturgical assembly join him in this act of worship, each participating according to his or her proper role within the one Body of Christ.

To answer your specific question, then, let me assure you that the Church certainly expects those in the state of mortal sin to reconcile themselves with Christ and His Church through sacramental confession as quickly as possible, but she also certainly expects them to continue assisting at Sunday Mass in the interim.

The best example of what I am referring to comes out with those who have divorced and remarried: Although they are not able to receive the sacraments of Penance and Holy Communion because of the ongoing mortally sinful nature of their second union, the Church most definitely encourages them to live up to all their other Christian obligations (including that of Sunday Mass) and to seek the grace needed to bring their lives into conformity with the values of the Gospel.

No contradiction

Q. In [a recent] issue of The Catholic Answer, *there seemed to be a contradiction between the article by Michael Gask, "Why It's Not Open-Season on Abortionists" and the Q & A response "Sharpshooter." Since these articles seem contradictory to me, I was wondering about the editorial policy of the magazine. Michael Gask would have done well in Nazi Germany, especially at Treblinka, in condemning the rebels at that death camp.*

A. I think we have a clear coherent editorial policy, and I see no contradiction whatsoever between the two pieces you cite. Mr. Gask makes the point that one of the very reasons why abortion-clinic violence is wrong — according to traditional Catholic morality — is that there is no assurance that any lives will be saved by killing one particular abortionist. The rebels at Treblinka (or in similar situations) had some reasoned expectations that: a) any guards killed by them would not be immediately replaced, thus leading to b) a well-founded hope of escape for at least some of the prisoners.

Careful thinking and the making of critical distinctions in an academic setting enable us to make intelligent and moral decisions when under fire. Name-calling and the mixing of apples and oranges do nothing for the pro-life cause or for one's own life in Christ.

Let us also remember that Mr. Gask made the crucial distinction that one may never directly intend the killing of the other person.

Marital abuse

Q. *Does the Church have any clear teaching on whether or not a husband has a right to make all final decisions in the name of obedience? Does a wife have a right to demand that her husband stop verbally abusing her and their children and to leave him if it continues?*

A. In my experience, when people start talking about "rights" within the context of the family, one has usually already gotten into problems. St. Paul consistently presents us with the image of Christ the Bridegroom desirous of demonstrating His love for His Bride, the Church, as the appropriate metaphor to govern family relations. Eagerness to show forth love does not rely on the assertion of rights.

Obviously, there will be times when a final decision must be made by one person, but I am not so sure that Christ offers us as absolute a formula on this as some of our Fundamentalist friends would hold. I know of many families in which "final decisions" are made by both spouses, depending upon the circumstances involved, and the competencies needed to resolve a dilemma or conflict. For example, would it make sense that the father automatically have veto power over financial matters if he can't balance a checkbook and is a compulsive gambler, all the while having a wife whose training and disposition qualify her to make such judgments? It seems to me that the deferring to one another in love, which St. Paul urges, takes all such scenarios into consideration.

As to spousal abuse (which, let's recall, can be visited on either spouse; women, after all, are not only victims but also perpetrators at times), permit me to make the following point. Abuse of any kind is out of place in a home where Christ reigns; it needs to be identified for what it is, brought to the attention of the guilty party who should repent of such behavior and seek all the required means to see that this never recur. Where malice or sickness seems to be insuperable, the innocent partner must safeguard his or her own welfare and that of any children.

Pornography

Q. There has been an on-going debate in our family over the use of pornographic material. I feel that because it exploits the use of sexuality, not to mention the person, that it is always wrong to read pornographic magazines or view such videos. Others in our family have advanced the idea that some people use it as a means to arousal, and that as long as the sexual act between the spouses is not interfered with, it is legitimate to use these "aids." What does the Church have to say about this issue?

A. Precisely because all pornography is degrading in and of itself, its use can never be justified. We also know from serial rapists, for example, that its regular use leads to other problems. If married couples require this type of external stimulation, I would suggest that they see a physician, psychologist, or counselor.

A fine line

Q. How do we stand as Catholics trying to maintain the virtue of charity in criticizing bishops and priests who do not follow the Magisterium without offending against the virtue of charity? I find it so difficult going to confession on a two-week schedule and confessing these offenses of the tongue on a continuous basis. Are we not obliged to protest in some way to save our beloved Church? Your comments would be very much appreciated.

A. Yes, it is a fine line, and with the confusion that abounds today, it is essential to be able to negotiate that line very carefully. St. Paul counseled the early Christians to "do the truth in love," which is easier said than done since most of us find it easier to gravitate toward truth *or* love, but not both at the same time. One must also seek to operate from pure motives and never out of a desire for revenge or to win an argument for its own sake. A great temptation for the person who gets involved in such matters is to become consumed by the process or the movement itself and to lose sight of the basic values that one originally sets out to defend. When someone is convinced that something wrong is being said or done, that person should try to correct the situation in the manner which is most effective and which causes the least amount of scandal. As you can see, this is a most delicate process demanding great prudence. Now, some people hear "prudence" and think that means keeping quiet. Prudence, according to St. Thomas Aquinas, is knowing exactly what to say or do in the present circumstances so as to achieve one's legitimate goals.

I guess what I'm saying is that running around like a bull in a China shop is no good, nor is a refusal to get into the fray for fear of public opinion or political considerations. The greatest saints in history and surely the greatest reformers (like Sts. Charles Borromeo, Ignatius of Loyola, Catherine of Siena, and Teresa of Ávila) knew the minefield they were getting into. They did what was necessary because of their love for the Church and also out of a sincere and intense desire to love the wayward in such a way that they were returned to the full and liberating truth of the Catholic Faith.

Counseling is needed

Q. My husband, children, and I all converted to Catholicism twelve years ago. My husband and I have always tried to instill high moral standards in our children, so you can imagine our shock three years ago when one of our daughters told us she was pregnant. She had the baby, kept it (couldn't bring herself to give it up for adoption), and we have helped her raise it. But it all gets worse. Then a second daughter got pregnant. She was adamantly opposed to having the baby at all, and we supported her in her decision to abort.

As a result, my husband and I are in the state of mortal sin. I cannot go to confession, I guess, because I'm not at all sorry for my decision and, if it happened again, I would do the same thing all over again. The first girl's child and she are not doing well at all, so why bring on a second disaster? Frankly, I consider my action to be one of self-defense — defense of myself and my daughter. Can we ever be forgiven?

A. The anguish of your situation comes out loud and clear in your letter. Although I do not know you, I sense a great deal of confusion, pain, and embarrassment — all of which are clouding your judgment and what is probably your basic moral sense as you attempt to justify your action and that of your second daughter. No matter how poorly your first daughter and her child are doing (and that is always a debatable and subjective evaluation), a fundamental Christian assessment is that to have lived is always better than never to have lived at all. Beyond that, it is always possible to improve one's quality of life for self or another if life is present. With no life (and having been instrumental in the taking of an innocent human life), no improvement is ever possible.

I would suggest that you contact a good and wise priest and/or your diocesan family-life or pro-life office for some needed counseling to aid you in coming to grips with what you have done and get you on the road to repentance. This is the only way you will be able to put this all behind you in an effective and moral manner.

Health care

Q. Our group medical coverage has added a new "benefit" — abortion coverage. I have real problems with this since I think I'm being forced to pay for the abortions of others. Is it morally permissible to continue enrollment in this medical plan?

Q. You have repeatedly written that those who cooperate in abortion are excommunicated. If President Clinton gets his way, won't we all be doing just that, in effect? Will Catholics then have to withhold their taxes in protest?

A. We need to resist all these plans with all our strength. Certainly, where alternative options exist, we should use them. As far as the proposed governmental health plan is concerned, we must make it eminently clear that Catholics will not accept any program that fosters abortion in any way: Our institutions will refuse to participate, as will individual Catholics. If the entire Catholic community (27 percent of the total population) mounted an effective protest against this immoral proposal, it would die aborning.

If it, God forbid, does become part of the so-called health-care package, then a question arises that each of us must answer for himself: Should I, as a practicing Catholic, register opposition to it at every level, including the withholding of taxes?

Speaking for myself, the answer is yes. But if we do our job at this stage of the process, more drastic action will not be necessary later on.

Rape and the pill

Q. Is it correct for me as a Catholic physician to offer birth-control pills to a rape victim to prevent pregnancy?

A. A rape victim has the moral right to stave off conception by any procedure that is not abortifacient. My understanding of the so-called morning-after pills is that they do not prevent conception; rather, they kill the fertilized egg after the fact and are thus immoral. Needless to say, a committed Catholic cannot participate in such a procedure in any way or for any reason.

Christian vs. Christian

Q. In [a recent] issue of TCA, you counseled against Christians going to court, but isn't this exactly what was behind the deceitful actions of bishops in covering up child-molestation charges with hush money, in-house counseling, and clandestine transfers? Our government is not hostile to the Church or Christians, so why shouldn't Catholics who have suffered at the hands of other Catholics seek legal redress? By the way, I am a prosecuting attorney.

A. Undoubtedly, you will recall the legal aphorism: *Nemo judex in causa sua* ("No one can be a judge in his own case"): I think it might apply in the present instance. While I would be the last to condone any kind of cover-up, I believe your statements are a bit too simplistic. After all, when a diocese has insisted on engaging in a full-blown judicial process, invariably the Church has been accused of not being "pastoral"; when the Church has been "pastoral" by providing counseling and justifiable compensation, she is charged with "cover-up."

As for your assertion that "our government is not hostile to the Church," I must ask with all due respect if you live in the same country as I. Not only is the society-at-large anti-Catholic, but this is ten times more true when it comes to the court system — and now the Clinton administration to the nth degree (see the question "Health care" on page 159 for more on attempts to force the Church to participate in this administration's passion for abortion).

Doubts vs. questions

Q. Is it a sin to doubt? When it comes to religious matters, are we as Catholics required to accept what we are told without question? It seems that doubt can sometimes be a good thing. Never to doubt seems to be very similar to being brainwashed. Please comment.

A. Your question seems to indicate that you are equating doubting with questioning, and I think the equation is wrong. If the act of faith is to be a truly human act, it needs to include the element of reason. In other words, faith is not and cannot be irrational. It is indeed a good thing to dissect the doctrines of our holy Faith in such a way that we seek to understand them as best we can with our limited human intellects. This is no more or less than what St. Anselm dubbed as *"fides quaerens intellectum"* ("faith seeking understanding"). This is a far cry from doubt or, even worse, rejection of revealed doctrine.

Cardinal John Henry Newman, the great English convert, put it best when he reminded us that "a thousand questions never equal a single doubt," for the simple reason that questioning done within the overall context of belief is itself a part of the act of faith. At a certain point in the searching process, we do have to be humble enough to admit that we have gone as far as possible and submit to divine revelation with the proper attitude.

Masturbation query

Q. You've said before that masturbation is a "serious sin." Is it a mortal sin in the laws of the Church?

About ten years ago I was teaching a course called "Christian Morality" to high school students. In our textbook, masturbation was discussed vaguely. I asked one of the priests in the school how I should teach it in relation to sin, and he told me "as long as it's not 'obsessive' it is OK." Well, taking that as my authority, that's what I taught. Now I feel as if I completely misled many young people into serious, possibly mortal, sin. Have I?

A. Masturbation is, objectively speaking, always grave matter. Particular circumstances can mitigate guilt. For example, as adolescents are becoming aware of their sexual identity, they may almost accidentally fall into the practice; once informed of the moral status of the act, they need to break off the behavior.

Another situation would be when masturbation has become

compulsive due to some other psychosexual disorder; the compulsion limits human freedom and thus diminishes culpability. Now, none of these mitigating circumstances should be taken as carte blanche for continuing an objectively disordered behavior, but such realizations should assist a mature believer in assessing the moral gravity of the acts in question. That person should also be helped to work out of the sinful behavior as quickly as possible through the assistance of a good confessor/spiritual director and/or a good Christian psychologist.

Godparental prudence

Q. What is the responsibility of lay persons to instruct their fellow Catholics on Church teaching? In particular, I am thinking of Humanae Vitae. *I would gladly leave such instruction to the priests and bishops, but I have yet to hear contraception and sterilization even mentioned from the pulpit, let alone condemned. My godchild's parents, my sister and brother-in-law, make no secret of their sterilization. I don't believe they really know it is wrong. Would I be wrong to destroy their "good faith" conscience, or is it my responsibility to witness to the Faith as a godparent? Surely the contraceptive marriage is hurting them, even if there is no culpability on their part. What will this example do for my niece?*

A. We have to approach delicate situations with prudence; if we come off like a bull in a china shop, we accomplish little or nothing. In all honesty, I don't see how anyone can legitimately claim ignorance of Catholic teaching on artificial contraception. I have often said that I think I could stand in Grand Central Station on any given day and ask the first five hundred non-Catholics getting off trains what that teaching is and not get a single wrong answer. So, if people outside the Church know the answer, how much "good faith" or "good will" is there on the part of a Catholic who pleads confusion or ignorance?

Perhaps the best way to raise the issue is to speak about the matter in reference to a person other than one who is present or to utilize one of the Holy Father's many allusions to the teaching as a springboard for your own discussion. If the teaching is handled in a dispassionate, third-party fashion, you will at least be able to get a reading on their attitude, and that should give you a solid clue as to how you should proceed, if at all.

Is cohabitation OK?

Q. My fiancé and I recently came across a perfect house and purchased it, together. Although we are not getting married for seven months, we are both now living in the house. Is it a sin for us to be living together now?

A. Although you don't mention it, I presume you are not living as husband and wife, for I am sure you know that would surely be sinful. So, let us assume perfect innocence on the part of both of you; is this situation good? I would respond in the negative for at least two reasons: First, you are putting each other in proximity to an occasion of sin. Human nature being what it is, we should take seriously our natural inclinations and not overburden our weak flesh with unnecessary temptations.

Second, no matter how pure your intentions and actions, few people outside could even imagine that a young couple today could be living together without resorting to conjugal relations.

Therefore, the sin of scandal is involved. Now, you can say that this is none of their business and that they have no right judging the two of you (and you are right to a certain extent), but you must also take responsibility for the impressions you create; given the sex-saturated society in which we live, I am afraid that your neighbors' conclusions about your relationship would not be unduly strained.

Why not rent out the house until you are married?

Never lose hope

Q. I am married outside the Church. My husband, who is non-Catholic, was married previously and will never seek an annulment. This raises so many questions for me. Since I cannot participate in the sacramental life of the Church, am I barred from the presence of the Holy Spirit? Is marriage after divorce an unforgivable sin since there is no possibility of confession and absolution? I attend Mass faithfully but do not receive Communion, even though my parish priest advised me to receive. I pray for the Holy Spirit to help me in prayer and daily life. Is this pointless since I am not in a state of grace? I would be ever so grateful for your advice and any recommendations for reading.

A. Your personal integrity and love for the Church are truly admirable. Let me try to hit upon some of your concerns.

First, there is no such thing as an unforgivable sin; however, we must be willing to give up the sin in order to obtain forgiveness. Therein lies the rub in regard to divorce and remarriage since, as I have explained before in these pages, each act of sexual intercourse in the second union constitutes a renewed sin of adultery. You clearly understand that, which is why you are (correctly) refraining from the reception of Holy Communion; it is a pity that your parish priest doesn't seem to understand it. A remarriage situation is more complicated than, let us say, an occasional lapse into illicit sex with a prostitute because it involves an ongoing relationship from which no exit is either envisioned or desired.

Second, your love for the Church and an already heroic approach give reason for hope. Perhaps one day the Lord will provide the necessary grace for things to change in one of two ways. He may move the heart of your present husband to seek a decree of nullity, paving the way for the validation of your union in the Church. Or He may give you both the grace to live as brother and sister, now or somewhere up the line, so that your access to the sacraments can be reopened. And so, you are not beyond the grace of God, Who can indeed work miracles in the lives of those who — although weak — love Him and want to do His holy will, even though they fall short all too often.

Third, get hold of a copy of Pope John Paul II's apostolic exhortation on the Christian family, *Familiaris Consortio* (available from the Daughters of St. Paul, 50 St. Paul's Ave., Jamaica Plain, Boston, MA 02130), in which he devotes a special section to the unique problems encountered by Catholics who are divorced and remarried. There you will receive the best encouragement possible from an understanding and loving father who is present to you in your difficulties.

The need for honesty

Q. I just wanted to thank you for your response to the question in [a recent] issue of TCA about masturbation. I accidentally discovered the practice at a very young age, and it became habitual. It has been, and continues to be, a struggle. I am thankful that your reader had the courage to ask the question and that you gave the Church's teaching clearly on this matter.

A. For many years now, I have seen that speaking the truth is, ultimately, always the most loving thing we can do. We need not be nasty or judgmental, but we must be honest — in reference to revealed truth, in regard to the true situation of people, and in terms of what they can and should do in response to divine grace. To do otherwise is to shortchange believers in the long run.

Marital question

Q. I have a friend who was married by a justice of the peace. He is a Catholic, but married a lady who was divorced and refused to seek an annulment; therefore, they could not have been married in the Church. As a result, he knows that he is not allowed to receive the sacraments. Years later, however, this lady joined the Church and now she goes to Communion every week. Is this situation correct? Surely since they both were married by a justice of the peace, there can't be different standards for the admission of the spouses to the sacraments. I'm confused; please comment.

A. My puzzlement is not just that the woman in question is receiving the sacraments, but that she was admitted to the Church, to begin with. If a potential convert approaches a priest for instructions, the priest must ascertain that the candidate has no impediments to the reception of the sacraments. Someone previously married with no decree of nullity and living in an invalid second union cannot be received into the Church unless and until the situation is remedied — if it can be. So, the basic question is how a priest justified the original action; unless you are lacking some critical data, I cannot understand it at all and must conclude that his action was completely wrong.

Mass obligation

Q. At what age am I no longer obligated to attend Mass on Sundays and holy days? I am sixty-five years old and not in the best of health.

A. The Code of Canon Law instructs us thus: "On Sundays and other holy days of obligation, the faithful are obliged to participate in the Mass. They are also to abstain from such work or business that would inhibit the worship to be given to God, the joy proper to the Lord's Day, or the due relaxation of mind and body" (Canon 1247). You will notice that no age is given for that duty; it is generally held to bind from the age of reason until death.

Now, of course, if one is incapacitated due to sickness or old age, the obligation is not in effect. The Code, however, advises that "if it is impossible to assist at a eucharistic celebration, either because no sacred minister is available or for some other grave reason, the faithful are strongly recommended to take part in a liturgy of the Word, if there be such in the parish church or some other sacred place, which is celebrated in accordance with the provisions laid down by the diocesan bishop; or to spend an appropriate time in prayer, whether personally or as a family or, as occasion presents, in a group of families" (Canon 1248.2).

In many places, the homebound also have the possibility of participating in the Mass by television. I would caution people, however, not to excuse themselves too lightly from the Sunday Mass obligation; it has often caused me great amazement to discover that senior citizens who claim they are too infirm to come to church on Sunday go to the hairdresser on Monday and to bingo on Tuesday!

Dormitory visits

Q. At most "Catholic" colleges and universities most students are housed in co-ed dorms, usually with males and females on alternating floors. Even in all-male or all-female dorms, visitation in the students' rooms is allowed until midnight on weekdays and 2 a.m. on weekends. Are not these living arrangements occasions of sin?

A. It seems to me that once we allowed any visitations in dorms, we had opened a Pandora's box; after all, at the risk of sounding crude, we have to admit that we know that people can engage in immoral behavior at any time of day or night; curfews and the like were merely attempts to put a more moral face on it all. The Church has always had a good instinct on human nature and has thus kept people away from "the near occasions of sin." I don't know whether we have lost that healthy sense of human nature or whether we honestly believe that human drives and instincts are different today (even though all the evidence is to the contrary); the worst possibility would be that we don't really care about sinful behavior. The critical point, however, is that — for my money — allowing for co-ed dorms is a disaster, as is allowing young folks to visit each other's rooms; any worthwhile social activity can and should be done in a public or at least semi-public forum.

Is astrology sinful?

Q. With the popularity of psychic and readings and astrological charts, I would like a definition of the Church's position relative to participation in either of these activities. At my own parish one of the priests said that it was a mortal sin to participate in either of them since they are avenues of the devil. I question the severity of this pronouncement. Some of the most popular psychics and astrologers are Christian and Catholic, saying that their gift is a gift from God everyone has if it is properly developed. What is your opinion? Please advise.

A. While the Church does not approve of either psychic readings or astrology (see the *Catechism of the Catholic Church* 2110-2117 on this matter), I think it also fair to say that most people who get involved in these things do it mostly for fun and do not take it all incredibly seriously. If that is the operative attitude, I don't think we can describe someone's participation as diabolical. The Church's difficulty with all occult practices is that they tend to become substitute gods and involvement with them can also bespeak a lack of trust in divine providence. Astrology is not a science, and its practitioners generally prey on the ignorant. While I would be willing to say that some psychics might indeed have a special gift from God (some saints were known for types of clairvoyance, for example), in the main we are also face-to-face with fraud and manipulation of the gullible. Hence, for all those reasons, I would strongly counsel Catholics to steer clear of all such things.

Validly married

Q. In [a recent] issue of The Catholic Answer, *we learned that our daughter, who just married a Jew, did not receive the Sacrament of Matrimony, even though a priest was present. How can they go about receiving the sacrament? Her husband is very open to learning about our Faith and goes to church with her every Sunday.*

A. I hope you did not misunderstand my response: Your daughter is validly married in the eyes of God and the Church, but she did not receive the Sacrament of Matrimony. Why? Because that necessarily involves two baptized believers. Therefore, the only way the union could be sacramentalized would be if her husband became a Christian.

Prison problem

Q. I am a Catholic and a prisoner seeking advice and counsel on a troubling and confusing subject. I was brought up as a Catholic, with all the traditional doctrines and ceremonies. Admittedly, I have faltered in the practice of my faith. However, I am now at the crossroads of my life, seeking atonement and spiritual enlightenment. In doing so, however, I am faced with a perplexing dilemma. Prison officials are demanding that I become an informant and disclose information I have obtained from assisting illiterate and poorly educated prisoners in their judicial proceedings. If I fail to comply, I shall remain in "segregation lock-up" until I die or am paroled. The Book of Daniel likens an informant to "one who eats the flesh of another." The Book of Sirach emphasizes the proper use of speech, which rules out gossip and "informing." And, in the New Testament, the informant is personified by Judas. Yet my only hope for release from segregation is to be an informant. Please help me. The prison chaplain supports the prison officials and recommends that I become an informant.*

A. I presume that prison officials are asking you to inform them about illegal and/or immoral activity on the part of other inmates. If that is so, then I think it is not only right to cooperate but that failure to do so would be immoral.

Clear, yet gentle

Q. I write with concern about my nieces and nephews who have legal marriages outside the Church. After a tragic death in our family, they now sometimes attend Mass and also receive Holy Communion. Delighted to see them at Mass, I haven't wanted to alienate them about their reception of the Eucharist. Is there a clear, yet gentle, way to explain Church teaching on this matter?

A. I presume by "legal," you mean "civil."

I concur in your judgment about having to broach the issue in a "clear, yet gentle, way," lest you alienate them further. I think the best angle to use is the simplest and most direct — namely, marriage outside the Church constitutes an ongoing and unrepentant state of fornication. St. Paul teaches that fornicators have no place in the kingdom of God, hence the rationale for the Church's exclusion of such individuals from sacramental communion. Now, that's the theology; knowing the people, you have to come up with the most appropriate manner in which to convey that information.

Confessional queries

Q. Many years ago, a person attended a communal penance service at which those attending were not told that mortal sins must be absolved individually. Until recently, he had never heard that communal penance and absolution did not absolve mortal sin. After so many years, when he can no longer remember what he might have been guilty of, and he always considered himself to be absolved, has he any responsibility to confess whatever he can remember? I am speaking of more than thirty years ago. Also, in our Rite of Christian Initiation of Adults (RCIA), a young woman who was baptized as an infant but had received no other sacraments or instruction is preparing to receive Confirmation and Communion at the Easter Vigil. She was told that she could attend the communal penance service [no individual confessions] as preparation. I had told her that she should prepare for and receive sacramental confession. If children are to be prepared for confession before Communion, should not adults, with more maturity and opportunity for the commission of serious sin, also be prepared if they have been baptized?

A. On the confession question, I would advise the man to approach the Sacrament of Penance at his earliest convenience, informing the confessor of the situation, confessing what he can remember, but not putting himself into a state of anxiety over it, either. After the situation has been handled in this way, he ought to be at peace and not worry about it anymore.

Regarding the woman to be received into the Church, your instincts are correct. Any baptized person who is going to be received into full communion with the Catholic Church must receive the Sacrament of Penance before receiving Confirmation and first Holy Communion.

Blessing battles

Q. A local Congregationalist minister, asked to explain her decision to sanction homosexual "marriages," responded, "Well, is it as wrong as blessing battleships?" Without much time to reflect, I replied that "two wrongs don't make a right." What would you have said to her?

A. Your off-the-cuff remark was rather on target, in my opinion. Beyond that, however, we do believe in a just-war concept; therefore, while all wars are regrettable, some are seen as either tolerable or even necessary. Now, I would never go so far as to bless the equipment that will be used to kill other human beings, even if they are our enemies. It is instructive that in the Old Testament we find that the soldiers of Israel were required to offer sacrifice in the Temple for all life they had taken, including that of their enemies — a salutary reminder that all human life is sacred and that our killing, albeit perhaps needed for national survival at times, is something that saddens the heart of God, the Father of all men.

Early departure

Q. A priest in a neighboring parish made this comment after Mass on Sunday: "I will not give absolution to anyone in confession who mentions leaving Mass early" because there are numerous people leaving Mass before the dismissal. Can a priest refuse absolution to a person who may have confessed a mortal sin for such a menial reason as leaving Mass early? Also, is there a point during the Mass before which it is a mortal sin to leave Mass early and after which it is a venial sin to leave early? In my instruction class in 1956, the priest mentioned that it was a venial sin to be late for Mass and a mortal sin to arrive after the Gospel had been read (and pretend that you had fulfilled your Mass obligation). I do not remember him saying anything about leaving early.

A. As much as I detest having people arrive late and leave early (usually the same people, coincidentally), it's more than stretching the elastic band to suggest that either could be a mortal sin. However, I also believe that we should not become legalists or minimalists who hold that as long as mortal sin is not involved that we have nothing to worry about. The Christian life is not a case of avoiding mortal sin but of loving God to the full — that means doing the maximum, not the minimum.

An occasional problem causing someone to be late or an unavoidable commitment demanding an early departure is not a sin. But tardiness for Mass and early "escapes" are generally ingrained habits of individuals, so much so that any parish priest can name for you the ten to fifteen people who can be counted on for this behavior pattern — one that needs to be broken because it is insulting to God and disturbing to priest and congregation alike.

If you want a standard for judging whether or not you have failed to uphold your Sunday Mass obligation, I would say that if you miss the First Reading, you ought to attend another Mass. Again, recall that I said earlier that this does not refer to situations beyond your control.

Three answers

Q. Three questions. How can my son, who is divorced, return to the sacraments? Also, could I get my grandchildren baptized without their parents' knowledge? Finally, is it a sin to have sex with your boyfriend, when your husband has died and you have to have it?

A. (1) If your son has not remarried, there is nothing to obstruct his access to the sacraments right now. (2) Barring the most unusual circumstances, no priest would baptize children against the will of parents, if for no other reason than the fact that the Code of Canon Law indicates that infant Baptism presupposes a reasonable hope that the children will be raised in the faith into which they are to be baptized. (3) Sex outside the covenant of marriage is objectively evil, no matter how much one thinks he or she "has to have it!"

Today's mentality

Q. My wife frequently threatens divorce because "irreconcilable differences" cause us to have a "dead marriage." She says that this releases her from her vow to stay together "until death do us part." Would you comment on this?

A. It sounds as though your wife has been infected by the mentality of "until death do us part, or problems emerge." If there are difficulties in the relationship — and every marriage has some — you both need to attend to them, if it's not already too late. Seek out a good Catholic marriage counselor; if your wife will not go with you, go yourself since something's better than nothing. If the differences are truly "irreconcilable," and were such from the beginning, that is the task of an ecclesiastical marriage tribunal to decide, not your spouse.

Civil duties

Q. For the last few months, I have been wondering what the Church's teaching is concerning a Catholic person who is an elected official, such as a magistrate judge, and conducts civil marriages in performance of his duties. I think that, as a Catholic, this person is committing a grave sin because in the eyes of the Church such unions are immoral. I have asked many of my Catholic friends, and they say it is okay because he is merely performing his civil duty as an elected official. I recognize that as an elected official he is fulfilling his duty, but I can't help feel that it is wrong for a Catholic to undertake such a duty. Would you please help me to understand how I should approach this situation?

A. First of all, the Church does not say that all civil unions are immoral — only those for Catholics. Second, inasmuch as a justice of the peace does not [and cannot] inquire into the religious affiliation of those who approach him for a marriage ceremony, he would have no way of knowing who is Catholic and who is not; therefore, he has no way of knowing whether or not such unions are problematic or not. Now, were he to know for sure about some person's Catholic identity, I think he would do well to abstain from performing the ceremony, giving it over to another official.

Sinful capability?

Q. Please help me to clarify something: I am fifty-eight years old, have controlled epilepsy, and a mild, borderline mental illness (also under control). Is it possible for me to commit sin?

A. Epilepsy has nothing to do with freedom of the will. Mental illness is another matter. However, you indicate that the mental illness is "under control," leading me to believe that you have the necessary faculties to engage in correct moral reasoning and to perform truly free, human acts. The best thing for you to do if you have genuine doubts along these lines is to discuss the situation with a Catholic psychiatrist and a well-informed priest.

Ten Commandments

Q. A local radio station featured a show on Roman Catholicism and a guest named David Hunt who claimed that the new Catechism *has changed the Ten Commandments. I couldn't believe that, so I looked and discovered that obviously the Vatican Council did in fact drop the whole second commandment dealing with idols. How can anyone change God's laws? By whose authority was this done? Certainly not God's! And why was this done?*

A. The text of the Ten Commandments as we have *always* memorized them as Catholics (so, nothing to do with Vatican II!) is a thumbnail or abbreviated version of the scriptural text. In truth, the Bible itself has two versions, one in Deuteronomy and the other in Exodus.

The Protestant enumeration of the commandments splits what the Catholic and Eastern Orthodox enumeration of the commandments subsumes into the first alone; the content is, however, the same.

In point of fact, the *Catechism's* treatment of the First Commandment does give the full scriptural text in number 2083 and then deals specifically with the question of "graven images" in numbers 2129-2132.

Racism is sinful

Q. I am a Mexican-American and am very active in my parish. How sinful is racism when it comes from your own parish priest?

A. Racism is sinful, no matter where it comes from. When the source is the parish priest, it is even worse for a number of reasons. First, a priest is to be a source of Catholic doctrine for his people — and it is clear that racism is totally repugnant to Catholic truth. Second, a priest is to be a source of unity for the parish, bridging gaps between groups and individuals.

Your original letter, much longer than what is reproduced here, indicates truly obnoxious behavior on his part. In the most charitable but also firmest manner possible, bring this to the attention of the dean and/or other diocesan officials. Be sure to document what you say with honest and objective examples.

TV trash

Q. I have been doing a lot of thinking about some of the trash that appears on our television screen. Most of the shows I no longer watch because I feel they insult our God. We never hear about these things from the pulpit. I would like to know if watching certain shows are sins for the viewers? Many shows that are exceptionally offensive have very high popularity ratings. Since some of the things they glorify in their shows are mortal sins, such as dirty jokes, extramarital affairs, etc., is it a sin (either mortal or venial) to watch these shows?

A. They are at least "near occasions of sin." To the extent that they arouse your passions and perhaps even move you toward sinful actions, they are sinful. But there is one additional consideration — namely, that we know *some* people are seriously tempted by these shows.

Therefore, out of a sense of Christian solidarity with them, we should refrain from viewing them and also to make a personal statement on the unacceptability of smut. If committed Christians refused to watch such garbage, the trash-purveyors would be out of business.

Discouraging scenario

Q. My daughter, twenty years old, informed me that she is a lesbian. I took her to our parish priest hoping that she would come out a little discouraged, but instead she came out encouraged. He explained that God wants everyone to experience love fully in this life, and that if she chose to love someone of the same sex, in this day and age, it is becoming more acceptable and, who knows, fifty years from now it probably would be acceptable. He also told her that he had two gay priest-friends. He did explain that God would want her to try to live a celibate life, and with one partner; to live with many partners would be a more serious sin. While he said that the Church would never bless homosexual unions, he did tell her to receive the Eucharist for guidance. I expected him to tell her that it is an abnormal condition that could be altered by staying close to Christ in the Eucharist. What can I say to my daughter now?

A. I am somewhat unsure of what either you or the parish priest has offered your daughter, largely because there seems to be some degree of mixing up of issues related to orientation and activity.

Surely, the pastor's statement that God wants the unmarried to abstain from sexual activity is correct, but it sounds as though he was counseling activity with one partner as a kind of "lesser of two evils" to sexual relations with multiple partners. Neither is morally acceptable. Instructing your daughter to receive the Eucharist regularly is fine, so long as it is understood that she is not in the state of mortal sin; perhaps he meant "strength" rather than "guidance."

I can't quite figure out your meaning for "an abnormal condition that could be altered by staying close to Christ in the Eucharist." Are you saying that receiving Holy Communion will eliminate your daughter's homosexual orientation? If so, that may or may not happen. Are you saying that the Eucharist could make the living arrangement less problematic? Again, that might or might not be the case.

My bottom-line advice is to eschew the living situation, which is simply an ongoing source of temptation to engage in objectively immoral acts. Friendship is one thing; this is something else entirely.

Orientation

Q. In the Catechism of the Catholic Church, *it is stated, regarding homosexual tendencies: "They do not choose their homosexual condition; for* most *of them it is a trial" (2358, emphasis added). If they do not choose the condition, is it not or should it not be a trial for all of them? Also, since the psychological genesis of the condition is unexplained, then how can the* Catechism *declare that "they do not choose their condition"? It seems to me that, with all due respect to the writers, they are stating an extra-compassionate, bending-over-backwards opinion, so as not to offend anyone. I suppose a pedophile could claim he did not choose to be that way. Isn't it strange that God's animal kingdom, with extremely rare exceptions, does not practice homosexual acts? I'd like your opinion, Father, on mentally competent people choosing or not choosing.*

A. Some people — of either a heterosexual or homosexual orientation — are not highly "sexed," by which I mean that they are not easily tempted toward sexual sins. I suspect that is what the *Catechism* is saying in speaking of "most," rather than "all," and that squares with my pastoral experience. I know of men who have known about their homosexual orientation for forty years and have never been seriously tempted to act upon their proclivity; others are constantly tortured by their desires for illicit sex. Once more, I have seen these same phenomena with heterosexually oriented individuals.

I don't think we have any "hard" data on just how many 'choose a homosexual orientation. You should note that the emended text of the *Catechism* drops out the very line to which you objected, thus reading: "This inclination, which is objectively disordered,, constitues for most of them a trial" (2358).

Regardless of the degree of freedom, the acts to which you refer, whether homosexual or pedophile, are never to be performed, being objectively evil. Personal culpability is not a matter for public discussion but for discernment in the internal forum.

Superstition

Q. At a family gathering, the subject came up that a CCD teacher told one of my nephews that the Church does not approve of the use of the Ouija board. He wanted to throw his away. I said "good for him," and everyone was suddenly against me. I told them it was the hand of the devil. They laughed and said it was a kid's game. Could you please tell me what the actual teaching about the Ouija board is, and why?

A. The Church has no specific "teaching" on the Ouija board, as such, but she does condemn divination and superstition (see the *Catechism*, 2110-2117). I tend to agree that for most, the Ouija board is "a kid's game," but at the same time, I have seen it produce an addictive effect and foster superstition. Therefore, I would not permit its use in my home.

Subsidiarity

Q. Please explain the Catholic social principle of subsidiarity.

A. Briefly put, the principle of subsidiarity holds that nothing should be done at a higher level of society that can be done at a lower level; in other words, social services should be offered by the person or agency closest to those being served. This principle ensures human dignity and guards against massive bureaucracies, which are divorced from real peoples' lives. The Church is especially sensitive on this score when it comes to the rights of the family, lest any intrusive element interpose itself within the sacred bonds of the family, particularly the parent-child relationship.

The *Catechism* discusses this theory of social doctrine in the context of human community and solidarity (1885 and 2209). The long and the short of it is that the Church has a healthy skittishness about excessive governmental involvement in human affairs. That should not be taken to suggest that we see no role for government in social services and the like, but it does imply that we should see at least "amber lights" when big government appears on the horizon.

Sabbath Day

Q. A friend of mine is looking for information on the Sabbath, as her son-in-law is a Seventh-day Adventist, and he tells her Catholics are celebrating on the wrong day. I have looked in the Catechism *and other sources for her but have found nothing. I would appreciate hearing from you regarding this matter.*

A. It's just a bit amazing for me to imagine that it took some Christians nearly nineteen centuries to discover that they had been worshiping the Lord on the wrong day!

In the early Church — before the formal split with Judaism — Christians went to the synagogue on Saturday and conducted their own eucharistic worship on Sunday. When the break was definitive,

Christians tacked the synagogue service onto the front of their own distinctive liturgy, abandoning Saturday worship in favor of Sunday, the day of the Lord's resurrection.

An incredible gift

Q. Every day teens are bombarded with information that tries to convince them that the way to happiness is through sexual experience. Although the message of the world is powerful, the message of the Gospel is even more powerful. But in order to appreciate the truth about love and sex, teens first have to know it. The book The Incredible Gift! The Truth About Love and Sex *is said to be entertaining and faithful to Church doctrine, guiding teens to discover that their sexuality is an extraordinary gift from God that needs to be protected and cherished, no matter what contradictory messages the world might impart. If you know of this book, would you comment please?*

A. The work you cite is excellent, and I highly recommend it for use in Catholic high schools for either a freshman morality course or for a senior course in Christian marriage. The work demonstrates how teenage chastity is not only critical for future happy marriages, but also explains how it is the essential seedbed for future vocations to the priesthood and religious life. It is published by Our Sunday Visitor and costs $8.95 (call 1-800-348-2440).

Chain prayer

Q. My wife had a very serious operation on her lower spine. She is still in much pain, and we understand the operation will take a long time to heal. The following letter arrived one day in the mail from a relative: "My daughter sent me this novena. It is not a chain letter. It is a novena to St. Theresa that began in 1952. It has never been broken. Within forty hours, send four copies of this letter to family members and friends, and mention my name (as I did my daughter's) at the top. On the day you receive it, say one Our Father and one Hail Mary. On the fourth day, watch what happens. This is a powerful novena, so please copy it exactly. Let me know what happens on the fourth day. Please do not break it."

I told my wife it sounded like a chain letter to me, and she never sent copies to anyone. Did I do the right thing?

A. You did the right thing. A rose by any other name is still a chain letter, and that is superstition, which is offensive to Almighty God.

Masturbation query

Q. A state university course on human sexuality treated the subject of masturbation. Does the Bible state specifically that this practice is wrong? It seems that it would have been mentioned along with lust, fornication, adultery, homosexuality, etc., if it were such a big deal. If it is not as serious as those specifically forbidden sexual practices, then might not promoting abstinence in this regard be placing an unnecessary burden on people — especially unmarried males — and cause them to walk away from the teachings of Jesus altogether?

From this class presentation I also have begun to worry about the relationship between forced abstinence and increased sexual desire leading people into forbidden sexual acts.

I'm confused; please respond.

A. Several points need to be addressed in your question.

First, Church teaching does not derive solely from Scripture. Our moral theology is grounded in biblical principles, to be sure, but the Bible is not like a big dictionary one consults and, finding nothing, determines there is no answer to the problem. After all, you will search the Scriptures in vain for issues like in vitro fertilization or use of the birth control pill. But that does not mean that there are not insights from the Bible which can help us forge a consistent and meaningful sexual morality.

The primary datum of Christian sexuality is the conviction that love and life are inextricably bound up with each other. Therefore, any genital act must be an expression of love (for another person) and be open to life — at one and the same time. Masturbation fails on both scores.

Second, I think you operate under a false impression when you say that allowing for masturbation will eliminate or make less possible other disordered desires. In my pastoral experience, I have found just the opposite: The more comfortable a person is with masturbation, the more likely he (or she) is to fall into other sexual sins. In truth, masturbation feeds the process.

Third, it seems that you have the notion that the male libido is so over-powering that masturbation is almost necessary. No clinical data exists to support that assumption. And I think your girlfriend would probably accuse you of sexism for the assertion!

Lesbian couple

Q. Recently I visited a Catholic church other than my own parish in my hometown. The young priest celebrated a beautiful Mass. At that Mass, there was a Baptism planned and administered to a baby boy. Everything was very normal and orthodox, except at the point where the priest introduced the parents of the child.

The parents were two women; the godparents, a woman and a man. I have seen these two women before and know that they are a lesbian couple. The priest did not address that issue, but just introduced them as the child's parents.

As a gay Catholic man myself, I don't see anything wrong with the orientation of the couple nor the fact that they are partners, as long as they adhere to the teachings of the Church in regard to chastity and celibacy. I believe the Church's teachings in this regard are very sound and beautiful: a gay person is called by God to a life of celibacy, which in my opinion is a beautiful and holy lifestyle.

My problem with the whole situation is not the Baptism itself (which was valid). My problem is the scandal that was caused when the priest introduced the couple as the child's parents, somewhat implying that the couple was legitimate.

Are there any regulations about this? What are your thoughts concerning the introduction of the two women as this child's parents?
A. I am in total agreement with you. The priest gave at least tacit approval to what one can only assume is a sinful union and, given the tenor of the times, one has the right to assume that this is the situation. The priest's action falls into the category of advocacy for a lifestyle that is personally problematic and destructive of family life and the social structure. And yes, that is scandalous. I should add that I would have the same judgment if the child's parents were heterosexuals who were either married outside the Church or not married at all.

Irregular unions demand private baptismal ceremonies, not public events which either embarrass the couple or end up legitimizing what is morally reprehensible.

Ghost tales

Q. I am an eleven-year-old boy and a student in a Catholic school. Once a month we are able to buy our choice of books from the Weekly Reader. Recently I bought a book titled Book of Ghost Tales to Haunt

You *by Bruce Coville. Would this book, and others like it, be okay for me to read? We looked in the* Catechism *and could not find an answer.*
A. If eleven-year-olds are using the *Catechism* as a reference tool, you know we're going to be in great shape in the coming decade!

At times, with all the New Age nonsense and the like, we have gotten a bit too skittish in my opinion on matters that are essentially harmless and even good, clean fun. I think ghost stories fall into that category. Common sense and a good grasp of the Catholic Faith are indispensable and infallible guides as to what types of entertainment are permissible — hard, fast rules are not always possible or desirable in areas like this. If one develops a preoccupation with ghosts and posits powers of them which contradict Church teaching, one is in difficulty; otherwise, I would not speak against the opportunity for a good scare.

Together Again

Q. Tom and Lisa, both Catholics, were married in the Church, divorced, but obtained no annulment. They each remarried, and these relationships both ended in divorce as well. They have now found their way back to each other and are currently living together. My sister says they are living in sin and need to be remarried in the Church or at least civilly; I disagree. Who is right?
A. You are. Since the Church does not acknowledge divorce, the civil decree means nothing, nor the civil unions. Therefore, in the eyes of the Church, it is as though they have merely been on an extended vacation from each other and now are resuming their relationship.

If they are serious now, I do think it would be a good idea to remarry civilly — for legal purposes — and also perhaps to renew their marriage vows in the Church as a way of healing the past and recommitting themselves to the future, this after receiving the Sacrament of Penance, which is certainly needed after years of living in invalid marriages.

Wedding plans

Q. My daughter plans to marry this summer. Her fiancé is not baptized and will not let any children they might have be baptized or raised Catholic, although he has agreed to attend a pre-Cana conference. My daughter says she will go along with his wishes. They plan to marry in a non-denominational chapel at the college from which they graduated. His uncle, a Unitarian minister, will officiate.

Please tell me my obligations as a Catholic in this situation. Could you please also give me some advice?

A. As I have said so many times in these pages, I do not see how a practicing Catholic can attend the invalid wedding of a child — as painful a decision as that would be. Have a heart-to-heart discussion with your daughter, making sure that she understands your rationale completely — and equally your love for her. Indeed, make it clear that your love (in the most ultimate and profound sense, which is intimately tied to your concern for her eternal salvation) is exactly what makes you take your stand. Let her know that you do not want to cut off communication or a relationship, but participation in either the ceremony or the reception would be hypocritical for you. Hopefully, she will be able to accept your decision, even as you have no choice but to accept hers.

Punishment from God?

Q. A friend and I were recently involved in a discussion about our Catholic position on birth control. My friend said that women are suffering and have had serious health problems as a result of using IUDs; therefore, he concludes this is a punishment from God. I asked him if the women who were having serious health problems with their silicone breast implants are having these problems because God is displeased with their decision to have breast augmentation. He said that such surgery is always sinful. We have been going around and around on this question for months. I hope TCA will settle the dispute.

A. I am generally nervous when people seek to attribute motives to God's activity or apparent activity.

First, all too often they confuse God's permissive will or the normal course of nature with God's direct involvement. I happen to believe that when you fool around with the natural way of doing things, you court disaster, whether that concerns birth control, unnatural forms of sexual intercourse, etc. Someone once quipped that God always forgives but Mother Nature never does. There's a strong element of truth in that. Second, when God allows evil to strike a person, it is always done to bring about a greater good. It frequently serves as a kind of "wake-up" call to evaluate one's behavior and thus is an invitation to bring one's life into line with the divine will. God's desire, then, is not to hurt His children but to bring them to their senses.

Regarding the specific issue of breast augmentation, I do not think an absolute answer can be given because many factors need to be considered, especially the rationale for obtaining such a procedure. No operation should ever be submitted to lightly; if a strange fixation on the size of one's breasts is the primary motivation (which also bespeaks a fascination with making oneself sexually appealing in a very gross sense), then I would probably judge the procedure wrong.

Sin and nature

Q. At a recent Sunday Mass I heard a priest say: "It's all right to sin." I was shocked and later asked him if I had understood him correctly. His explanation was that it is natural for us to sin. Would you please comment on this idea? It seems all wrong to me.

A. I think your priest spoke inaccurately. Sin is certainly a part of the human condition, but it is a deformed human condition to which it belongs. Our original nature did not incline us to sin. Once the original sin was committed, it became a part of our personal baggage to have this propensity toward sin, which is traditionally called "concupiscence" (cf. the *Catechism of the Catholic Church*, 1264).

St. Paul spoke about this difficulty in his Epistle to the Romans (7:18-20) when he sadly noted that he found it difficult to do the good he wished to perform and easy to do the evil he sought to avoid; he was describing not only his own life experience but the general human condition. God, however, does not want us to wallow in sin; on the contrary, He sent us His own divine Son precisely as a way out of the morass of sin and alienation. Jesus provides us with a twofold help: His example and His grace, both of which are intended to enable us to live holy lives. We are to model our lives on Christ, the perfect Man.

There is a sense in which one can say that a person needs to be "comfortable" with his sinfulness if, by that, one means not becoming overwhelmed with one's sins to the point of despairing about either reform or salvation. That is not the same thing, however, as being complacent and accepting of a disordered approach to life.

Lesbian relationship

Q. I am in a real dilemma about my daughter and our relationship. She is a practicing homosexual, and lives with her partner. At first I wasn't aware of her lifestyle, but as situations made it too obvious to deny, she admitted it. She knows how I feel, although my husband and I still treat her as before; however, the uneasiness is a part of me.

When we go back home to visit, we stay at their house, but this bothers me. They don't show physical affection in front of us, but the way I feel about it, I don't know what to do, if anything. There is no question of her not knowing how I feel, because I have been very open. In one of our conversations about her religious neglect, she told me she felt she was going to heaven — and I told her only because of all the praying I do for her conversion. In another conversation I also told her that her lifestyle is an abomination. I told her I have given her over to St. Joseph to bring her back into the Church, and even put a little statue on her piano.

Here's where my dilemma comes in. Should we be staying with her on our visits? Should we welcome her and her "friend" into our home? I know to deny these visits will put a strain on our relationship, even to the point of her probably not speaking to us. I'm sure she will be hurt and her friend, outraged, since she has a lot of influence on our daughter. I don't want to lose our daughter, but at the same time, I want to do what the Church would require of us in this situation. Any help would be most appreciated, especially your prayers for her.

A. The home visitations require some nuance. When you go to their home, do they sleep together? If so, I would not be involved with that, if I were you. When they come to your home, do they sleep apart? If so, I would welcome them. My norms as a parent would be essentially the same for her as they would be for a heterosexual child living in an invalid marital union.

It seems to me that your conversations with your daughter have been very frank and loving; her continued association with you likewise shows maturity and openness on her part. Build on that foundation.

Welcome immigrants

Q. Why was the pope railing about immigration to a country full of immigrants already?.

A. I don't think the Holy Father "railed" about immigration, but he surely did call us Catholics to be sensitive to the needs and rights of immigrants, many of whom are also our brothers and sisters in the Catholic Faith.

I often remark that I am astounded when I hear otherwise good, devout Catholics speaking with hostility about immigrants, if for no other reason than the fact that none of us were on the Mayflower. I do not think the United States should simply throw open its borders, but I do believe that generosity and a welcoming attitude are part and parcel of our American tradition. Furthermore, my own experience is that most of the jobs that immigrants are doing would not be of the slightest interest to the average American.

For a fine discussion of this whole topic, I would refer you to a document from the U.S. bishops' Committee on Migration: "One Family under God," available from the publishing division of the United States Catholic Conference for $1.95. This statement is a very precise reflection on the theology that should form our attitudes and policies. The bishops here refuse to allow themselves to become mouthpieces either for the left wing of the Democratic party or for hard-core capitalists.

Euthanasia permit?

Q. Our doctor has told us that the law requires him to obtain our signature for his records in regard to the acceptance or refusal of surviving measures to be used if our hearts should stop. Isn't this the same as consenting to euthanasia? Is it against the Faith to sign this consent form?

A. Without seeing the form in question, it is not possible to judge its moral acceptability; the problem is that so many documents like this exist right now, with some being completely in keeping with Catholic moral principles while others are but thinly veiled contracts for euthanasia, as you suggest. To get an accurate reading on it, I would suggest sending it to your state Catholic Conference's pro-life activities office or the similar agency within your diocese. The Human Life Resource Center at 11244 S. Western, Chicago, IL 60643 would also be of assistance to you.

Perhaps it would likewise be helpful to recall this insight from the *Catechism of the Catholic Church*: "Discontinuing medical procedures that are burdensome, dangerous, extraordinary or disproportionate to the expected outcome can be legitimate; it is the refusal of 'over-zealous' treatment. Here one does not will to cause death; one's inability to impede it is merely accepted. The decisions should be made by the patient if he is competent and able or, if not, by those legally entitled to act for the patient, whose reasonable will and legitimate interests must always be respected" (2278).

Another excellent document to study has been produced by the American bishops' pro-life office: "Faithful for Life — A Moral Reflection," dealing specifically with abortion and euthanasia. It is available for $2.95 from the United States Catholic Conference.

Sunday sports

Q. My fifteen-year-old son plays baseball in the summer. While we do not actively seek out baseball games played on Sunday, sometimes in the course of a state tournament, Sunday games do get scheduled. What are your thoughts on playing sports on Sunday? Would you consider this a violation of the Third Commandment, even if you have fulfilled your Sunday Mass obligation?

A. I have problems with sporting events being scheduled in conflict with Sunday worship services. For a government school district or a municipal team to do so would be tantamount to civic interference with the free exercise of religion. Needless to say, Catholic schools should never have games or practices on a Sunday morning, regardless of whether or not team members have had an opportunity to fulfill their Sunday Mass obligation.

So what about Sunday afternoons or evenings? I don't think we should develop into latter-day Puritans on this score. Both the Code of Canon Law (Canon 1247) and the *Catechism of the Catholic Church* (2184-2188) make it clear that what is forbidden on the Lord's Day are activities which obviate that joy and relaxation which are proper to it. Generally speaking, sporting events would not come under that stricture.

Moral Math 101?

Q. If one feels an obligation to get involved with pro-life organizations yet does not, would this sin of omission be venial or mortal? I always vote pro-life and occasionally contribute monetarily to different organizations, but is this enough to fulfill my obligation?

A. One cannot come to moral judgments like this on the basis of a slide rule or other means of mathematical calculation. Many personal factors have to be considered: family obligations, financial resources, other Church and community responsibilities, etc. A decision of this kind can best be handled by consultation with one's regular confessor or spiritual director. And for one interested in making genuine progress in one's life in Christ, spiritual direction is essential.

Sacraments for abortion advocates?

Q. Pro-choice Catholics multiply. Catholic politicians advocating "choice" co-exist comfortably with the hierarchy. They receive Holy Communion from their bishops. They are even permitted to speak after Mass. Today's accommodation by our hierarchy to a more pluralistic tolerance ought to make even TCA retreat from its monolithic tone on abortion. Or would you suggest our bishops are mere "wimps"? As always, give it to us straight!

A. While appearing to advocate a hard line on this issue, your own speech evinces signs of caving in to the culture as you speak of these folks as "pro-choice" — which is their rhetoric; I prefer to talk about their being "pro-abortion" which cuts to the chase. That said, I don't think the Church in this country can ever be accused of being weak on abortion; if anything, our opponents make the very opposite claim, namely, that we are shrill and intractable.

As regards giving Holy Communion to pro-abortion politicians, I must say that I would not do so, but I think that many bishops (and priests) feel that carrying the matter to that extent would have a negative impact on the whole cause. In some sense, that then becomes a situation calling for a prudential judgment, involving multiple circumstances.

For example, if I deny Senator Jones the sacraments, will that bring him to repentance? Will it enhance the teaching authority of the Church? Will it make fence-sitters sit up and take notice? Will it drive a wedge even further between the Church's Magisterium and people of good will who might seriously misconstrue the action? Would this action be "too little (or too much) too late"? In other words, might this have been effective had it been tried twenty years ago, but not now?

To raise these questions and to struggle with finding adequate answers is not "wimpish" in my considered judgment — and I do hope you think this answer "gives it straight!"

Home sale

Q. My husband and I recently had to sell our home and encountered a moral dilemma. Many married couples came to look at the house; however, none came through with an offer to buy it. An unmarried couple came and was most anxious to buy the house. We did not want to sell to them because we felt that it would be cooperation in their sin (living together). For a while we put them off and consulted four different priests about the moral thing to do in this situation; we got three different answers. One said that what was done with the property after it was sold was not our concern — we were selling property, nothing more. He distinguished this case from rental of the property, in which case we would have a say in how it was used. Another priest said that we should not sell it to this couple because we would feel guilty. Yet a third priest said that we had to answer the question "Am I cooperating in the sin?" We prayed about the situation, but the prospects for selling the house became no better. In the end, we sold the house to the unmarried couple. I still can't help wondering if we did the right thing morally. Am I in a state of mortal sin for selling the house to that couple?

A. I agree with the advice of the first priest — and for all the reasons he gave you. While we should not cooperate in evil, the cooperation in this instance is incredibly remote. If you didn't sell the house to them, it would not have forced them to break up their immoral living arrangement; hence, your house did not really facilitate the sinful relationship.

While I think your action was blameless, objectively speaking, it is regrettable that you did it in the final analysis thinking that you were doing something wrong and only to close the deal! Perhaps there is some sin at that level and, beyond that, maybe this can put you on alert for similar behavior in the future.

Tithing

Q. Why does the Catholic Church not talk about the "tithe" as Protestant churches do? Should we tithe as Catholics?

A. Tithing is giving a tenth of one's income (usually based on gross income) to the Lord; the practice springs from the injunction found in Leviticus 27:30. While the Church does not generally stipulate the precise amount a devout Catholic ought to give to his parish, diocese, the universal Church, and other works of charity, the notion is that when one gives to Christ and His Church, one should give "sacrificially." But what does that mean? My pastor in grammar school used to say that one had given sacrificially when he had given until it hurt — and then gave some more! In other words, we don't give God the leftovers; we give Him the first fruits.

Catholic giving patterns are the very worst of all religious groups in the United States; part of the difficulty stems from a residual immigrant mentality which reasons thus: "My grandmother gave a dollar a week to our parish; my mother gave a dollar a week. And I give a dollar a week." The fallacy, of course, lies in the realization that when Granny gave a dollar a week, it may well have been even 20 percent of her income, while a dollar today is nearly meaningless.

We have also lulled Catholics into believing that the way to raise money for the Church is through silly schemes like bingo and bake sales. Put very bluntly, if we are not willing to support our own programs and institutions, why should we expect others to do so?

I have always said that I find it rather sad that nearly penniless immigrants were able to build up a system of parishes, schools, hospitals, and orphanages unparalleled in the history of the Church, and now the most affluent Catholic population in history is unable to maintain this network. That concern has likewise troubled the American hierarchy, moving them to produce a pastoral letter on this entitled, "Stewardship: A Disciple's Response." I recommend it to you.

Divorce/Remarriage

Q. Enclosed is an excerpt from our parish bulletin that introduces the concept of the "internal forum" solution to the problem of participation in the sacramental life of the Church when one has remarried after a divorce (with no annulment). Is the information contained in the article accurate? Is this the current teaching of the Church? If so, does the "internal forum" solution require the couple to live together as brother and sister?

A. The teaching authority of the Church has consistently indicated that this procedure is pastorally inadmissible. Pope John Paul II deals with it in *Familiaris Consortio*, and Cardinal Ratzinger devoted an entire document to the necessity of maintaining the Church's traditional discipline in regard to sacraments for those in irregular unions, that is to say, they cannot receive the sacraments.

The rationale is very easy to apprehend: A previous bond (maybe even one for each partner) exists, so that the second union is not a true marriage but really an on-going state of adultery. Why? Because each act of sexual intercourse takes place in the context of the still-existing marriage bond from the earlier valid union(s), one is thus committed to an unrepented condition of adultery, thus obviating the possibility of receiving either the Sacrament of Penance or the Holy Eucharist.

Living together as brother and sister, on the other hand, is a possible pastoral solution for the divorced and remarried, since a couple would not thereby engage in the acts proper to marriage.

Aquinas misquoted

Q. Somewhere I heard an alleged quote from St. Thomas Aquinas to the effect that governments which allow abortions (a sin against the natural law) were to be resisted by "any and all means." Assuming this were accurate, it would appear permissible to steal from the government and use the funds to oppose abortion. However, Veritatis Splendor *tells us that it is never lawful to do evil in order that a greater good may come of it. Was St. Thomas misquoted? Perhaps it should be "any and all legitimate means" — if it is quoted from St. Thomas at all. Can you please comment?*

A. I am not familiar with the citation you try to offer; in truth, it doesn't ring true for many reasons, the first being that governments in Aquinas's day did not pay for abortions.

You are correct in writing that *Veritatis Splendor* does not permit one to perform an evil act to bring about a good effect — and that is the teaching of St. Thomas. I suspect that what you really have in mind is what Aquinas envisions in terms of not accepting laws which do not conform to the natural law. One "does not accept" them principally by refusing to obey them and by working to correct them.

Masses for magazine?

Q. The journal titled Christ to the World, *published in Rome* "cum approbatione ecclesiasticus vicariatus," *states that priests may defray the cost of a subscription "by agreeing to celebrate a certain number of holy Masses, which we can assign them at their explicit request convalidated by their Ordinary (with his stamped seal)." It goes on to say that "a subscription by surface mail — five holy Masses" and "by airmail — seven holy Masses."*

How is this different from simony?

A. As I read this material, I see it as an attempt to provide priests in mission lands with little or no financial resources with the possibility of obtaining this journal. I suppose it works something like this: People have sent in Mass intentions and stipends, which are thus available to these missionaries. Let's say the standard stipend is $5 and the subscription is $20; therefore, by taking four intentions, the priest — in effect — has earned the subscription. Canonically speaking, I find nothing wrong here — no different, for example, than for a priest to have earned $20 in Mass intentions and then paying for the subscription directly. I do agree that it takes quite a bit of piecing together to come to that conclusion and, on that score, I would hesitate to establish such a program.

Trafficking in Mass stipends is to be avoided at all costs, according to the Church, but also even giving the appearance of such a practice; it cost us dearly in the Middle Ages, and we don't need another Reformation to set the record straight again.

Sharpshooter!

Q. If it is not outside the scope of your words of wisdom, I would like your answer to the following situation.

A man atop a building is shooting down onto a busy street, killing people right and left, with utter abandon. A sharpshooter arrives. He could easily shoot the man and end the slaughter. Would he be permitted to do this?

A. Rather than relying on my own "words of wisdom," allow me to cite some passages from the *Catechism of the Catholic Church*: "Someone who defends his life is not guilty of murder even if he is forced to deal his aggressor a lethal blow: . . . Legitimate defense can be not only a right but a grave duty for someone responsible for another's life, the common good of the family or of the state. Preserving the common good of society requires rendering the aggressor unable to inflict harm. . ." (2264-2266).

Putting it all together, one can say that the sharpshooter is defending the lives of the innocent; if he thinks he can stop the perpetrator without killing him, he ought to do so. If that is too risky, then he has the right to kill him — all the while intending to save lives rather than take even this one.

Here again, the *Catechism* is instructive, falling back on St. Thomas Aquinas's distinction: " 'The act of self-defense [in this case, the sharpshooter is acting on behalf of defenseless victims] can have a double effect: the preservation of one's own life [or that of helpless innocents]; and the killing of the aggressor. . . . The one is intended, the other is not' " [St. Thomas Aquinas, *STh* II-II, 64, 7, corp. art] (2263).

Perfect contrition

Q. In the Act of Contrition, why do we say, ". . . but most of all, because I have offended Thee. . ."? It seems to me that statement reflects perfect contrition, which is certainly desirable, but makes me uncomfortable because it seems at times I am being dishonest with God. Could you please clarify?

A. You are right in intuiting that the prayer offers sentiments of perfect contrition to Almighty God. Here's what the *Catechism of the Catholic Church* says about this form of sorrow for sin: "When it arises from a love by which God is loved above all else, contrition is called 'perfect' (contrition of charity). Such contrition remits venial sins; it also obtains forgiveness of mortal sins if it includes the firm resolution to have recourse to sacramental confession as soon as possible" [cf. Council of Trent (1551): *DS* 1677] (1452).

On the other hand, "The contrition called 'imperfect' (or 'attrition') is also a gift of God, a prompting of the Holy Spirit. It is born of the consideration of sin's ugliness or the fear of eternal damnation and the other penalties threatening the sinner (contrition of fear). Such a stirring of conscience can initiate an interior process which, under the prompting of grace, will be brought to completion by sacramental absolution. By itself, however, imperfect contrition cannot obtain the forgiveness of grave sins, but it disposes one to obtain forgiveness in the sacrament of Penance" [cf. Council of Trent (1551): *DS* 1678;1705] (1453).

In sum, the Church puts the words of perfect contrition on our lips to move us in the desired direction. As the First Epistle of St. John says, "perfect love casts out all fear" (4:18), and that should certainly be the goal of the Christian life. Simply because we have not arrived at that level of spiritual maturity, that should not cause us to feel "uncomfortable," let alone hypocritical, so long as we keep the goal in view and keep striving for it.

Confession confusion

Q. In a Rite II Communal Penance Service, the priest told the people that they must confess their mortal sins by type and number. He further instructed them that if they had only venial sins, they should either acknowledge generally that they are sinners or indicate an area in which they are having difficulty. Does a person who has no mortal sin to confess, and does not even confess a single venial sin specifically, validly receive sacramental absolution? I realize that confession is not the only means for remitting venial sins, but I wondered in this situation whether or not a sacramental absolution actually took place.

A. It would appear to me that your priest was seeking to have "matter" for confession by asking penitents to identify "an area in which they are having difficulty." At times, priests mean well by indicating the lack of necessity for an integral confession (according to species and number) for venial sins but end up confusing people. The simplest thing to do, in my experience, is just to announce what he did about mortal sin and let people have enough common sense to take it from there.

Annulment question

Q. In a recent issue of The Catholic Answer *there was a question put to you about a Catholic woman who was married to a non-Catholic who would not seek an annulment. Consequently, she could not receive the sacraments because she was committing adultery. In part of your answer, you said that the Lord may give them both grace to live together as brother and sister.*

My husband and I are in the same situation. I am the non-Catholic and we are presently going through the annulment process, but it doesn't look good.

If the annulment is not granted, but we live together as brother and sister, can he return to the sacraments? In other words, if we have no sexual relations, can he then go to confession and resume receiving the sacraments? It hurts me to know that our relationship is presently keeping him from Communion because it is important to him. We both believe that the Lord put us together. I am trying hard to understand the reasoning of the Church. Your insight into this question would be a great comfort to me.

A. Your love for him is quite moving; that kind of sensitivity and openness to God's will surely can go far to make the heroic sacrifices you seem prepared to make. As Our Lord said to the scribe, "You are not far from the Kingdom of God!" (Mk 12:34).

I don't think the Church's reasoning is a problem for you; I suspect it's a matter of trying to put head and heart together. In that case, ask God's Holy Spirit to help you accomplish that task. Perhaps prayer to St. Joseph would also be helpful; after all, he and Our Lady also lived as brother and sister.

For a good, pastoral discussion of your situation, see what our Holy Father says on this matter in his apostolic exhortation on the family, *Familiaris Consortio*, especially number eighty-four.

Co-ed wrestling

Q. What is your advice about the prudence of co-ed wrestling teams in high school? Most of the Catholics that I have spoken with — both clergy and laity — agree that boys and girls should not be wrestling with each other in competition because it involves improper touches on the body. Others see nothing wrong with it. Am I a prude — or just prudent?

A. Having spent more than fifteen years of my life in high school teaching and administration, I cannot begin to imagine co-ed wrestling! Such a practice clearly reveals a lack of common sense; of course, all too often people are driven by ideology more than a genuine concern for the welfare of youngsters. In this instance, it seems like the move to question or deny sexual differences is more important than providing teenagers with wholesome athletic experiences.

Astrological signs

Q. Our son is a kindergarten student in our parish school, where they recently celebrated "spirit week," which had the theme of "St. X School — the Center of the Universe." Each class presented an astronomical constellation or heavenly body and sang an appropriate song.

To my astonishment, however, I also discovered that each child had been given a button to wear, on which was printed his name, birthday, and astrological sign. Even more amazing, the week ended with a final program on astrological signs and the singing of "The Age of Aquarius."

When I called the principal, a nun, she said that it was "harmless" fun and no one took it all seriously. Isn't this really a problem to foster such things in a Catholic school?

A. I think that the involvement of most folks with astrology is relatively harmless, but that does not mean that we should be teaching children about it and perhaps even giving the appearance of advocating such practices. The *Catechism of the Catholic Church* forthrightly condemns consultation of astrologers, horoscopes, etc. in paragraph 2116.

Is sin obsolete?

Q. What has happened to the concept of sin and punishment? Daily I see people doing things I had been led to believe were wrong, and doing so with impunity. Are they less guilty than I because the Church now shies assiduously away from the mention of sin and its consequences, engendering in people the idea that in doing what they feel is right for them they are doing no wrong? I, on the other hand, grew up with clear ideas of right and wrong and was taught the consequences of my actions.

A. The Church has not shied away from sin and punishment. All one need do is look at the documents of the Second Vatican Council, Pope John Paul's apostolic exhortation *Reconciliatio et Paenitentia* (Reconciliation and Penance in the Mission of the Church Today), and his book *Crossing the Threshold of Hope* to discover that the Church continues to believe in the reality of sin and the possibility of eternal damnation.

The difficulty comes at the local level, where all too many priests and teachers think that their popularity depends on "lightening up." I do not think every Sunday homily ought to be an exposure to "fire and brimstone," but the truth about sin and its consequences formed an essential core of the preaching of Jesus Christ. Our failure to hand on the content of the Faith as He gave it to us is blameworthy.

How will God judge people who have not been properly formed by their pastors and teachers? Because God is merciful, we have reason to hope. However, I would not want to be in the shoes of the shepherds who have short-circuited the full Gospel of Christ. The Hebrew prophetic works are full of denunciations of priests who shirked their responsibilities, and we have no reason to think that God has changed His mind in the interim.

Scrupulosity

Q. My question concerns whether a person in good conscience may buy goods or services that refer to the evil one in the brand name or with more subtlety, the fall of man? Examples of this would be Red Devil Paint, the Dirt Devil vacuum cleaner, and the Apple Computer Company symbol that has a multi-colored apple with a bite taken out of it. I am worried that buying any of these products seems to be a form of rejecting God. Is this being overly scrupulous?

A. Yes, I would imagine that you are letting scrupulosity take free rein here. If anything, I suppose that naming products and the like after the devil can be likened to the Psalmist's portrayal of Leviathan and other false gods as playthings of the one true God. What does annoy me, however, is Guaranteed Overnight Delivery, with its acronym of GOD.

Reveal past sins?

Q. I am a convert of several years and am embarrassed to take my question to my confessor. I took my sacramental preparation seriously, fasted and prayed, and my entrance into the Church through Baptism has brought me incomparable joy. Since my Baptism, I have been very active in the Church: attending daily Mass, leading the Rosary, making holy hours, etc. This has brought with it the company and friendship of many devout people who seem to look up to me.

I had committed many mortal and venial sins before Baptism, and I understand they were washed away at that time. As I have become close to certain people, they have confided to me stories of their past. I cannot tell anyone my secret past for fear that my image would be ruined, and the distrust of "holy" people would be aroused.

Should I reveal my own past to my special friends and to my confessor? It will dampen everything I have done since my conversion, their belief in me will be shattered and people will feel they have no one to turn to or to trust. I am honestly a different person and feel that my pre-baptismal days should not count against me.

Please give me your advice about this matter.

A. While I do not belong to that school of thought which encourages people to "let it all hang out" or to tell one's whole life story in the first encounter, I cannot help but wonder where we would be if St. Augustine or St. Francis of Assisi or St. Ignatius Loyola thought like you. In other words, they shared their sometimes sordid pasts with others to demonstrate the power of God's grace to effect a change in one's life. I don't want to come off as judgmental (especially since I have no personal knowledge of you), but it does seem that you are awfully concerned about serving as a kind of icon and that the human adulation that comes from such a pedestal existence is very attractive to you. In that context, I would remind you of the scriptural warning that "pride goes before a fall."

Finally, if others would think less of you because of past sins, that says more about them than it does about you.

In the final analysis, whatever you choose to reveal or to keep to yourself should be motivated by genuine Christian love for the other and not influenced by a desire for human respect.

Chastity is key

Q. I am quite puzzled by the behavior of my confessor. I am a homosexual male. For many months, I went to confession to this priest and mentioned various liaisons I had; he gave me the usual advice about avoiding the near occasions of sin, gave me a penance, and then absolution. Recently, I have become involved with one man and have thus given up all the promiscuity. Now that same priest seems on the verge of denying me absolution — unless I abandon the relationship.

To make matters even more muddled, a "straight" friend of mine has had the exact opposite experience with this priest. He used to sleep around with lots of girls, and the priest was very firm with him; now that he is dating one girl seriously (they're talking about engagement) and going over the line with her occasionally, the priest still discourages the activity but is rather compassionate. What gives here?

A. I am sure you can appreciate the fact that a priest hundreds of miles away is not in any position to make an iron-clad judgment on the confessional practice of another priest, who has the obvious and necessary advantage of knowing the situation up-close, but I would venture the following.

It appears that your confessor gave you good pastoral advice about your earlier promiscuous lifestyle. His upset now comes from a different angle: When you were involved in so-called casual sex, it may have been somewhat easier for you to avoid such eventualities. Now that you are involved in a romantic way with this other man, putting aside the sinful activities may be much more difficult. In all likelihood, that is what your confessor intuits and thus his reaction.

With your friend, however, his promiscuous behavior has ceased, and he is now apparently in something of a committed relationship which may end in marriage, whereas yours never can.

I understand the logic of your confessor — although I would be equally firm with your friend, precisely because I think that premarital chastity is the best predictor and guarantee of marital chastity.

Sexually active?

Q. We are workers in a Catholic home for developmentally delayed teenagers. Most of the program's participants have the mentality of five-year-olds in the body of twenty-year-olds. The home's policy is not to admit pregnant girls. Should one become pregnant after entry, she is discharged. It isn't possible to supervise the girls at all times. As a result, the parents — all of whom are Catholic — insist that their girls take oral contraceptives to prevent pregnancy. Isn't this against Church teaching? Surely if a child is conceived it would be better to put it up for adoption. How can a Church-affiliated home operate with such a policy?

A. I don't see how it can. If the home is cooperating, the bishop of the diocese ought to be brought into the drama.

Frequent confession

Q. A friend of mine tells me that she never goes to confession because she doesn't want to brag that she has no sins! She goes to Mass every Sunday and receives Holy Communion. She hasn't been to confession in years. I had always understood that confession was necessary at least once a year and that it is better to confess even more frequently. If I am correct, then perhaps it would be helpful for some people if you could give some guidance about what to confess in the absence of mortal sins.

A. The Scriptures tell us that even the just man sins seven times a day (Prv 24:16). Now, scrupulosity must be avoided at all costs, but modern man seems to have become a master of self-deception in denying the existence of sin in general and of his being a sinner in particular. Pope John Paul II has often spoken of the loss of the sense of sin both in the Church and in society. But try as hard as we might to eradicate the awareness of sin, sin still impinges on us every day. Therefore, we are no healthier for the denials.

Church law presents us with the minimal expectation: namely, that we must utilize the Sacrament of Penance at least once a year if we are aware of having committed any mortal sins. That is, however, the bare minimum, and good Christians are never content with minimalism. It is good and important to use the Sacrament of Penance well and often — even for lesser offenses against Almighty God. And the interesting fallout, among other things, is that this process of self-examination and self-accusation sensitizes one even more to the need to love God and neighbor with all one's heart, soul, and mind.

Human nature being what it is — prone to sin and eager to excuse the self — we should not be surprised to discover that people who rarely utilize the Sacrament of Penance have a difficult time identifying any sins, whereas those who go to confession more often never seem to run out of material.

Confession is good because: (1) it makes us pause to look at ourselves in an objective manner; (2) it provides us with spiritual counsel from a disinterested third party; (3) it assures us of Christ's forgiveness; and (4) it confers grace to lead the Christian life, helping us to avoid sin in the future.

Medicinal masturbation?

Q. I am a woman and have a nerve-and-sleep disorder. I have found that masturbation (about twice a month) relaxes me and enables me to get more sleep. I have confessed this to three different priests, each of whom assures me that it is not sinful. Is their advice correct?
A. It is obvious you do not consider their advice correct, or else you wouldn't be asking me!

Masturbation is an objective evil, and an evil means can never be pursued even for a good end, as you have undoubtedly heard on countless occasions. If you have not already done so, obtain the services of a good physician and perhaps also those of a Catholic psychotherapist, who will be able to assist you in dealing with your disorder in a productive and moral manner.

Author critiques critique

Q. Dear Father Stravinskas,

I recently received a photocopy of a page of what I presume was a rather recent issue of The Catholic Answer. *[The questioner] raised some questions about my article "Why Sunday Mass?" — part of the "God's People Alive" bulletin-insert series. The answer given, I think, was simplistic and missed the point of the article: to give people reasons for celebrating Sunday Eucharist.*

Despite the answer, "The author is wrong on both scores," I affirm that I was not wrong on either score. One cannot be wrong on what he does not say. Not quoting a canon or waving "mortal sin" does not make me "wrong." The article simply tries to provide further motivation for the fulfillment of the canonical responsibility. Your answer could easily have pointed that out, rather than seeming to agree with the questioner and undermining the credibility of the article. We're in the same Church and about the same mission. We need to reinforce one another as often as possible.

Your answer further missed the point of the article in citing a canon precluding those in mortal sin from "receiving Communion." The point of the article was to encourage people to come to Mass, not to encourage them to come to Communion. Though people in mortal sin are, according to the canon, precluded from receiving Communion, I don't think we want them to feel excluded from Sunday Mass.

With a little more perceptiveness and a little less contentiousness, your answer could have picked up this point too. You could have even taken a minimal amount of effort and called me at the phone number given at the bottom of the article to get a clarification before you published your broadside. I would hope, perhaps unrealistically, that you might in the interest of truth and charity bring these observations to the attention of your readers.

Fraternally yours in the Lord. Fr. Ron Luka, C.M.F.

A. Father, I have read and reread your original article, and I still believe I was both accurate and fair in my assessment. By the way, the person who sent in your piece was upset because you appeared to countenance and even encourage reception of Holy Communion by those not properly disposed. I agree with her.

While your article in general was an encouragement to attend Mass, you became quite specific in handling the Communion issue, and it was clear that you saw no reason for people to abstain from the Eucharist if in the state of sin. Let me quote from your original article: "Some stay away from Eucharist because they feel an inconsistency between some aspect of their life and the Eucharist. . . . But the Eucharist is not a reward for good living just like [sic] food isn't a reward for accomplishment (unless you're a laboratory mouse). The Eucharist is the means, the food, the nourishment, the healing to help us live more faithfully. We come to Eucharist in our sinfulness. . . ."

That, Father, is not Catholic teaching. In fact, even your present letter hints at this by your parenthetical statement that one must not receive Holy Communion in a state of mortal sin, "according to the canon," as though there might be an alternate valid source of information and conscience formation. In point of fact, there is, and that is the entire Catholic tradition of moral theology.

While I always seek to support a brother-priest, I regret to say that I cannot do so when he is manifestly wrong and leading others in a direction other than in a full communion of mind and heart with the Church and the Church's official teachers, namely, the pope and the bishops in union with him.

A time for healing

Q. Several years ago, our daughter was diagnosed with an obscure disease from which she was not expected to recover. Since the doctors did not know the cause of the disease, they could not tell us whether or not we could expect the same problem with other children that we might have. My wife and I were not practicing our Faith and, in weakness and doubt, decided not to take further chances; my wife underwent a sterilization procedure.

We have since returned to the Church and regret having taken this course of action. This year, my wife underwent surgery for the reversal of the sterilization, but it failed. I am tormented with the knowledge that we cannot right the wrong we did those years ago. I can't help feeling that our marriage is profane in the sight of God. I am always troubled with doubts about whether or not the next Communion I make will be sacrilegious. I pray that God will release us from this sin and heal our marriage, but I will understand if He does not. What should we do now?

A. I think you and your wife need to sit down with a good priest to discuss the situation. Of course, if you have not already confessed the sin of sterilization, that should be done. Once the sin is confessed and absolved, there should be no more concern about it. There does not seem to be any basis that God would consider your marriage "profane" on account of this.

You obviously have a very sensitive conscience (it's not clear if your wife shares that condition with you), but that should not be allowed to evolve into a scrupulous conscience. You and our wife made a noble effort to undo the damage and failed, through no fault of your own. It is now important to trust in God's love and mercy, leaving the past to the past and committing the future to His compassionate love.

Liturgy

Children's Masses

Q. The enclosed article appeared in our diocesan newspaper. Is it proper for this music teacher — a Lutheran — "to design new music and re-do the text" to make the Mass a foot-stomping, hand-clapping experience for young people? Is the idea of different types of Masses for children a sound idea? How will they ever learn to appreciate the Mass for what it is, if the form keeps changing to entertain them? Would you please comment on this?

A. The sacred liturgy should not be "entertaining" for anyone; it should be appealing, pleasing, and uplifting but those are very different categories from that of entertainment.

On the first front, it should be observed that no one may "re-do" the texts of the liturgy. In the fitting of text to music, it may be necessary to repeat certain words or lines, either for the sake of the music itself or to emphasize particular ideas in keeping with the musical setting, but that is not a change in the original text.

As for so-called "children's Masses," I am unalterably opposed to them for a variety of reasons. The first is that the "children" who seem to enjoy them the most are usually over the age of forty, that is, religious educators and even priests who are reliving lost or forgotten childhoods. Most child psychologists would hold that one does not help children grow into adult activities by providing them with dumbed-down versions of the real thing. For example, comic book editions of Shakespeare's plays are not worthwhile preparation for reading the Bard's true works. One need only watch little ones in action to see that when left to their own devices, they do not try to act like babies; they instinctively seek to imitate adults.

Children require an introduction to the Church's life of worship, but that takes much effort over a long period of time. Quick fixes like children's liturgies do not have any positive or long-lasting effects, in my judgment.

Mass additions

Q. My present pastor likes to add his own words to the eucharistic prayer. He doesn't leave anything out that is in the text, he just augments it. Is this acceptable? He is a sincere man, but the practice bothers me — perhaps I'm just not used to it.

A. Changing the liturgical text does not simply mean leaving things out; it also involves adding things. One bishop made the comment recently that a conductor can do violence to a symphony by leaving out some of the composer's original notes or by adding notes not in the original score. In either instance, what is performed is not the work of the composer, is it?

The task of the celebrant is certainly to make the Church's words come alive, but to do so by fidelity to the text, not by altering it. Richard Burton became a great Shakespearean actor, not by deleting problematic passages, but by studying them and interpreting them in such a way that his audiences came to appreciate them for all their meaning and beauty. The responsibility of a priest is no different.

Crucifix covered

Q. In our church there is a traditional, life-size crucifix hanging on the wall behind the altar. It is the only crucifix in the church. This past Lent it was covered with a purple cloth for the entire season. I've always thought that Lent was the time to meditate on the sufferings of our blessed Lord. Covering the crucifix — or perhaps my resentment at having it covered — made this more difficult for me. My pastor could give me no explanation for why this had been done. The pastoral minister and chairman of the liturgy committee, a Sister of Charity, replied that I should consider it a form of fasting! Is it a good practice to deprive the faithful of this beautiful portrayal of God's love during the Lenten season? What are the Church's regulations for the covering of images?

A. The French have a proverb which translates as "the more things change, the more they remain the same."

An immemorial custom called for the veiling of images (crucifixes included) during Passiontide (the fifth and sixth weeks of Lent). About twenty years ago, the American bishops noted that the practice should be eliminated. In the past five years or so, I have noticed that the earlier tradition has gradually been creeping back. The purpose of the veiling was done to introduce a starkness to our worship as we approached the final days of the holy season, and I think it had a very salutary effect. Therefore, I would be pleased to see its return.

Taking your concern, I would say that looking at the veiled image could remind you that your sins blind you to the love revealed in the Savior's act of self-offering, and that you should see in that an invitation to cleanse yourself of those sins so as to behold the Lord in glory on Easter more worthily.

New wording at Mass

Q. Some priests at Masses said in our area are using altered forms: "The Lord is with you" instead of "The Lord be with you" and "The Holy Gospel according to the tradition of John, Luke, etc." I find these changes disturbing. Are they permissible? What is the rationale behind either of them?

A. We begin — once more — by repeating that no one has the right to change existing liturgical texts, no matter how awful we may think they are or how beautiful we may imagine our own reconstructions!

On the first matter, the text as given by the Church is not a declarative statement; it is a wish or a prayer that the Lord might be with the liturgical assembly. No priest can assume that the Lord is, in fact, with each and every member of the congregation, since personal sin holds each and every one of us at bay, to varying degrees. The same psychology of declaring everyone holy is behind inviting everyone to receive Holy Communion, whether or not all are objectively worthy to do so (that is, no mortal sin, observance of eucharistic fast, etc.).

A similar mentality moves homilists to "canonize" the deceased at funerals. All such efforts are unwise and pastorally counterproductive because they cause people to become complacent and self-satisfied with their less-than-perfect lives. The Gospel of Christ calls us to on-going perfection.

The second deviation is serious, too. It seems to question the authenticity of the Gospel texts. If the proclaimer of the Gospel does not intend to convey this impression, he should stop saying what he is saying; if he does question the Gospel's authenticity, he should not be proclaiming the Gospel. In 1964, the Holy See issued a document "On the Historical Truth of the Gospels," which deals with the historical veracity of these works and on their having been composed by the apostles or apostolic men under the inspiration of the Holy Spirit.

Souvenir hosts?

Q. At Mass today the children made their First Holy Communion. The ushers handed out to everyone, presumably as a souvenir, a small plastic-bag with a label of a cross, and three hosts inside the bag.
I assume that the hosts were not consecrated, although nothing was said to relieve any fears.

I know that the hosts are nothing more than flour and water until they are consecrated; nevertheless, it troubles me knowing that most adults will toss them into the trash can or a drawer and most children will play with them. It does not increase a sense of reverence for the Eucharist. Is this practice out of line, or is my thinking? Please comment.

A. I have never heard of such nonsense! Making one's First Holy Communion is not like going to a wedding reception and taking home a piece of the wedding cake! You are absolutely correct in linking it to a lost reverence for the Blessed Sacrament. Whether or not the motivations were good or bad, the results can only be bad, and send confusing mixed signals about the whole affair.

No leaven allowed

Q. Is it permissible at any time to use leavened bread for the celebration of the Eucharist in the Latin Rite?
A. No. Canon 926 says: ". . . in accord with the ancient tradition of the Latin Church, the priest is to use unleavened bread in the celebration of the Eucharist whenever he offers it."

Altar girls

Q. I am a priest presently having a major conflict with my bishop over altar girls. He is attempting to force me to have them. When I brought up the fact that the Roman document had not yet been entered into the Acta, he referred me to the December 1994 newsletter of the Bishops' Committee on the Liturgy, which asserts that it is indeed now in the Acta, and hence valid law. It seems so hard to get to the truth in this debacle. Just what are my rights here?
A. For the benefit of the uninitiated, let's go over some of the terminology here.

The *Acta Apostolicae Sedis* is the collection of all official documents of the Holy See which, after their issuance, are incorporated and then — and only then — obtain the force of law. The Bishops' Committee on the Liturgy, refers to the altar-girl decision having been entered into the *Acta*, but that is not quite the case. Only the first part of that document has found its way into the *Acta*, namely, the decree of the Pontifical Council for the Interpretation of Legislative Texts from 1992 (which simply told us that the Code of Canon Law in and of itself says nothing for or against altar girls, which we already knew). The second half, from the Congregation for Divine Worship and the Discipline of the Sacraments in April of 1994 is not yet in the *Acta*. Therefore, the implementation decree has no status.

I should note that the normal "turn-around" time from the promulgation of a document to its entrance into the *Acta* is usually about three to four months. For the first half of this particular document, it took more than two years, while the second is nowhere in sight. Canonists in Rome and elsewhere cannot figure this out. Beyond that, I have checked with authorities in Rome and have been informed that no one in Rome ever envisioned their "permissive" legislation being turned into "prescriptive" legislation. In other words, just as the Holy See is apparently willing to defer to the pastoral judgment of the diocesan bishop, it is assumed that he will have similar confidence in the pastoral judgment of his priests.

If you have serious problems of conscience about this, I would have a heart-to-heart conversation with the bishop. If he refuses to take your concerns into account, you always have the right to appeal to the Congregation for the Clergy and the Congregation for Divine Worship, should you believe that your rights are being violated.

Baptismal sprinkling

Q. Is the Sacrament of Baptism valid when the water is sprinkled, rather than poured, on the head?

A. Three methods of Baptism have been used historically: infusion, immersion, and aspersion, that is, pouring, submerging, and sprinkling. The first two continue to be viable options, while the Church hesitates in regard to the last because of concern that there is no real guarantee that the water does ultimately land on the candidate's forehead; furthermore, the act of sprinkling is not very expressive of the cleansing which the ritual should evoke.

The Real Presence

Q. A recent article in Extension *magazine about the Eucharist states that Our Lord's Presence in the Eucharist is sacramental, not physical. I have always been taught that at the moment of consecration, the bread and wine truly become the physical Body and Blood of Christ — the same Christ Who was born of the Virgin Mary, died on the cross and sits at the right hand of the Father. If this is what the Church teaches, then how can the Lord's presence in the Eucharist be simply sacramental?*

A. Your gut instinct is correct, but the author's theological expression of that Catholic instinct is more correct. The presence of Christ in the Eucharist is a real and true presence so that, as you say, the whole substance of the bread and wine is transformed into the substance of the Lord's Body and Blood. His Body and Blood, however, are present sacramentally — not physically in the normal meaning of the word; Christ is present in His glorified Body, not His physical (i.e., earthly) Body, being present to us in the Eucharist as He is to the angels and saints in heaven. "Simply sacramental" does not mean "unreal" or "spiritual," and for that reason, I would never modify "sacramental" with "simply," for sacramental presence is the most profound form of presence possible. Nor would I say that Christ's presence in the Blessed Sacrament is "non-physical;" better, "trans-physical" or "supra-physical." Why? Because there are elements of physicality to it, but the Eucharist transcends the categories of space, time, etc. (as does the life of heaven).

With great care, Pope Paul VI taught in *Mysterium Fidei* in 1965: "Christ is present whole and entire in His physical 'reality,' corporeally present, although not in the manner in which bodies are in a place" (no. 46). In all likelihood, this is what the author was trying to say; either he didn't express it as well as he might have, or you misunderstood what he was saying.

Peace isn't 'flowing'

Q. In my parish, the organist has begun playing "Peace Is Flowing Like a River" every Sunday during the sign of peace. She sings and gets everyone else singing too. I feel she has inserted this song into the liturgy without authority. Not only am I tired of singing this same song every week, but it seems as if there is hardly a quiet minute any longer to recollect oneself before receiving Holy Communion. I don't believe that

our pastor cares one way or the other. What is allowable in this case?
A. The sign of peace does not call for any singing (except for the greeting itself, which may be chanted), and that part of the Mass should not become an end in itself, unduly protracting the liturgy. Your concern about the same tune being used week after week is also valid. If you think the pastor really doesn't care, approach him with a few like-minded parishioners to ask him to have the organist stop doing this.

Consecration question

Q. When do the bread and wine become the Lord's Body and Blood? When the priest makes the sign of the cross over them? When he repeats Jesus' words?
A. The *epiclesis* is the calling down of the Holy Spirit to effect the change in the elements; in the Latin Rite, this precedes the words of institution/consecration, while it follows in the Byzantine.

The *Catechism of the Catholic Church* says the following: "The Eucharistic presence of Christ *begins* at the moment of the consecration and endures as long as the Eucharistic species subsist" (1377, emphasis added). I think we can point to the words of institution as providing the starting point for the transubstantiation and allow for its having been "sealed" by the epiclesis (which follows rather than precedes in the East).

Deacons at Benediction

Q. You have mentioned that an unordained person may not give a blessing with the Eucharist at Benediction. During Lent in our parish last year, a permanent deacon held the Way of the Cross — even though we have four full-time priests — and concluded with the Benediction. Is he ordained to do this or not? The exact duties of a permanent deacon still confuse me. Can you help to clarify this situation?
A. You rightly recalled that I said a "non-ordained person" may not give Benediction, but a deacon is ordained. He may, therefore, proclaim the Gospel at Mass, distribute Holy Communion, solemnly baptize, and witness marriages. In dioceses where preaching faculties are given to deacons, they may also deliver the homily.

Benediction questions

Q. In Europe, where I was born and ordained, I never saw the practice whereby an altar boy incenses the Blessed Sacrament during the actual blessing at Benediction. The priest has just done so prior to the Benediction, so why the repetition? Also, is it permissible for one who is not a priest to incense the Blessed Sacrament?

A. I have never seen this *not* done — anywhere in the world: North America, South America, Europe, and Africa!

Many things are repeated in liturgical rites. In point of fact, during an entire Eucharistic devotion, the Blessed Sacrament would normally be incensed upon exposition, during the *Tantum Ergo,* and then during the benediction proper — all as signs of reverence for the Lord and, quite appropriately, when He as our High Priest blesses us.

On your final question, yes, it is permissible. Thus, if a non-ordained person is commissioned to expose the Blessed Sacrament for adoration in the absence of a priest, the rite directs him to incense the Blessed Sacrament at the proper times. A non-ordained person, however, may not give the blessing with the Eucharist.

Chalice veils

Q. In the General Instruction of the Roman Missal, Number 80 says: "The chalice should be covered with a veil, which may always be white." Has this changed? Most use no veil, and those who do use one use the color of the day. Please explain.

A. Let's take a close look at the text: a) the law requires a veil, and b) the presumption is that such a veil would be the color of the day but, that lacking, it may always be white. The purpose of the chalice veil is to accord a special dignity to that vessel which will contain the Blood of Christ. Given our heightened awareness of the Book of the Gospels and some of the truly magnificent ornamentation found on these volumes, does it not make sense to operate in the same way with this sacred vessel?

Casual consecrations?

Q. In our archdiocese, the majority of priests don't follow the rubric that directs the priest to hold the host or chalice "a little above the altar" during the words of consecration and to show the consecrated elements to the congregation afterward. Instead, these priests begin showing the host or chalice immediately, turning from side to side while they rather casually say or even paraphrase the words of consecration. This is so widespread that I think there must be something behind it. Do you have any idea what it is?

A. "Casual" and "paraphrase" are serious problems in the liturgy. Even if the priests in question intended nothing mischievous by their actions, they should refrain from personal idiosyncrasies that distract people from the act of worship underway and subsequently attract attention to irregularities, which in turn fuel speculation about personal motivation or ideology. Like a broken record, I repeat: "Stick to the text, Father!"

The lector's duties

Q. Is there a particular format that the lector should follow when introducing the Mass?
A. I am in a bit of a quandary about your question, inasmuch as the only real function of a lector is to proclaim the Scripture readings and, absent a deacon or cantor, read the petitions of the general intercessions. Some parishes continue a practice from the 1960s that had "commentators" giving a kind of blow-by-blow description of the liturgical action. I find this to be excessively verbal and intrusive for what is both an art form and prayer.

One of the ideas behind the use of the vernacular was that the faithful would be able to understand all of the liturgical texts without such interference. Some liturgists seem to operate from the principle that the average person in the pew is too stupid to comprehend the rather clear meaning of the texts of the liturgy and requires constant interpretation from so-called experts. This is demeaning and unnecessary at the same time, in my estimation.

Ave Maria passé?

Q. I was lamenting the fact that we seldom hear the Ave Maria *in church anymore. The organist to whom I was speaking said that the* Ave Maria *is no longer "liturgically correct"! Can this be the case? I would like this clarified. Thank You.*
A. It depends. A hymn should be selected because of its appropriateness, that is, how it relates to the feast, the sacrament, or other event being celebrated. Therefore, we don't drag out musical pieces just because we like them or because a slot needs to be filled. This is true of any musical selection, not only the *Ave Maria*. Honesty compels me to admit that many parish music directors are more apt to apply the standard of "liturgical correctness" to the *Ave Maria* than they are to most of the other options they choose for the sacred liturgy.

Greeter gripe

Q. At our church we have "greeters" who stand at the doors leading into the church; they shake the parishioners' hands and greet them as they walk in. On Holy Thursday I walked into the church with my hand extended to the lady standing at the door and said, "Good evening." Instead of taking my hand, she said, "Kiss of peace!" grabbed me by the shoulders, and planted a kiss on my cheek. I found this a very inappropriate gesture and was uncomfortable with it. She greeted everyone in the same way. After Mass I told one of the priests what had happened. He was uninterested and said as he was walking away, "Tell her that." Was I wrong in stating how I felt or in asking him for help? Was this greeter's behavior appropriate?

A. It seems the Church can never find a happy medium: Either we behave like unfeeling robots and don't acknowledge anyone else's existence in church or we turn everything into a '60s love fest. I have no problem with the idea of ushers greeting people (especially newcomers) at the door of the church, but hugging and kissing do not go in our Anglo-Saxon culture and I think that needs to be respected. Wouldn't a polite and warm "Good evening. Welcome to St. John's" do the job?

And no, I don't think you were wrong to ask the priest to do something about the inappropriate behavior. If he started it all, he should be prepared to deal with the aftermath; if he wasn't the initiator, he should have told you the right person to contact to ensure that the greeters are making people feel comfortable, rather than uncomfortable!

'Inclusive' language

Q. Recently I have noticed attempts in our seminary at "inclusive" language in communal celebrations of the Liturgy of the Hours (according to the books approved for use in this country), especially in the intercessions. For example, if the text says "beloved brothers," is it permissible to change it to "beloved brothers and sisters" or change "men" to "people"? I thought that unless an option is indicated for alternate wording, as in certain places in the Roman Missal, the printed text was to be used without alteration.

A. You are correct, and I have received numerous inquiries about this from seminaries and religious houses. So let me stake out the territory rather carefully.

This exact problem was addressed on November 18, 1992, by Bishop Wilton Gregory, then head of the Bishops' Committee on the Liturgy. At the communal celebration of one of the hours of the Divine Office, those presiding simply used the texts as found in the Breviary. The next day, some bishops rose to say that they had found the procedure offensive and even embarrassing since certain phrases in those texts did not reflect so-called inclusive language. Bishop Gregory responded to their comments by noting that no one, including the bishops, had the authority to alter any of the prayers, Psalms, etc. Therefore, he said, everyone "is required to use only the officially approved texts for liturgical celebrations." No adaptations were possible, even using the guidelines which the bishops themselves had approved since those guidelines were intended for those officially deputed to change existing texts, which texts then had to be presented to the full body of bishops, obtain a two-thirds majority, and receive the confirmation of the Holy See.

Some argue that the intercessions of Morning Prayer and Evening Prayer, for instance, are a different story since the General Instruction for the Liturgy of the Hours specifically envisions the possibility of adding or changing such texts. The reader should look more closely because the Instruction says that such modifications are the province of the episcopal conference and no one else (cf. no. 184). Bishop Gregory did ask the assembly of bishops to determine if they wanted to provide interim norms for such modifications, but no such resolution was forthcoming. And so, unless and until the liturgical books are so changed, no one has the authority to alter the prayer of the Church or to ask, let alone demand, that anyone else do so.

Foot-washing petition?

Q. I have enclosed a letter that I received from the general editor of the Paulist Press Ordo, *in answer to my inquiry about the notation that "the group whose feet are washed should represent a cross-section of the local community." What is your reaction to his comment that you were obviously unaware of the petition of the American bishops to permit women for this rite?*

A. I am not aware of any petition from the American hierarchy to the Holy See seeking permission for women to be included in this rite because there never has been any such petition! The editor does acknowledge that the Circular Letter on Holy Week forbids the inclusion of women, but then goes on to note that the competent Roman congregation is still studying the matter. Where does he get such information? And even if it were being "studied," does that in any way permit us to go counter to the legislation?

Often, people assume that because a matter is being "studied," it will result in a change in the law or discipline. When Pope John XXIII and Pope Paul VI had the birth-control issue "studied" for years, note the study resulted in a strong restatement of the traditional teaching. We have no right to anticipate an answer, lest we cause confusion and scandal.

When to say creed

Q. When do we profess our faith at Mass? Why is it different each Sunday?

A. The Nicene Creed follows the homily and precedes the general intercessions; it should be the very same every week, which is the whole point of the profession of faith. The only legitimate deviation is that the Apostles' Creed may be substituted if a Mass for children (that is, when the vast majority of those in attendance are of grammar school age) is being celebrated.

Reverence gone awry?

Q. Recently I was reprimanded by my parish priest because I always genuflect before receiving Our Lord. At the time of receiving Holy Communion, the priest hesitated for a while before giving me the Sacred host. After Mass he referred to this genuflection as creating a "catastrophe" and an expression which has been outdated for the last twenty years. I found the whole situation most uncomfortable. Is my action improper?

A. The 1967 instruction *Eucharisticum Mysterium* [no. 34] notes that the faithful may receive Holy Communion either standing or kneeling. If they kneel, no other form of reverence is needed; if they stand, an appropriate acknowledgment of the Real Presence (profound bow or genuflection) should be given. I can see that genuflecting when no one else does so can "create a catastrophe" in the sense that people behind you might not expect the gesture, and they could trip over your leg. Of course, if the priest had everyone follow the norm, there would be no problem. In the meantime, it might be wise to be a bit more careful, so as not to give him fuel for the fire. I should also say that, if your description of his behavior is accurate, he was off-base theologically and also in terms of being both priestly and gentlemanly.

Praying twice

Q. I thought Our Lord was teaching the apostles to pray when He gave them the "Our Father." If this is the case, then why do we have to sing it at Mass? Is it wrong or right to sing it?

A. St. Augustine tells us that "he who sings well prays twice." Some people will note the adverb "well" and argue that on that very score they should not sing! But the Church, following the example of Jewish liturgy, has always regarded singing as integral to worship. Along with the *Sanctus*, the Memorial Acclamation, the Great Amen, and *Agnus Dei*, the *Pater Noster* should normally be sung since the solemnity of the action of singing highlights the importance of these key parts of the Mass.

Reading the missal

Q. I have been told by both the priest and the director of religious education in my parish that my habit of reading the Liturgy of the Word from my missal along with the lector or priest is not in keeping with the reform of the liturgy by Vatican II. The only references I can find in the Constitution on the Sacred Liturgy pertain to the proclamation of the Word, but do not prohibit the use of a missal. Would you comment, please?

A. Since they told you that liturgical law does not permit or at least frowns on reading along with lector or priest, why not ask them to produce such a document of the Church? Be sure that it is an ecclesiastical text and not merely the opinion of some self-styled liturgist. Of course, in reality, they will be able to produce no such text for the simple reason that there is none.

In an ideal world, it might be nice for people to focus their attention on the lector without the use of a worship aid, but reality impinges all too often. Sound systems are not always good; lectors are not always articulate; people have difficulty hearing; some have problems internalizing a message that they can hear but cannot see. So, why not take human nature into account and allow for what is eminently reasonable, and what the Church herself permits and even encourages?

Furthermore, educational psychologists tell us that the more senses a person uses in learning, the better the hold on the material; hence, seeing and hearing the Word of God make for a double impact.

Some people object to the use of a missal by the faithful because it makes the congregation wise to the alterations being foisted on them from the sanctuary — all the more reason to keep those missals.

Gloria timing

Q. Could you please inform me if there is a regulation on where the Gloria of the Mass is to be sung? May it be sung as a processional or entrance hymn, or only after the Penitential Rite of the Mass, where it has traditionally been placed?

A. The Gloria belongs exactly where you said it belongs — and nowhere else.

Mass participation

Q. I read in one of your previous answers that the offertory prayers are the private prayers of the priest. I have hated music during this part of the Mass because I was distracted from offering myself on the paten and offering all the souls of family and friends in the chalice. How can I really take part in the Mass if I do not make the offering with the priest? Somehow I believe that if the offering is only the priest's, I am being excluded. I would prefer to be given the privilege of making the offering with him.

A. Not all people participate in the liturgical action in the same manner. The diversity of roles in the Church is especially reflected in the liturgy. The way in which the lay faithful participate in the offertory (really the preparation of the gifts) is by performing the communal action of the entire assembly, by joining in a hymn, prayerfully listening to a musical piece, or responding aloud to the prayers of the priest. St. Paul teaches us that the hand cannot be the foot in the natural order, and that it cannot be so in the supernatural order, either (cf. 1 Cor 12:12-31).

Several prayers of the Mass are the private prayers of the priest, offered in his role, either as the *alter Christus* or as the head of the Body of Christ, which is the Church. This should come as no surprise since, as Vatican II reminds us, the ministerial priesthood and the priesthood of the faithful "differ essentially and not only in degree" (*Lumen Gentium*, 10).

Temporal needs

Q. Is it liturgically proper to have the Mass interrupted after the Creed and before the Canon — sometimes for up to eight minutes — for the purpose of presenting the temporal affairs of the parish and of the congregation? It gives the impression of splitting the Mass in two; and personally, I find it difficult to recapture the frame of mind proper for worship. Please comment.

A. I'm not sure what you mean here. Are you referring to the parish announcements? If so, the General Instruction of the Roman Missal informs us that they are to be brief (eight minutes is not brief, and they surely should not be a restatement of what is already in the bulletin) and are to be done after the Post-Communion Prayer, before the dismissal. The point you have identified sounds like the preparation of the gifts, and I couldn't even guess why that should be a spot for anything but the preparation of the gifts.

Liturgy of the Hours

Q. While recuperating from a cold and looking for something to read, I stumbled upon my late mother's pretty much unused Divine Office, published about 1963. This notion of liturgical prayer that's on your own (so to speak), but still in unison with the entire Church, including many of our separated brethren, offers something that enhances the experience of the Mystical Body of Christ. Do you think the Divine Office has the potential for getting us more involved, first, in praising God (an area most of us are probably short on); second, in actually participating in the liturgical prayer of the Church; and, finally, in living the Catholic life in our day-to-day world, as opposed to some sort of spiritual life that is separate and apart from the way we go about our daily life? Is the return of the laity to the Divine Office, if only by the psychological effect of forcing ourselves to be aware of the supernatural during the day, part of the key to catholicizing culture?

Practically, I'm sure that the book I have is out of date. Could youplease tell me what the current version of the Divine Office is and where I might find it? Thank you.

A. You touch on a number of important points. Taking the last first because it is the easiest, let me offer two possibilities for laity: *Christian Prayer* (which contains Morning Prayer, Evening Prayer, and Night

Prayer), published by Catholic Book Publishing Co., and the full Divine Office in four volumes, *The Liturgy of the Hours*, published by the same house.

Throughout the centuries the Church has desired that all the faithful (not just clergy and Religious) pray the Liturgy of the Hours. In my boyhood, a remnant of that desire was fulfilled with Sunday Vespers (evening prayer) in many parishes. Ironically, when Vatican II made a strong call for renewed participation in the Divine Office by the whole Church, even Vespers seemed to disappear from most parishes. In the past few years, I have seen a resurgence of interest in the Liturgy of the Hours on the part of many younger clergy and laity. It is not unusual to find parishes where Morning Prayer and Evening Prayer precede the celebration of Masses celebrated in the morning and evening. Such a practice is most praiseworthy and thoroughly reflects the mind of the Church.

As you correctly note, this form of prayer is the highest possible next to the eucharistic sacrifice itself, because it is truly the worship of the whole Church, even when prayed by an individual alone. (Granted, this is not the most desirable manner of celebration but practical considerations are not unimportant, especially when performing a work to which one is not obligated, strictly speaking.) The Liturgy of the Hours is essentially psalmody (the very prayers Our Lord used), with massive doses of other scriptural passages and readings from the Fathers of the Church. The prayer of adoration is paramount here, with the prayer of petition taking a back seat (for a change). I have been praying the Divine Office since adolescence and never cease to receive new insights into the prayers and into the God-man relationship.

Baptisms by immersion

Q. Where can I obtain information about the practice of celebrating Baptisms during the Mass on Sunday? In my diocese, wading pools are replacing beautiful baptismal fonts. The priest stands in the water and submerges the infants and small children (stripped of all clothing). The naked babies are then held high for the welcome of the parishioners with cheers and clapping. Adults are also submerged. What is the history of this practice? Is it authentic?

A. Not everything that is permitted makes sense to implement in every parish. Prudence goes a long way but is often in short supply today.

Yes, it is true that in the early Church the Sacrament of Baptism was administered by immersion. Early baptisteries were really similar to wading pools and catechumens had their clothes removed, which is one of the reasons deaconesses (unordained female ministers) existed: to tend to the needs of women. But when whole families began to be received into the Church as the normative practice, along with their infants, the earlier method changed to accommodate the new situation. Infant Baptism is not easily administered by immersion, and certain practical problems also exist (like natural bodily functions sans diapers!). To advance a practice simply because it was done in the early Church is the kind of antiquarianism condemned by Pope Pius XII in *Mediator Dei*; the age of something is not a decisive factor in determining something's worth. It seems to me that people need to be consistent. How often we hear folks push for Baptism by immersion or married clergy because the early Church had them, but those same people do not seem so eager to return to things like public penance, which was also the norm in the early Church. Beyond that, we must realize that the large parish communities of the modern era are a far cry from the tiny, discreet, and nearly homogenous communities of a millennium ago; what could be done at that time with no difficulty takes on mammoth proportions in this day and age. Finally, the minute the circus or theatrical element enters into liturgy, we know that we are not on sacred ground but shaky ground and should react with great caution.

Missalette questioned

Q. In the Sacred Congregation for Divine Worship's circular letter Eucharistiae Participationem, *issued to the presidents of the conferences of bishops on April 27, 1973, it is stated that introductions are "among [the] elements favoring a fuller adaptation that are within the power of the individual celebrant. . . ." These introductions "are ways of leading the faithful to a more thorough grasp of the meaning of the sacred rites or certain of their parts and to an inner participation in them. . . By their very nature such introductions do not require that they be given verbatim in the form they have in the Missal. . ." (no. 14). The problem is this: The J.S. Paluch Company seems to interpret this reference to include the Orate, Fratres, and the Ecce Agnus Dei. It seems to me that the rationale expressed is that any text which invites a response from the congregation must be considered open to adaptation. Please comment.*

A. The document lists the introductions which are intended: "The comments introducing the faithful to the day's Mass before the celebration, to the Liturgy of the Word before the readings, and to the Eucharistic prayer before the preface, the comments concluding the whole rite before the dismissal." You will note that neither the Orate, Fratres, nor the Ecce Agnus Dei is noted in the list of possibilities; hence, I do not know why missalette companies print alternatives to these texts and why those publications are then given ecclesiastical sanction.

Signs of the cross

Q. Why are there three signs of the cross made before the reading of the Gospel?

A. The three signs of the cross at the beginning of the proclamation of the Gospel correspond to the prayer that the Lord would be in our minds, on our lips, and in our hearts as we hear the Gospel. In the Eastern rites and in several religious congregations, the triple sign of the cross is not used; a single, standard sign of the cross is made (which is probably the more ancient gesture at this point). This then explains why at the *Benedictus, Magnificat,* and *Nunc Dimittis* of the Divine Office, these canticles are accompanied by a sign of the cross — they are Gospel canticles and the traditional gesture is used to introduce them.

Homily time

Q. Recently I visited a parish where a visiting priest read the Gospel, gave a short homily, and then began telling the parishioners about a parish self-evaluation that was going to be conducted. After briefly outlining the evaluation process, he called upon a lay woman who continued to discuss the self-evaluation. Was this correct? I thought that the time after the reading of the Gospel was to be used only for the homily (reflecting on the readings), and that announcements, etc. were to be made after the communion prayer and before the final blessing. Please comment.

A. What you suggest is the preferred practice, however, the Church does envision certain occasions when, after a brief homily, a talk can be given on a topic of importance to the parish community or the overall life of the Church. For instance, it is not uncommon on Right-to-Life Sunday to have pro-life speakers address the congregation or to have seminarians make a pitch for priestly vocations on Good Shepherd Sunday. Under controlled circumstances and when ideology or political agendas are not involved, this type of occasional deviation is not problematic.

In the example you offer, I would have preferred that such a talk be done after the distribution of Holy Communion, but I don't think one can say that what was done was rubrically incorrect. I should stress, however, that the homily (even if abbreviated) can never be omitted, and that the homily must be delivered by an ordained minister.

A liturgist responds

Q. I would like to comment on two answers you gave in The Catholic Answer. *First, I cannot believe that any Catholic priest would suggest that only a "representative" of the faithful be "allowed" to receive the Eucharist at Papal Masses. I do agree with your opinions that these Masses become a social event and lose the proper reverence for celebrating the Eucharist. I too was at Yankee Stadium in 1979 for the Papal Mass. As a liturgist, may I suggest that instead of the Eucharist, papal liturgies should consist of a Liturgy of the Word or Evensong? In doing this, people will be exposed to other liturgical rites of the Church, which can be celebrated without the logistical nightmares of distributing Communion.*

Second, in reference to confessions during the Sacred Triduum, *the Roman Missal states clearly: "According to the Church's ancient tradition, the sacraments are not celebrated today (Good Friday) or tomorrow" (p. 140, no. 1). Now the Holy Father says we can; no wonder there is confusion! Personally, I feel that a priest should* always *be available for confession; however, as you know, people always wait until the last minute to do things, so it is an issue of education and flexibility. Here we do not celebrate the Sacrament of Penance publicly during the* Triduum, *but our priests will hear confessions if someone asks them.*

I think you are doing a great job in clearly explaining the Catholic Faith to your readers, and I encourage you to keep up the good work.
A. Thanks for the compliment. While I agree that Catholic liturgical life has been diminished by "Massing" people to death since the Council and that exposing people to other liturgical forms (like the Divine Office) has great merit, I would disagree that papal events should not include

Mass. After all, the Church is never more the Church than when she gathers to offer the eucharistic sacrifice, and certainly, at an ecclesiological level, the fullness of Catholic life is never more visible than when Christ's faithful are at the altar in the company of the visible head of the Church, Christ's vicar on earth. What a shame it would be to exclude Mass from such an ecclesial experience.

Second, as desirable as the reception of Holy Communion is, it is not essential that each and every member of the congregation receive; indeed, many cannot or should not receive for a variety of reasons. Therefore, I stand by my original statement in that regard.

As far as confessions during the *Triduum* are concerned, I must say that I never understood the passage you cite as being a ban on the Sacrament of Penance during that period. I always think of it as referring to the Easter sacraments, namely, Baptism and Confirmation, along with one's first Eucharist. And so, according to my interpretation, the Holy Father has not changed horses in mid-stream; he has simply given the correct understanding of that rubric, which had been distorted by some liturgists who wanted to downplay the importance of the Sacrament of Penance. As a parish priest, I would also have to disagree that being available for an appointment for confession is the same as being available in a confessional at a particular time. People are most reluctant to "bother Father" when he does not seem to be truly available, let alone interested. After your nice remarks, I hope you do not construe my rejoinders as ungracious!

Inclusive lectionary?

Q. My parish uses a lectionary published in Canada, written in "inclusive language." My pastor claims the book was approved by Rome. Is this true? He concludes that if it is permissible for use in Canada, it is likewise so here. Please comment.

A. First of all, the lectionary in question was never approved by Rome because the Canadian hierarchy never submitted it for such approval, although they are required to do so. How that situation continues, I have no idea.

On the second point, your pastor is equally misinformed. Approval of the Holy See for a particular work is given only to the hierarchy that requests it, not for the universal Church or even for all countries using the same language as the country making the request.

No matter how the cake gets sliced, that lectionary should not be used in the United States.

Sign of peace

Q. My friend has been told twice by a priest at his parish that it isn't proper for him to kiss his girlfriend during the sign of peace at Mass. My friend has approached other couples who aren't married and who kiss at that time (even in the front row) and none of them has been similarly cautioned by this priest. He says he has kissed his mother, sisters, aunts, nieces, and cousins (most of whom the priest does not know) without any comment. He is sure that the priest is only picking on him because he is white and his girlfriend is black. I have seen them, and they are neither impassioned nor immodest. Both are devout Catholics and would like to know what the guidance of the Church is. Can they dismiss the priest's instruction as racist, or is he right even if he is selective in its enforcement?

A. I have no way of knowing if the priest in question is selective in his enforcement or racist, but I do object to people kissing at the sign of peace on principle. Why? Not because I'm a prude, because I'm not, but because it is importing a secular symbol of love to a liturgical context. The "kiss of peace" which is proper to the liturgy is a uniquely sacred gesture (an embrace at the shoulders and elbows and an accompanying bow); kissing connotes either familial and/or erotic love and/or affection. These latter dispositions are not wrong in themselves and in the right place are even holy signs, but the liturgy is not the right place or time. I should also add that I find a handshake at that point in the liturgy equally inappropriate for two reasons: it, too, is a secular sign; and among close friends and especially relatives, it is stilted and artificial and, therefore relatively meaningless.

For a point of comparison, let me suggest that my opposition to kissing and handshaking is paralleled by my opposition to secular greetings like "Good morning!" serving as replacements for sacred greetings like "The Lord be with you."

Unbelievable hymn

Q. I intended to become Catholic, along with several friends, because I understood the Church to be the defender of the historic Christian Creeds. Apparently, I was wrong. A hymn used at the local parish, "As a Fire is

Meant for Burning," states "so the Church is meant for mission, giving glory to God's name. Not to preach our creeds or customs, but to build a bridge of care, we join hands across the nations, finding neighbors everywhere." If this is an accurate expression of the relation of the Church to the Creeds, then I shall discontinue my instruction. Please help me.

A. You shouldn't discontinue instructions; the parish should discontinue the hymn, which is silly at best and bordering on heresy at worst. Inane sentiments like those expressed in the song seek to create dichotomies where none should exist. Believers are not forced to choose between believing the true Faith and being charitable toward their neighbor. In point of fact, a wholehearted acceptance of the historic creeds leads one to become engaged in the spiritual and corporal works of mercy.

Just how central doctrine is to our life should be apparent from the production of the new *Catechism of the Catholic Church*. While I would urge you to continue your study of the Catholic Faith, I would also offer a caution: If you speak to someone in authority in your parish about that song and get no satisfaction, that might be a good hint that your instructions will not be all that beneficial there either, and it would be wise to look for another parish in which to learn the fundamentals of the Faith and be received into the Catholic Church.

Liturgical tampering

Q. Instead of simply repeating the quote from Vatican II prohibiting liturgical tampering, why not cite Canon 846.1?

A. I cite Vatican II because it was an ecumenical council and because so many self-described "liberals" try to claim it for themselves. Of course, the citation you offer is equally good.

The readings at Mass

Q. I use The Vatican II Sunday Missal, *St. Paul Edition, with the scriptural text from* the New American Bible. *At Mass, words are often substituted, added, or deleted from the readings as given in my missal by the lectors or priest. I have asked my pastor about this, and he said that he is using the text of the revised* New American Bible. *Also, in a handbook for lectors, I have seen it implied the* New Revised Standard Version *is approved for the readings at Mass. Are the readings in the missal allowed to be changed in this way?*

A. The revised *NAB* is an approved text for Mass, but there is no lectionary based on it yet available. So where has your priest found it, unless he's simply using the Bible directly? That's possible but improbable, due to the hassle involved in finding passages, especially when the lectionary calls for skipping from one verse to another. Ask him for a further clarification.

Alleluia, again

Q. Some time back, an archbishop took you on for your statement that the Alleluia should be sung and, if not, ought to be omitted. You then agreed with him, but you were actually correct, to begin with. In the revised lectionary (1981), we find Number twenty-three, which says: "The Alleluia or the verse before the Gospel must be sung. . . ." It does not, however, leave the option for its recitation at all; it must be sung, period.

A. Thanks for your sturdy defense of me, but I did not perceive His Grace's letter as a personal assault. Your letter did cause me to go to the original Latin for the directive you cited, where we find this: " '*Alleluia*' *et versus ante Evangelium cantari debent. . . .*" (emphasis added). My own instinct suggested that the line would be better translated by "should" or "ought," rather than "must" — which is just a bit too strong. I consulted several Latin dictionaries, all of which confirmed my judgment (with only one offering "must" as an option at all, and that in second or third place).

Logic also helps out here. The Alleluia is hardly the most significant part of the Mass, and if parts like the Memorial Acclamation and the Great Amen *should* be sung, why *must* this be sung? Once again, we are confronted with the International Commission on English in the Liturgy trying to outdo the *Missale Romanum*.

For readers interested in an accurate translation of the Ordinary of the Mass, with a commentary providing the rationale for the English texts, I invite them to order a study copy from the St. Gregory Foundation for Latin Liturgy, 21 Fairview Ave, Mt. Pocono, PA 18344; the cost is $10 each, plus $1 postage.

Eucharistic exposition

Q. Could you please advise us what is necessary for the exposition of the Sacred host for adoration? Is it proper for the exposition to take place using a glass dish that contains several hosts? Where might we find the Church's directives regarding exposition?

A. Exposition of the Blessed Sacrament may be done solemnly or simply. Solemn exposition involves the placement of the Sacred host in a monstrance; simple calls for the ciborium to be placed in the doorway of the tabernacle.

A glass dish is an inappropriate vessel for the sacred species under any circumstances. This issue is addressed in the General Instruction of the Roman Missal (No. 290).

A 'rite of passage'?

Q. Was the Sacrament of Confirmation ever supposed to be a "rite of passage"? This seems to be the current thought. Is this what Jesus intended the sacrament to be? Would you please comment.

A. The *Catechism of the Catholic Church* notes that "there is thus a certain resemblance between the stages of natural life and the stages of spiritual life" (1210), so that the sacraments of the Church have a certain parallel to various aspects of natural human life: birth, growth, etc. In that sense, Confirmation fits into the scheme in that way.

Some catechists in the past two decades, however, have turned this sacrament into something very different from what either Christ or His Church ever intended. They place such stress on Confirmation as an adult moment of decision for Christ or the Church as to make that kind of human action decisive for understanding either Baptism or Confirmation. To make the connection, it is critical to read what the *Catechism* itself has to say: "Although Confirmation is sometimes called the 'sacrament of Christian maturity,' we must not confuse adult faith with the adult age of natural growth, nor forget that the baptismal grace is a grace of free, unmerited election and *does not need 'ratification' to become effective*" (1308, emphasis added).

Faith knows no borders

Q. Is it improper to render the First and Second Readings in two languages at Mass?

A. I suspect that you mean this: Is it proper, for example, to proclaim the First Reading in Spanish and the Second Reading in English? There is nothing wrong with that. I think it would unduly prolong the liturgy if both readings were done in both languages. In some older ethnic parishes, it was common practice to do that with the Gospel and even the homily, so that the Gospel would be read in both languages and was followed by the homily in both languages. I am not aware of situations where one could not get away with doing everything only once in one language or the other. Furthermore, the homily should be able to tie together any loose ends that slipped through the cracks.

While we are on the question of language in the liturgy, let's move beyond the Liturgy of the Word to the Liturgy of the Eucharist.

I recall receiving an inquiry some years ago from a newly appointed bishop who was concerned about the appropriate language to use for the eucharistic prayer; he was going to a very polarized diocese and was afraid that praying the canon in English would tell Hispanics he didn't care for them, while using Spanish would signal "Anglos" that they could not expect him to be their bishop too. I asked him if he had thought about using Latin, and he replied that he had even forgotten that it was an option! The Church had great wisdom in maintaining a so-called dead language for many reasons, not least of which was and is becoming yet again the need to maintain unity among various (and, sometimes, conflicting) cultural groups. When I had the pastoral care of a parish that was traditionally Lithuanian (in which lived many second- and third-generation folks ignorant of Lithuanian, as well as many Portuguese and even a smattering of Italians), we followed this procedure at the principal Sunday Mass: hymns in Lithuanian; Gloria, Credo, Sanctus, and Agnus Dei sung in Latin; first two readings and Psalm in Lithuanian; Gospel, homily, and general intercessions in English; recited Ordinary parts in Lithuanian. On important feasts, especially when there would be only one Mass, the eucharistic prayer was done in Latin, with some English and Portuguese hymns used.

If people find such arrangements annoying, they need catechesis on what it means to belong to a universal Church. All Catholics should feel welcome in any Catholic church anywhere in the world; ethnocentricity is totally out of bounds for anyone with a truly Catholic heart. Blessed George Matulaitis, archbishop of Vilnius, once reflected on a similar dilemma in his time saying: "Christ commissioned us to preach the Gospel, not to teach languages!" In other words, while political entities may question what language should be used within secular borders, that is not an ecclesiastical question, precisely because the Church, although located within a civil state's borders, has no borders herself.

Lector seating

Q. In our parish, Mass is celebrated with reverence (basically); however, there is a lot of movement in the sanctuary. The repositioning of chairs helped somewhat, and the distractions were decreased. Now a new assistant pastor has come who has convinced the pastor that the lector should not be seated in the sanctuary, but should come forward out of the congregation. He said this was called for in the documents of Vatican II. Is this true? I find all of the motion of commentators, cantors, and lectors to be a terrible distraction.

A. There are no hard and fast rules about the location for the lector. My own predisposition is to have the person come forward immediately after the opening prayer, after having genuflected to the Blessed Sacrament and bowed to the altar and the celebrant. My reasoning is that this function is a true lay role, and the proclaimer of the Scriptures ought to be seen as coming forth from the congregation; this is also my rationale for having lectors wear lay clothes, rather than choir robes or albs. Both of these procedures are, by the way, those used at papal Masses in St. Peter's Basilica.

As far as noise and distraction go, I don't know why that should happen; at least, I've never had such difficulties at any Masses in any of my parishes.

Holy Communion forms

Q. I am writing in regard to your answer on the questioner's "wheat host allergy." I was under the impression that it was mandatory to receive the host, the Body of the Lord, and that receiving the Precious Blood was optional. So, are those who would receive only under the form of wine really receiving Communion?

A. The normal method of receiving Holy Communion in the Roman rite is under the form of bread alone. One may also receive under the form of wine, either by intinction (the Sacred host dipped into the Precious Blood by the priest) or by directly drinking from the chalice. In the Eastern rites, Holy Communion is normally administered under both forms, by intinction.

In the whole Church, however, it has always been acknowledged that certain circumstances may require one to receive one particular way, and this is doctrinally possible because Our Lord is present — whole and entire — under each form. Therefore, one does not receive "more" of Christ by receiving one species rather than another or by receiving both species. Thus, the following scenarios suggest themselves: The woman with the wheat allergy would receive only under the species of wine; an alcoholic, only under the form of bread; someone unable to take solid food, only under the form of wine; etc.

Too hot for Creed?

Q. In celebrating Sunday Mass, one of our priests omits the Nicene Creed. When asked about this, he said it was customary to do so in his former parish during the summer because of the heat. Is this permissible?
A. No, it is not. If he's so concerned about the heat, let him shorten his homily (but not eliminate it!).

Sign of reverence

Q. Recently I have noticed more and more people merely bowing when reverencing the Blessed Sacrament, instead of genuflecting. At times, the bow is no more than a nod of the head. This is true also of some of the clergy, both during and outside of Mass. One of my friends has said that the Catechism *(1378) now allows for either bowing or genuflecting. What's the story?*
A. We must remember that the *Catechism* was written for the universal Church, not just for the Roman rite. It takes into consideration the practice of the Churches of both East and West; therefore, the mention of both gestures of reverence for the Eucharist. But do not miss that the *Catechism* does speak of a "profound" bow, not a nod of the head! If one wants to discover the discipline explicitly set for the Roman rite, one must consult documents dealing with that rite. In doing so, one learns that the gesture is still a genuflection, replaced by a bow only when physical conditions do not allow for the former.

As for the priest during liturgy, it could not be any clearer that he is to genuflect on three specific occasions: after the elevation of each eucharistic species, before presenting the Sacred host to the congregation ("Behold the Lamb of God. . ."), and any time he (or any other minister) passes before the tabernacle.

Concelebration query

Q. Sometimes at Masses with large numbers of concelebrating priests those at the end of the line cannot receive the Precious Blood because it

227

has already been consumed by those ahead of them. Does this invalidate the Mass for that priest? What if he accepted a stipend for that Mass?

A. Reception from the chalice for concelebrants is normative but not an absolute; therefore, if the supply of the Precious Blood ran out, a concelebrant would have truly concelebrated and, yes, could rightly accept a stipend for that Mass. Of course, massive concelebrations invite problems like this; careful advance planning should be practiced.

Consecrated or not?

Q. At the majority of Masses I attend, not enough altar bread is consecrated, resulting in reliance on additional hosts from the tabernacle. One Sunday after Mass, I observed a layman open the tabernacle and refill the ciborium with altar breads. Would these be consecrated at the next Mass if they are still in the tabernacle? Or are some people receiving unconsecrated hosts? Also, is the term "unconsecrated host" appropriate or should "host" be used only when referring to the consecrated species?

A. Unconsecrated hosts do not get consecrated by osmosis; they must be in a vessel on the altar during the eucharistic prayer, with the celebrant having the intention to consecrate them. What you describe is a grave violation which must be brought to the attention of those in authority.

Strictly speaking, you are correct in saying that the word "host" ought to be kept for the consecrated species since it comes from the Latin *hostia*, which means "victim." That is why the more careful among us speak of "altar breads" for them before their consecration.

Anoint the healthy?

Q. If a caregiver is present when a priest gives the Sacrament of the Sick to someone who is ill and he says, "I'll give it to you, too," does that mean that all sins and the punishments due to sin are forgiven without first going to confession?

A. The question is why the priest would want to anoint the caregiver to begin with. The Sacrament of the Sick is for those who are gravely ill (see the *Catechism of the Catholic Church*, 1527-1529), which would suggest that such a person would hardly be in a position to tend to the needs of someone else, at least in the normal course of events.

All too often this sacrament has been abused in recent years. I can understand a priest's invitation to those in attendance to receive Holy Communion with the sick person (assuming all are in the state of grace or are willing to receive the Sacrament of Penance), but not what you describe.

Mass 'itinerary'?

Q. I am not comfortable with the almost universal practice of the priest beginning Mass without announcing what options he is going to use. As a result, throughout the Mass participation by the people is practically impossible. The following is the announcement I make: "We will celebrate this Mass for the intention of. . . . You will find the proper parts of this Mass in your missalette on page ___. Where we have a choice of parts in this Mass, we will take the third choice. In the fourth Eucharistic prayer we are told that those go home with extra merit who take part in the Mass. Let's all go home with extra merit by all taking part in every way we can: singing, responses, prayers, etc., and meaning every word we say." Would you have any criticism of my practice?

A. I think your goal is meritorious, Father, but I strongly disagree for several reasons. The first is practical. If I intend to use the fourth eucharistic prayer, I would then have to use the fourth penitential rite, yes? But there isn't any!

Second, the Church did not produce the several options to "go together." In other words, there is no logical or necessary connection among Penitential Rite A and Eucharistic prayer I and the first memorial acclamation.

Third, and most importantly, the liturgy is an art form; announcements about pages and options reduce the event to a ride on a subway car, in which we are given the itinerary at the outset and all along the way. Can you envision the diva at the opera launching into a guided tour of the work before singing her first aria?

My own pastoral/liturgical experience of more than eighteen years convinces me that the average congregation can follow quite well without pedantic introductions and on-going commentary, which not only destroy the artistic element, but also go a long way toward eviscerating the sense of the sacred.

One last item: If people need to be told in advance where the propers for a particular feast are, for example, that ought to be done by a commentator, leader of song, or lector before the liturgy actually begins.

Triduum confessions

Q. In spite of what you have said, my pastor insists that confessions are not to be heard during the last three days of Holy Week. What can I show him to convince him he is wrong?

A. During one of the 1993 *ad limina* talks to American bishops, the Holy Father said this: "Advent, Lent, and *the days of the Sacred Triduum* are especially appropriate times for evoking conversion and celebrating the Sacrament of Penance" (emphasis added). "The days of the Sacred Triduum" are precisely the days your pastor says are off-limits to confessions; the pope says otherwise.

Intinction

Q. My pastor just put a notice in the bulletin that says the following: "We have been instructed by the Archdiocese not to distribute Communion by intinction [dipping the host into the chalice]. A number of people have asked about this. There is a chance, with this practice, that the Precious Blood will drop to the floor. Our eucharistic ministers have thus been instructed not to allow people to receive by intinction." Yet you say this is a viable option. Please explain.

A. Communion by intinction is indeed "a viable option" and cannot be proscribed by local liturgical authorities. Reading the directive carefully, however, I detect something different here.

Intinction is the procedure whereby the minister of Holy Communion dips the Sacred host into the Precious Blood and then places it directly onto the tongue of the recipient. The letter, on the other hand, is talking about another procedure, namely, that the communicant who has apparently already received the host from a minister then proceeds to a chalice and dips It therein himself. That is self-communication and is strictly forbidden (cf. *Inaestimabile Donum*, no. 9). Diocesan authorities are right in prohibiting such action. However, they should not have given it the name of intinction (which is a proper method of Eucharistic distribution) but rather "self-intinction" or "self-communication," which is not correct.

Not entertainment

Q. In our parish during Mass, the words of the hymns are projected onto the wall. The words of many songs are changed for purposes of "inclusivity," including "God language" ("She" is often used). I have objected to the music director and gotten nowhere. What's my next step?

A. My first objection is the projection of the texts of the hymns onto the wall, which smacks of a 1960s hootenanny or a piano bar more than worship. In and of itself there is nothing inherently wrong with the procedure. After all, holding a book is not a more sacred action than reading the same words off a wall. The problem is the image conveyed and the linkages established; we must always guard against ever offering the impression that the sacred liturgy is in any way connected to secular entertainment.

I cannot understand how people can imagine that they have the right to change the words written by another person, whether we like what they have written or not. No one would dare (I hope) attempt to change the words chosen by Shakespeare, so why change the compositions of hymn writers?

As far as "inclusive language" for God, especially as that affects the use of the feminine pronoun, that is completely beyond the pale. While we know that God has no gender, the Sacred Scriptures do indeed use the masculine pronoun for God and never the feminine. Furthermore, the Bible consistently refers to God as "Father." Although Scripture does posit feminine qualities of God, not even once is God referred to as "Mother" or any other feminine title.

A sign of confusion?

Q. Might there be a practical limit to the time spent on the sign of peace at Mass? A venerable and saintly priest in our parish is so loving of the congregation that he hugs the first three persons in each row all along the aisle.

It seems to me that the words, "Let us offer each other the sign of peace" [emphasis added] suggests that we don't have to receive it from the celebrant but from each other. The procedure I described delays the action of the Mass by as much as twenty minutes. Isn't this an abuse?

A. It certainly is an abuse, and the priest in question errs in several ways.

First, the priest should never leave the sanctuary once the sacrifice has begun. Second, it is a mistaken clericalism to assume that the peace can only be extended to the liturgical assembly by direct contact with the celebrant. As you correctly note, the directive is to offer the peace to each other and not in some sort of derivative manner. In point of fact, the peace that is exchanged is a peace that is in the midst of the people.

Third, to spend twenty minutes on a single part of the Mass — and one that is optional, to boot — is rather ridiculous and betrays a genuine lack of comprehension about what it is that we are doing in the liturgy. The focus has been shifted to man and away from God, whether or not that is the explicit intention.

Blasphemous view?

Q. The enclosed editorial from Maryknoll *magazine argues that Mary's action in conceiving Jesus and giving birth to Him were priestly actions, enabling her to say more than anyone else, "This is my Body. This is my Blood." I think this is shocking and even blasphemous. Of course, the priest goes on to challenge Rome to begin ordaining women. What should be said in response?*

A. I fully agree with your assessment. As I followed the letters to the editor, it was clear that many others had the same reaction. What sounds pious and even logical on the surface is, upon deeper investigation, shallow and politically motivated.

It also reflects a tremendous confusion between the natural and supernatural orders of reality. Simply because a woman can rightly and proudly proclaim that the child of her womb is truly her body and blood, that is no reason to hold that she can do so sacramentally, just as the priest can say those words sacramentally but can never apply them to the natural order.

A separate liturgy

Q. Our parish has adopted the practice of dismissing the children from the Mass for a separate Liturgy of the Word. My questions are these: Is this appropriate? Should the Mass be interrupted to re-seat the children? Do the adult facilitators have to participate in another Mass? Frankly, none of this makes any sense to me. Would you please enlighten me?

A. It is permissible to provide a separate Liturgy of the Word for children; whether it is advisable is another matter entirely. Pedagogically, I find no merit in the approach. If we watch little children left to their own devices for but a few minutes, we discover them imitating adults in terms of dress, occupation, and speech; the last thing they want is to be treated as children. If that is the nature of the beast, why are some religious educators and liturgists refusing to take this kind of data seriously? Pastorally, I would find the procedure most distracting and disruptive.

As far as adult facilitators go, I suppose that if participation in the separate Liturgy of the Word (followed by the Liturgy of the Eucharist) fulfills the Sunday obligation for those children who have attained the use of reason, then it must do the same for the adults.

Missed 'manners'

Q. During the summer, we attend a 6:30 a.m. Mass at which there are usually about thirty people. The priest and an extraordinary minister distribute the hosts, and the chalice is left on the altar for us to "help ourselves." The priest is annoyed that I bow before receiving, and one day right then and there he said, "Do we have to go through this everyday?" He also later upbraided me for always receiving from him, never from the lay person and never from the chalice. What should I say to him?

A. You are correct on every score. Under no circumstances may people "help themselves" (cf. *Inaestimabile Donum* [Instruction on Certain Norms concerning Worship of the Eucharistic Mystery], no. 9). The General Instruction of the Roman Missal mandates a bow or genuflection if one receives Holy Communion standing, as does *Eucharisticum Mysterium* (Instruction on the Worship of the Eucharistic Mystery, cf. No. 34b); given the number of people at Mass, one cannot even begin to justify the use of extraordinary ministers, and so your refusal to give credibility to the abuse is meritorious. Give your priest a complimentary copy of the liturgy documents, especially Pope John Paul II's *Inaestimabile Donum* and *Dominicae Cenae* (Letter on Mystery and Worship of the Holy Eucharist), as well as a book in common courtesy befitting a Christian gentleman and a priest. Both of these Church documents are available from the Daughters of St. Paul, St. Paul Books and Media, 50 St. Paul's Ave., Boston, MA 02130.

Sunday Vespers

Q. Why have Sunday Vespers been suppressed in the parishes?

A. I have no idea, especially since the Second Vatican Council made an explicit call for an even broader celebration of the Liturgy of the Hours. Thus do we read in *Sacrosanctum Concilium*:

"Pastors of souls should see to it that the principal hours, especially Vespers, are celebrated in common in church on Sundays and on the more solemn feasts. The laity, too, are encouraged to recite the Divine

Office, either with the priests, or among themselves, or even individually" (no. 100).

My own observations lead me to conclude that the Liturgy of the Hours has been making something of a comeback in the past few years. Many priest-friends of mine have reinstituted Vespers, for example, on the Sundays of Advent and Lent, for starters. Yet other parishes make available Lauds (Morning Prayer) before daily Mass.

Passion for the passion

Q. There seems to be a lack of emphasis placed on the passion and death of the Lord in the Church these days. I'll give two examples from my own parish this past Lent: (1) During the Stations of the Cross, a fifteenth Station — The Resurrection — was added. Our parish priest says it is because we cannot leave Jesus in the tomb. I have always thought of Lent as a time of sacrifice and denial leading up to the Resurrection; including this new Station seems to de-emphasize the sacrifice made by Our Lord on Calvary. (2) On Good Friday, we used to venerate the image of the Crucified Christ. Now, we have been told to kiss the cross. Some members of our parish have refused to venerate the cross. Are they wrong not to do this? Shouldn't we honor the body of the Crucified Christ on Good Friday?

A. In general, I agree with your basic point that all too many people on the contemporary scene downplay the Lord's passion and death. They fail to appreciate the insight of classical spirituality, *post crucem, lucem* ("after the cross, the light"); in other words, it as only after experiencing the Cross that one can hope to enter into the light of glory.

On the first matter, inasmuch as the Stations of the Cross are not a form of liturgical prayer, they are open to various adaptations. We have seen this, for instance, with the present pope's inviting different authors each year to produce a text for the Good Friday Stations in Rome, and even using some stations that do not correspond to the usual fourteen. For decades now, a fifteenth station has been added as optional, to commemorate the Resurrection. While not wrong theologically, I think it ill-advised from a psychological stance.

On your second concern, please realize that "the cross" referred to in the Good Friday liturgy is to have an image of the Crucified Lord's Body on it; a legitimate confusion can occur because the Latin uses "*crux*" ("cross"), but the reason is that Latin has no word for "crucifix."

If, however, you want pictorial proof of what should be done, obtain a photo of the papal Good Friday liturgy, wherein it is clear that a crucifix, not a cross, ought to be used. The only exception to the veneration of a crucifix is if a relic of the True Cross is available; then it may be used.

Kneeling norms?

Q. Positions always seem to keep changing in our parish. When the gifts are brought to the altar for the offertory, does it matter which element is carried on which side of the aisle? Also, we have been instructed to stand after the Great Amen until after having received Communion, when we are asked to be seated. I always thought that we were supposed to kneel after the Lamb of God and also to spend some time in thanksgiving after having received Holy Communion on our knees? Are there any hard-and-fast rules for this?

A. As far as the position for the gifts in the offertory procession, there are no rules; the only goal is to get them to the altar in a dignified manner.

Neither the General Instruction to the Roman Missal nor the American norms indicate congregational posture for the time frame you mention. Therefore, local options are possible.

Inconsistent?

Q. Our parish liturgy committee has taken away all decorations from around the tabernacle, they say, to bring out the penitential nature of Advent. They intend to do the same for Lent. Are they correct? It seems odd to me, however, that they continue to decorate around the various statues. Isn't this inconsistent?

A. Yes, I think it is inconsistent. Advent's focus is not so much penitential (in the way that Lent is) as it is expectant: a spirit of anticipation that includes, necessarily, the removal of personal obstacles which get in the way of our "receiving Christ with joy," as the liturgy puts it. Joyful expectancy, then, is the overriding attitude of the season.

Lent, on the other hand, is much more clearly penitential. In both cases the Church desires that our personal practices and our liturgical worship be somewhat muted. Therefore, we are not only encouraged to perform penances but also to avoid parties and the like, at a personal level. Our liturgical life should also be without great display (weddings are discouraged, the Gloria is suppressed, purple vestments are worn, flowers should not be used, nor should musical instruments — unless the singing of the congregation requires this kind of support (cf. *Musicam Sacram*, no. 66).

If the parish liturgy committee wants to lead the community in a wholehearted observance of these sacred seasons, that is certainly laudable, but it should not become a matter of picking and choosing which elements will be affected and which will not.

Polka Masses?

Q. Recently, at a neighboring parish, I attended a "Polka Mass" as part of a weekend Germanfest. At the Mass, it was announced that the Holy Father not only approves of Polka music as part of the official liturgy, but recommends it. Please comment.

A. Liturgical music is to be sacred music, which by definition refers to music that is composed specifically for liturgy and used only within that context. Polka Masses thus fail on both scores. Absent any comments by the pope about this phenomenon, I can only conclude that the person who told you about his approval is engaging in wishful thinking.

A clear distinction

Q. In our parish, the sanctuary has as many people as does the nave of the church; it seems as though everybody and his uncle have a reason to be there. Our former pastor said this was not permitted, but the present man seems to like to be surrounded by a crowd. At the Lord's Prayer, the entire gang of extraordinary ministers comes up and stands by as though they are concelebrants. What's right?

A. Your former pastor was correct. Part of the problem is the terminology in English. What we generally refer to as the "sanctuary" in English is known in Latin as the *presbyterium*, that is, the place where the priests function. If we used that word in English, the inappropriateness of what you describe would be apparent to all. The Order of Mass (no. 257) indicates that the area surrounding the altar is the area reserved for the priest; in 1981, the Congregation for Divine Worship and the Discipline of the Sacraments also handled this question and noted that "only the celebrant who presides remains at the altar."

Practically speaking, what should all this mean? Lectors and altar boys, for example, should be positioned at chairs and kneelers at a distance from the area immediately surrounding the altar. If extraordinary ministers of Holy Communion are used, under no circumstances should they stand around the altar; they should be communicated from the same general area as the other ministers of the Mass. Even the deacon should not stand in such a way and place as to suggest that he is a concelebrant.

I know that some will find this all rather offensive and label it "clericalistic." But the Church herself makes the point that the relationship of the ordained priest to the Eucharist is qualitatively different from that of anyone else in the Church, and that this distinction must be clear in the celebration of the sacred liturgy.

The 'offering prayer'

Q. Where does the term "anaphora" come from? Why is it used as another name for the eucharistic prayer?

A. The Greek verb *anaphorein* means "to offer," and "the offering prayer" in the East is called the "anaphora," which is, as you note, the equivalent of the eucharistic prayer in the Latin rite.

Gloria and Credo

Q. At the local Newman Center, the priests often omit the Gloria and the Credo from the Mass. One of the priests I have spoken to says that the Gloria is not supposed to be used unless it is sung, while the recitation of the Creed seems to be left to the initiative of the individual priest. This is not the practice in my home parish, and I cannot find any mention of dispensing from saying either prayer in the missal I have. Could you please comment on who is correct?

A. The Gloria is recited on all Sundays of the year, except during Advent and Lent; the Credo is to be recited on all Sundays. There is no discretionary element involved.

Feet vs. hands

Q. Last year on Holy Thursday the priest dispensed with the washing of the feet of twelve individuals and instead invited the entire congregation to come forward and have their hands washed! Is this variation allowed? It seemed very odd. Would you please comment?

A. Once more, we find ourselves encountering people who think they can improve on the Church, and, as often happens, it gets silly, in addition to being disobedient.

The washing of the feet is an optional rite of the Holy Thursday liturgy, but there is no option to replace it with something else. The choice of "hand washing" is particularly ridiculous since it is a completely different symbol: The foot washing signifies Christ's humble service to His apostles; hand washing (even in Mass every day) represents a desire to be cleansed of sin; in the context of Holy Week, one is driven to consider Pontius Pilate who tried to wash his hands of the guilt of Christ's blood!

Liturgical unfaithfulness

Q. You are frequently called upon to address liturgical abuses and to be a "voice crying out in the wilderness," reminding priests of their obligation to obey universal Church discipline. According to St. Thomas Aquinas, in his Summa Theologiae, *"a man incur[s] the guilt of falsehood who, on the part of the Church, gives worship to God contrary to the manner established by the Church or divine authority, and according to ecclesiastical custom." Since the Second Vatican Council's Constitution on the Sacred Liturgy declared that "No person, even if he be a priest, may add, remove or change anything in the liturgy on his own authority," it would seem that even the apparently innocuous (but deliberate) alteration of isolated words in the prayers of the Mass shall render the offending priest guilty of falsification of the worship rendered to God in the most August Sacrifice of the Mass — hardly a minor offense.*

What is the opinion of modern moral theologians on the moral gravity of unfaithfulness to liturgical texts, of disobedience to liturgical directives, and of irreverence in the celebration of the Mass? Would you comment, please?

A. I think your question is excellent and opens up some fruitful discussion on an aspect of this thorny problem not frequently considered, namely, the sinfulness of departures from the officially approved liturgical texts. I see the potential for sin to arise from disobedience to legitimately constituted authority; pride (in that one pits his own opinion over the collective wisdom and discipline of the Church); scandal (due to the amazed reaction of the faithful); disunity (since the worshiping assembly is being deprived of praying with the Church throughout the world); and, all too often, heresy (since texts or practices introduced frequently have a heterodox dimension to them).

Once again, the Angelic Doctor has something to teach us; I hope liturgy classes in seminaries and diocesan clergy conferences begin to take up this question with renewed vigor.

Mass commentaries

Q. My parish has a very annoying practice: Every Sunday the lector gives a long introduction to the Mass before announcing the entrance hymn; then, there is another commentary, normally about a paragraph in length, read before each of the lessons from Sacred Scripture, including the responsorial psalm. These are not improvised by the lector, but are provided by the parish. It seems to me that the type of material that constitutes these commentaries should be covered in the homily. What is the regulation regarding such commentaries? Could this be considered preaching by the laity during Mass?

A. Nothing you describe is liturgically prohibited, but I do think it's all ill-advised because it makes liturgy (which is an art form) into a didactic event— excessively verbal and cerebral. Furthermore, I thought the notion behind having a vernacular liturgy was based on the presumption that the congregation could then understand everything without the very kinds of commentary that seem to be creeping into parish celebrations around the country. I agree with you: A good homily should be able to tie together all the loose ends.

Linguistic query

Q. In the Preface of the Mass, the response to "Let us give thanks to the Lord our God" is: "It is right to give Him thanks and praise." However, some of the Sisters in my convent say, "It is right to give God thanks and praise." I presume we are referring to Jesus, God the Son, when we say "the Lord our God"; therefore, we should not substitute "God" for "Him." I think some sisters do not want to use the masculine "Him" for God. I do not think they should tamper with the liturgy to suit their own liking. Please comment.

A. Actually, Sister, we are not referring to God the Son there but to God the Father. Remember: The entire eucharistic prayer is directed to the First Person of the Blessed Trinity.

Of course, your intuition is correct, namely, that some of your Sisters have an allergic reaction to the masculine pronoun for God and a particularly strong aversion to the title of "Father" for God as well. Aside from their illicit changing of liturgical texts, we are also obviously involved in doctrinal deviation. Naturally, it makes sense — when we don't like a particular doctrine, we try to shy away from it. That is exactly why the adage applies: *Lex orandi, lex credendi*, which sets up the connection between prayer and belief.

In my experience, people do not normally go to the trouble of changing a text unless there is something especially bothersome to them contained in it. That is why all liturgical deviations are potentially dangerous, and most today are actually so.

Sacrament prep

Q. This time at the end of the school year brings another opportunity for sacramental preparation — and anxiety. I am not a professional liturgist or theologian; I volunteer my time for the preparation of the children in the CCD program for the Sacraments of Penance and the Holy Eucharist. Our pastor has latched onto some strange ideas, some of which he attributes to the RCIA; I wonder if you could clarify a few situations.

(1) According to the Directory for Masses with Children, immediately after the opening prayer, the children leave the church and go to the hall where they celebrate the Liturgy of the Word with their teachers. It is one of the teachers who gives the "homily" to the children. With the ones preparing to receive different sacraments, the homily is supposed to be related in a special way to their preparation. This is a regular occurrence involving all of the children in the parish.

(2) The children come back to the church at the time of the Creed. At this point, the pastor dismisses the children preparing for First Penance and First Communion, citing the practice of the ancient Church which only allowed the "faithful" to remain for the offering of the Eucharist. He says this will make the Liturgy of the Eucharist more meaningful to the children on the day of their First Holy Communion. I've been able to find some reference to this in the preparation of candidates for Baptism in the early Church; however, it doesn't seem to be retained even in the present RCIA. In any case, isn't this mixing apples and oranges? Children preparing for First Penance and First Holy Communion are not catechumens. I always thought that Baptism made one a part of the "faithful."

240

(3) Isn't this idea of a children's Liturgy of the Word bad pedagogy? It seems to me only to feed a desire to make the Scripture "relevant" to all ages. What do you think? If all of this continues, I might withdraw as a teacher, because I think it presents faulty Catholic teaching to these young children about the importance of attending Mass.

A. Your first scenario has me in a quandary: If this is truly a Mass for children, when the children go to their classes for the Liturgy of the Word, who's left in church with the priest? And what is he doing in the interim? If it's just a regular Sunday Mass with children present (but not in the majority), then the norms for Masses for Children do not apply at all.

Regarding the second item, your pastor is making a distinction that the Church does not. You are certainly correct that baptized children are not catechumens. Beyond that, the Code of Canon Law tells us that everyone who has attained the age of reason (that is, seven years) is bound to attend the eucharistic sacrifice on Sundays and holy days of obligation (cf. Canons 11 and 1247). The practice in your parish obviates the fulfillment of that obligation.

As for your third query, I would say just this: The Scriptures ought to be "relevant" to all ages, but in different ways. A ten-year-old and a fifty-year-old can both go to a ball game and come away fulfilled and enriched, but both did not get the same thing out of the experience. Both did, however, obtain age-appropriate satisfaction. I think the analogy holds for Sunday worship as well. We should not "dumb down" the sacred liturgy.

Seminarians' roles

Q. Seminarians are involved in planning one Sunday Mass at our college church each week. There are always men who have received the ministries of lector and acolyte present; however, they do not always function as such. Normally, a lay college student does the readings, while the installed lectors sit in the pews. When it was suggested that some of the college's extraordinary ministers of the Eucharist assist with the distribution of the chalice at that Mass, we were told that it would not be proper since there were instituted acolytes present. Is that a double standard? If the appropriate installed minister is present, should he perform the function before anyone else? If it doesn't really matter, it seems that allowing the college students to function as lectors

241

and not as extraordinary ministers is nothing more than tokenism. Please advise.

A. I would tend to agree with your college's policy. As I noted in an earlier question, reading the Scriptures at Mass is a genuine lay function; distributing Holy Communion is not. This point was made by Pope Paul VI himself in his 1976 letter to Catholics in this country for our bicentennial observances.

While we're talking about seminarians' roles, let me put in my oar on a related matter which often emerges in our mail, namely, seminarians assigned to weekend parochial duty, finding themselves not permitted to distribute Holy Communion because this would dislodge laity. This is a pure and simple abuse. If lay people are properly trained as extraordinary ministers of Holy Communion, they should realize that seminarians come ahead of them in the "pecking order," and if they truly love the Eucharist, the Church and the priesthood, they would rejoice in the availability of future priests to perform this sacred task.

Were they to take umbrage at the presence of a seminarian, their own faith commitment could logically be called into question, and certainly the quality of their formation as extraordinary ministers.

Amice use

Q. A friend of mine is a Franciscan — a fine young priest — but he never wears an amice with his Mass vestments, saying that it is now optional and that he likes people to see his Franciscan cowl as part of his vestments. I think he's wrong. Could you settle this?
A. Admittedly, in the grand scheme of things, this is not a major issue, but you are right and he is wrong. Let me explain.

The directive on the use of the amice indicates that it need not be worn if the alb is such that it covers the priest's street clothes. For a secular cleric, that means covering the Roman collar; for a religious, the habit. The cowl is certainly part of the habit. I find it particularly annoying to see a brown or black cowl resting on various colors of vestments (with Dominicans, the white looks no different from an amice). While vesting, such religious should put the cowl on their heads, cover it with an amice, proceed with the rest of the vestments, and then lower it once the chasuble is in place.

Mass irregularities

Q. This morning I attended a weekly Mass offered in the basement chapel of a building attached to the main church. There were five of us present, all ladies in their seventies and eighties. Our pastor arrived, did not add one thing to his very casual attire (he never wears a Roman collar), joked with us and began the Mass. After the Gospel reading, for which none of us stood, we had a general discussion that included some politics. Father then continued the Mass. We actually stood for the Our Father, which dispelled my suspicion that maybe these old ladies couldn't stand, and I shouldn't embarrass them by doing so myself when the Gospel was read. Father read it, still sitting.

I feel strange about Father's sitting through the whole service in his street clothes, except for the Our Father. I was happy to receive Our Lord, but my sadness over this worry caused me to finish the Mass in tears. Is the pastor too far out of line on this one?

A. It sounds as though the poor man has a serious problem. If talking to the bishop has been tried and hasn't changed anything, pray for him.

Both forms

Q. Could you please explain why it is permissible to receive only the consecrated bread or only the consecrated wine, preferably answered by quotes from the Bible?

A. Let's take your last comment first. While Catholics have a profound reverence for the written Word of God, we do not worship the Bible. Therefore, the implication that only the Bible can settle a matter does not hold water; the suggestion that such is required reflects the worst kind of Fundamentalism. Even the Protestant Reformers did not subscribe to that theory. Luther, for instance, maintained that silence on certain issues in the Scriptures can offer Christians total freedom.

Now, we should be in a better position to handle your concern — because the Bible really says nothing about receiving Holy Communion under either one or both forms, as such.

The Church has always maintained that receiving the Eucharist under one or two species is receiving the whole Christ. Why? Because the Risen Christ is present under either form; therefore, receiving under the form of bread alone, under the form of wine alone, or under both forms brings one the same Christ and the same grace.

In the Latin rite, it is common to receive only the species of bread, but at times people receive only the species of wine (e.g., someone with a wheat allergy or one who cannot ingest solid food).

In the Eastern rites, it has always been the practice to communicate the faithful under both forms (by intinction), but, even there, infants are given their First Holy Communion at their Baptism by means of a spoonful of consecrated wine. One can see, then, the practice of the Universal Church through the centuries attests to the validity of single-species communication. That having been said, receiving both species reveals the fullness of the eucharistic sign.

Holy Thursday

Q. I was always taught that the emphasis on Holy Thursday was on the Holy Eucharist, and now I learn that the emphasis is placed on the washing of feet, on service to others. Would you please explain when the emphasis shifted to service?

A. It did not shift; the element of service has always been there.

The *Missale Romanum* tells us on Holy Thursday that the celebrant's homily ought to include three aspects of the day: The institution of the Holy Eucharist, the institution of the sacred priesthood, and the importance of fraternal charity, exemplified in the washing of the feet. In other words, all three go together in our meditations on that evening, just as they went together in the Lord's celebration of that Last Supper of His.

Anyone who wishes to separate one from the other, elevating it and implicitly denigrating the others, is acting contrary to the intentions of the Church and the clear example of Christ Himself.

Pecking order

Q. Is there still a hierarchy to how extraordinary ministers of Holy Communion are to be picked? I once read that the "pecking order" was: seminarians, male religious, female religious, lay men, lay women.

A. Yes, *Immensae Caritatis* does have that "pecking order," and while I am unaware of its having been revoked anywhere, I am equally unaware of anywhere it is enforced!

Preaching aids

Q. I am a seminarian taking some homiletics courses and am amazed at how little there is by way of decent preparation sources for preaching.

I don't want someone else's work, but you would think that after two thousand years, we would have something so that the wheel doesn't have to be reinvented every week. Do you have any suggestions?

A. There is much on the market, but the essential word in your letter was "decent," so the gap is narrowed, unfortunately. If you want worthwhile sources, read the homilies of the Fathers of the Church; the exegesis and preaching of men like Sts. Augustine, Leo, and John Chrysostom are unparalleled. St. Thomas Aquinas also produced some valuable commentaries. In our own time, the Navarre Bible has pulled together many of the classical sources in each of its commentaries on the individual books of the New Testament.

When I was getting started with preaching and giving other types of talks, I happened upon the writings of Monsignor Arthur Tonne, who churned out volume after volume of homiletic aids throughout his long priestly life (he's still quite active, even in retirement). A sampling of his material includes the following, all in paperback: *Talks on the Sacramentals, Prayer, Precepts and Virtues, Stories for Sermons* (eleven volumes!), *Five-Minute Homilies on the Gospels of Cycles A, B, C, Wedding Homilies, Feasts of Our Lady*, and *Jokes Priests Can Tell* (eight volumes). All of Monsignor Tonne's works are characterized by good common sense born of decades of pastoral experience and fidelity to Church teaching. He may be contacted at: 520 N. Freeborn, Marion, KS 66861.

hosts at Mass

Q. We have just gotten a new priest who insists on consecrating at every Mass, rather than using what is already in the tabernacle. Is this some kind of implicit denial of the Real Presence?

A. No, your priest is simply doing what the Church wants him to do; and this is not some type of new-fangled theology. As far back as the time of Pope Pius XII (and even before), the Holy See reminded priests of the importance of consecrating altar breads which would be consumed by the congregation at that particular Mass. In his encyclical on the sacred liturgy, *Mediator Dei*, Pope Plus XII explained the rationale well: "They should be commended who, when present at Mass, receive hosts consecrated at the same Mass, so that it is actually verified: 'That as many of us as, at this altar, shall partake of and receive the most holy Body and Blood of thy Son, may be filled with every heavenly blessing and grace" (no. 121). This same point is made in *Sacrosanctum Concilium* (no. 55) and in *Eucharistiae Sacramentum*, which notes: "By receiving Holy Communion during Mass, we participate more perfectly in the celebration of the Eucharist. This is more clearly signified by this sacrament when the faithful receive the Body of the Lord after the priest's communion from the same sacrifice. Accordingly, fresh hosts should, as a general rule, be consecrated in every celebration of the Eucharist for the communion of the faithful" (no. 13).

Now, this is not a hard and fast norm, hence, "as a general rule." In other words, it should be the usual procedure, but circumstances could dictate otherwise. For instance, if enough hosts have not been consecrated, it only makes sense to go to the tabernacle and communicate the remaining faithful from the reserved Sacrament.

Or, it may be that too many hosts have been consecrated at another Mass, and they would not be consumed in a timely manner by distribution to the sick; therefore, it would be prudent to use them before too long an interval passes. But good pastoral planning should obviate this occurrence on a regular basis.

As far as the Real Presence is concerned, it is good to recall that the Church reserves the Blessed Sacrament for communion to the sick and for adoration. The tabernacle, then, should not be regarded as a kind of storage receptacle for weeks or even months on end.

Simply put, there should never be an overabundance of hosts in the tabernacle. None of this denies the doctrine of the Real Presence; in fact, it affirms it by underscoring the relation between the reserved Sacrament and the Sacrifice at which it was confected.

Confirmation query

Q. In our diocese our bishop is implementing the reception of Confirmation at the same age as the reception of Holy Communion (seven or eight years). The final step of this plan will have the Sacrament of Confirmation administered by the priest, instead of by the bishop. I recall reading an article on the Sacrament of Confirmation based on the new Catechism *which said that the reason the Sacrament of Confirmation was separated from the Sacrament of Baptism in the Roman rite is to allow ample opportunity for the bishop to administer the sacrament. In addition, the bishop is advised not to delegate his responsibility readily.*

If this information is correct, and I am aware of it, and nevertheless

I allow my child to be confirmed by my priest, am I guilty of assisting my bishop in defiance of Rome? What are my alternatives or responsibilities? Any assistance you can render would be most greatly appreciated.

A. I have no problem with the idea of moving Confirmation to the age of reason; in fact, I actively support it for many reasons, not least of which is that it restores Confirmation to its proper position after Baptism and before Eucharist, which order is maintained in the Eastern Church. Your analysis of the bishop's desire to delegate authority to administer the sacrament (rather indiscriminately, it would seem, from your description) is quite correct and consonant with Church law.

I find it hard to believe that the Holy See has given him permission to proceed in this manner; therefore, in your shoes, I would submit this all to the nuncio in Washington and to the prefects of the appropriate Roman dicasteries: the Congregation for Divine Worship and Discipline of the Sacraments and the Congregation of Bishops. Dealing with it now will eliminate the need to confront the problem as a *fait accompli*.

Purple Passiontide

Q. I am a Catholic of the Eastern rite and have a question concerning a traditional Latin-rite practice. I remember when I was growing up that the statues were covered with a purple veil at the end of the Lenten season. Since the statues are not merely decorations, but rather aids to prayer, the practice seems strange to me. Could you explain the meaning behind the covering? Is the practice still done today?

A. The universal Church maintains this tradition but does leave it to local episcopal conferences to determine the practice for their own regions. In the United States, the bishops voted to eliminate it over two decades ago. It seems to be coming back, however, over the past five years or so, perhaps for two different reasons. The first is that we have so many ethnic parishes that should and do preserve the liturgical norms of their own country, that is, the precise purpose of such personal parishes. The second seems to be coming from younger priests who think the custom of veiling the statues heightens the experience of Passiontide and helps the faithful focus more fully on the mystery of the Lord's suffering and death, which was the rationale behind the custom.

Mass at home

Q. Not too long ago my sister had the good intention to have a "home Mass" said at her place for all of my family. While her intention that we all might grow closer was nice, I was rather upset at the whole way the Mass was said and by the actions of the priest. First, he arrived without any vestments or vessels; therefore, Mass was said in his street clothes, with regular table wine and unleavened crackers in two wine glasses provided by my sister. At the time of Communion, cracker crumbs went all over the floor. Was this a valid Mass? If so, was it a sacrilege for the crumbs to fall everywhere at Communion time? What are the regulations for "home Masses"?

A. Whenever Mass is celebrated outside a sacred place, vestments and vessels are still required. If improper matter was used for the Mass (either the bread or the wine), the validity of the sacrament could have been affected. If what you describe is an accurate depiction of events, it certainly was sacrilegious and reprehensible. The only difference between a "home Mass" and one celebrated in a church is that the permanent fixtures of the church building are lacking; all other rubrics remain intact.

Tabernacle veils

Q. Some time ago, you answered a question concerning chalice veils. Is there any regulation regarding tabernacle veils, which are fast disappearing?

A. *Eucharistiae Sacramentum* (1973) indicates that a veil is to cover the tabernacle in which the Blessed Sacrament is reserved and that a lamp is to draw attention to that spot. There were exceptions to the norm on veils very often in the past; for instance, when a tabernacle was of exceptional beauty, it was permitted to forego the veil. The 1983 Code of Canon Law only mandates a lamp (Canon 940).

I must say that I like the maintenance of the veil because it links it more directly to the ark of the covenant.

Different Agnus Dei

Q. In our parish, in addition to the usual singing of the Agnus Dei three times, five additional titles for Jesus are added, e.g. King of Kings. Is this an acceptable practice?

A. Yes, it is. The General Instruction of the Roman Missal envisions this on occasions when the fraction rite will take longer than usual [cf. no. 56]: I see no difficulty with this, so long as the first, second, and last invocations are addressed to the "Lamb of God."

Passover and Mass

Q. I have been studying the Jewish feast of Passover in my attempt to learn more about the Last Supper and so come to a deeper appreciation of the Mass. As a result, I have some questions about the connection between the two: (1) One of the rubrics of Passover mandated by God Himself was to burn any of the Passover lamb which was not eaten that day in their holy meal. I see a disharmony between this rubric and our reserved sacrament of the Holy Eucharist. Please comment. (2) I have also learned that it was customary to have a child ask the celebrant the meaning of the feast. I thought it would be wonderful if we would have a designated child ask the celebrant of each Mass the meaning of a particular action of the priest; for instance, "Father, why are you breaking the host?" and the priest would have to answer. So that this would not be too disruptive, certain rules would have to be made. I think it would make the children more attentive and teach the whole assembly things they never knew or have long forgotten. What do you think?

A. While there are clear parallels between the Jewish Passover and the Christian Eucharist, there are also differences. For example, the Passover is a home celebration, while the offering of the eucharistic sacrifice is generally not such. The Passover is a once-a-year celebration, while the Eucharist is daily. Beyond that, we do not seek to mimic the Passover but only to appreciate what is in common.

Last of all, if liturgy is an art form (which it is supposed to be), it should speak for itself; that naturally presupposes that the work of catechesis has been properly done in advance of a liturgical service. Didactic intrusions into the liturgy are artistically offensive but, even more, disruptive of an attitude of prayer.

Divine Praises

Q. A parishioner of mine maintains that the Divine Praises should be prayed while the Blessed Sacrament is still exposed and before the blessing. I have never seen a ritual for Benediction, except what is given in the missalettes. Is there a ritual for Benediction with step-by-step directions? Why should the Divine Praises be used after the blessing?

A. The directives themselves allow for a variety of options, even in the older ritual. Therefore, it is permissible to pray the Divine Praises before the blessing or to do so as the priest returns the Blessed Sacrament to the tabernacle.

About-face?

Q. I have always been taught that Vatican II required the priest to face the people while celebrating Mass. I have also read Monsignor Klaus Gamber's book in which he states that the priest should not face the people while celebrating Mass. Has there been any official clarification about which practice is correct?

A. *Turned Toward the Lord* is the title of the book to which you are referring. While I have problems with some of Monsignor Gamber's analyses of the liturgical reform, I think his chapter on the direction of the celebrant for the liturgy is superb.

In reality, the Council said not a word on the question at hand and the rubrics of the current Mass actually presuppose that the priest will be facing not the people but East. I have already discussed this matter in previous issues of TCA and so do not want to rehash that material. What is new in the discussion, however, is that the Congregation for Divine Worship in the May 1993 issue of its official journal *Notitiae* took up the question in an editorial and had this to say:

"The positioning of the altar 'versus populum' [facing the people] is certainly something desired as a result of current liturgical legislation. However, it is not always an absolute value above every other. It is necessary to take into account those cases in which the sanctuary does not allow for the placement of an altar oriented toward the people, or when it would not be possible to preserve the former altar with its ornamentation in such wise that another altar turned toward the people would stand out as the principal one. It is more faithful to the liturgical sense, in these cases, to celebrate at the existing altar with the back (of the priest) to the people than to maintain two altars in the same sanctuary. The principle of having one altar is theologically more important than the practice of celebrating facing the people."

Dialogue homilies

Q. Are homilies that involve a dialogue between the priest and members of the congregation permissible? Can the homily be given from the main aisle of the Church? I thought the rule was that the priest should remain at the pulpit.

A. The only possibility for "dialogue homilies" would be for Masses with children, where such an option is specifically treated. The place for the homily is to be either the chair or the pulpit, since the location should reflect the dignity of the event. In the General Instruction, we read the following: "The homily is given at the chair or at the lectern" (no. 97).

Lest a priest say, "But that doesn't say you *can't* deliver the homily from the center aisle," let me hasten to remind him that rubrics tell us what *should* be done, not what should *not* be done. In other words, simply because the General Instruction does not explicitly ban homilies in parking lots or rest rooms does not thereby allow for those options; the idea is that telling where something is to be done automatically excludes other possibilities.

Lutheran Eucharist

Q. I have a videotape of the Tridentine Latin Mass which has a commentary explaining that the Protestant reformers, in their opposition to the doctrines of the Real Presence and the eucharistic sacrifice, developed their communion services. Martin Luther is identified as one of the reformers. All I can remember hearing while in a Catholic school was that Martin Luther was excommunicated for his views on indulgences — nothing about the Holy Eucharist. Do Lutherans believe as we do regarding the Real Presence in the Holy Eucharist? What religion is it that has the Eucharist as only a symbol of Christ's presence?

A. You are correct that Luther's original problem with the Church stemmed from aberrations connected to indulgences; however, as in most situations, a battle on one front leads to others. Luther was most reluctant to attack the Catholic doctrine of the Eucharist because he saw it as verifiable from both Scripture and Tradition. Calvin and Zwingli, on the other hand, had rather thoroughly spiritualized the meaning of the Eucharist. If one reads the correspondence among the various reformers, it becomes clear that Luther's "moving off the dime" in regard to the Real Presence was done only under serious pressure and perhaps even as an attempt to slap the pope once more. Even at that, his eucharistic doctrine never went beyond "consubstantiation," the theological position that the bread and wine co-exist with the Lord's Body and Blood. The Catholic doctrine of transubstantiation maintains that the entire substance of the bread and wine are transformed into Christ's Body and Blood, leaving only the accidents or appearances of bread and wine.

Protestant theologies of the Eucharist cover the entire spectrum from theories that Christians are simply involved in a memorial meal when they gather for the Eucharist, to the idea that if a transformation occurs, it happens due to the faith of the recipient, to very "Catholic" notions which would be common among certain "high church" Anglicans and Lutherans.

A word of caution about theological terminology: It is incorrect to refer to other Christian bodies as other "religions." Anyone who is baptized and subscribes to the Apostles' Creed is a Christian; if he is not a Catholic, we should speak of his affiliation as membership in a particular tradition or confession, but not another religion.

Sign of the cross

Q. I once read that making the sign of the cross before receiving the Holy Eucharist was an acceptable acknowledgement of the Real Presence. In your answers regarding signs of reverence before receiving Communion you have never mentioned it. Could you please give me some advice in this matter?

A. The liturgical norms call for an act of adoration before reception of Holy Communion; in our tradition, that is either a genuflection or a profound bow. Making the sign of the cross is an acknowledgement of the Triune God or one's salvation through the cross of Christ, but that has no necessary connection to the Eucharist.

Liturgical advice

Q. I am the liturgical planning coordinator of a large parish. As a volunteer, my job is to run the committee that plans all of the liturgies and then works with those responsible for implementing these plans, such as lectors, musicians, etc.

My problem is that I have a hard time finding instructional material. I subscribe to both Today's Liturgy *and* Modern Liturgy. *While both of these publications run some worthwhile articles, they also suffer from the "Trendier-than-Thou" disease — if it's new, it must be better! Can you recommend any publications for my use? Also, you have written in the past about Tenebrae services that you have incorporated into your*

Lenten program. Do you have any sources for a Tenebrae service that I might be able to incorporate into our parish?

A. A sign of the malaise in liturgical circles is that most of the publications exhibit the deficiencies you describe. *Notitiae* is the official journal of the Congregation for Divine Worship in Rome, but articles could be in anything from Latin to French to English. Frankly, I think all you really need is the proper liturgical documentation and some common sense.

As far as the rite of Tenebrae is concerned, you would probably do well to contact a local Episcopalian parish since they seemed to retain this rite longer than we, or else consult the old Latin rite and make any necessary adjustments. Since this is not a formal, liturgical ceremony any longer, such adaptations would be permissible.

Catholic-Jewish wedding

Q. Recently a friend of the family married a Jew in a Roman Catholic ceremony that was performed by her parish priest. It is my understanding that the ministers of the Sacrament of Matrimony are the husband and wife. Actually to receive the sacrament, is it not necessary then for both parties to be baptized Christians (at least)? If my understanding is correct, then I'm puzzled how anyone of the Jewish faith can receive the Sacrament of Marriage. Please comment.

A. For marriage to be a sacrament, it is necessary that both spouses be baptized. Therefore, the union between a baptized and a non-baptized would be a valid union if performed according to all the norms of law but would not be sacramental.

Laity's prayers

Q. Can people participating at Mass whisper the prayers of consecration intended for the priest only? Also, when several priests are concelebrating Mass, I hear many people praying out loud with the priest the prayer just before Communion. Please comment.

A. I have come across what you describe on a few occasions; it is not correct, but I think it is usually not done in bad faith or as a way of asserting that the laity can indeed validly confect the Eucharist. Generally, it is most likely a misplaced piety or even confusion because of hearing a large number of others (concelebrants) saying prayers out loud. It would probably be pastorally wise for the priest to call this deviation to the attention of the congregation every so often and remind everyone that while all must participate in offering the eucharistic sacrifice fully, the modes of participation differ according to one's vocation.

This might also be an opportune moment to note that concelebrating priests are not to pray out loud; the Latin rubrics indicate that their participation should be done *submissa voce*, which means in a low voice (not silently, either), so that the voice of the principal celebrant can be clearly heard over the collectivity of all other voices.

No aberration

Q. I am a Byzantine-rite Catholic. In the Liturgy of Saint John Chrysostom, purification of the chalice takes place directly after Holy Communion. While serving as an acolyte, I was instructed by the deacon during the purification to pour the unused portion of unconsecrated wine from the cruet into the chalice containing the Precious Blood. While most of the consecrated species was consumed, clearly some remained. After the mixture occurred, the whole (of the contents) was consumed by the deacon. Is it licit to mix unconsecrated wine with the Precious Blood in either Western- or Eastern-rite liturgies? Does "particle" theology apply to the Precious Blood, though perhaps under a different name? If so, how can one licitly mix unconsecrated with consecrated species, or am I being too rigid?

A. I don't know why the deacon would not have consumed the entire contents of the chalice *before* asking you to pour in unconsecrated wine, but I don't really see a problem with what was done. Certainly you must know that in the East when Holy Communion is brought to the sick, the consecrated bread is intincted with unconsecrated wine.

I guess what I'm saying is that while I would not have utilized the procedure your deacon did, I don't perceive any doctrinal or liturgical aberration, just a strange order of doing things.

Fraction rite

Q. What is the theological significance, if any, of the "fraction rite" in the Mass? In nearly every church that I have been in (and I have been in scores of them around the country, both conservative and liberal), I have noticed no particular reverence given the hosts being broken during the fraction rite. In fact, it appears that the immediately preceding Rite of Peace nearly always overshadows the fraction in significance, by priest and laity alike. During large concelebrations the fraction rite seems almost scandalous as priests and bishops often hurriedly and sloppily break the large Frisbee-sized hosts for distribution. Is the fraction rite merely one of practical function? The term "rite" suggests that it is not. Please comment.

A. I do not know what you mean by "no particular reverence given the hosts" at the fraction. Aside from a respectful and discreet breaking of the host, what would you have in mind? Of all the liturgical abuses that I have unfortunately witnessed over the years, I must say that I cannot recall even one involving this rite, and so I find myself at a loss in responding to your specific concern.

Yes, the rite has significance beyond the practical. Its first meaning "completes," in a sense, the consecration in that it "shows forth" the breaking of the Lord's Body or His death — that event which the words of institution proclaim and effect. The action is also intended to signify the sharing of the "many" of the liturgical assembly in "the one loaf" of the Lord's Body, pointing toward our unity in Christ.

Sacrament or sacrifice?

Q. I am having some difficulty understanding the Sacrament of the Holy Eucharist as presented in the new Catechism of the Catholic Church. *Paragraphs 1322 through 1332, as well as later paragraphs, seem to present the sacrament, properly speaking, as the memorial and sacrifice of the Lord's passion and resurrection, i.e., the eucharistic celebration, as opposed to the consecrated species, which is what the sacrament was properly linked with in the Catechism of the Council of Trent. My problem here is the confusion between the Eucharist as the whole liturgical action versus the Eucharist as the species of the Body and Blood of Christ. Is the Church teaching that this sacrament is proper to both meanings?*

I notice some pastors are consistently using the phrase "First Eucharist" to designate what used to be known universally as First Holy Communion. If this sacrament is not, properly speaking, the species of the Body and Blood, but of the whole eucharistic liturgical action commemorating Christ's passion and resurrection, how can one celebrate the sacrament of First Eucharist, when one has been celebrating the sacrament of Eucharist since Baptism? Is not First Holy Communion still the more proper phraseology for the reception of the sacred species by a baptized Catholic for the first time?

A. Let me handle your question by beginning at the end.

I agree with you that it is a misnomer to refer to one's first reception of Holy Communion as one's First Eucharist. As you correctly note, a child of seven has presumably been participating in the Eucharist for many years before receiving Our Lord for the first time in Holy Communion; it reflects an unfortunate conflation of eucharistic theology, whereby one presumes that everyone who attends a celebration of the eucharistic sacrifice will automatically receive; or, worse yet, that one's participation is tragically flawed if one has not received. Granted, the Church encourages us to receive Holy Communion frequently, but always with the understanding that such receptions are "worthy," that is, the recipient is not conscious of having sinned mortally (cf. *Catechism*, 1415).

Now, on to your first point. I do not read the *Catechism*'s treatment of the Eucharist as you do. I think the authors are describing the process of the Eucharist, while you are more interested in one phase of that process. Holy Communion, whether received or reserved, is the end of the eucharistic process — which is a totality. The sacrament (or the species) obtains its meaning from the total process, which consists of all those other "moments" which we call "epiclesis," "anamnesis," "sacrifice," etc. Hence, I see no contradiction between the present treatment of the Eucharist and that found in the *Roman Catechism* from the Council of Trent.

Which cycle?

Q. At our parish on the Sundays during Lent, our liturgy committee insists on changing the readings from the B or C cycle of readings to the A cycle. They claim the A cycle readings are the only ones that relate to the catechumens. Because of this, it has been many, many years since any of our parishioners have heard about Moses and the burning bush or any of the other wonderful stories in the B and C cycles. Is this proper?

A. The readings of the A cycle for Lent may always be substituted for those of the other two, but let me make a few observations to put things in context.

First, if the concern is the instruction of the catechumens and their ritual entrance into the Church with the appropriate ceremonies during Lent as part of their experience of the Rite of Christian Initiation of Adults, then I would presume that this is happening at only one weekend

Mass and not the entire schedule of Masses. If the various candidates were spread over several Masses for instance, I would consider this to be pastorally inappropriate; ideally, it should occur as part of the principal Sunday Mass.

Second, if it is taking place at only one weekend Mass, then I would not have the concern that you do since other options exist and then the normal cycle would be followed for the remainder of the schedule.

Third, as much as I value the three-year cycle of readings, it would be good to recall that it is not an absolute value in and of itself. After all, from at least the time of the Council of Trent until 1970, the Church of the Latin rite had only two readings (rather than three) in an annual cycle. However, not only do I prefer the much richer presentation of God's Word which the revised lectionary makes possible, but I also believe that the mind of the Church is that we avail ourselves of this opportunity, unless serious reasons dictate otherwise.

Ciborium update

Q. In [a recent] issue of TCA there was a question about the location of the ciborium during large Masses. You questioned the practice of the deacon holding the ciborium and about the practice at St. Peter's in Rome. Yes, deacons do hold the ciborium if they are to distribute Holy Communion. Your readers should also bear in mind that those distributing (whether priests or deacons) are not concelebrating: it is the Pontiff who is the celebrant, and it is he who consecrates. Therefore, I would assume that this would hold for other Masses celebrated in like manner.

A. Thank you. I had forgotten that the priest-distributors in St. Peter's never concelebrate.

Latin Masses

Q. What is the official position of having Latin Masses? We recently attended a wedding Mass at which all prayers, except the readings, were said in Latin. It was explained that this was a Nobis Oro *Mass; however, I was under the impression that this type of Mass was reserved for only very small and private groups.*

A. Whoever told you the title of the Mass was mistaken; he probably meant *Novus Ordo* (New Order), but there is no such reality, liturgically or canonically speaking. There is only one normative Mass for the

Roman rite, and that is found in the Roman Missal of Pope Paul VI.

It is not necessary to have permission for the celebration of Mass in Latin according to the *Ordo Missae* promulgated after the Second Vatican Council. The Council's *Sacrosanctum Concilium* (Constitution on the Sacred Liturgy) makes it clear that the norm intends the celebration of the Mass in Latin: "Particular law remaining in force, the use of the Latin language is to be preserved in the Latin rites" (no. 36, ¶11). Another paragraph of the same section goes on to allow the "competent, territorial ecclesiastical authority . . . to decide whether and to what extent the vernacular is to be used" (no. 36 ¶13). Since the use of the vernacular is a permission granted by the local ecclesiastical authority and then confirmed by the Holy See — and not considered the norm for the Latin rites — no permission is needed for the celebration of the Mass in Latin.

Should any doubt remain, however, it is only necessary to consult the Code of Canon Law, wherein we read the following: "The Eucharist is to be celebrated *in the Latin language* or in another language, provided the liturgical texts have been legitimately approved" (Canon 928, emphasis added). There must, however, be an accuracy to our speech. Many use the term "Latin Mass" when referring to the celebration of Mass according to the so-called Tridentine rite which was in use until the time of the post-conciliar reforms. The Holy Father granted permission for the celebration of the Tridentine Mass in a 1984 indult under certain conditions. While the provisions of the indult have been expanded following the Holy Father's letter, *Ecclesia Dei*, the permission of the local ordinary is still necessary for celebrations according to the Tridentine missal.

Happy birthday?

Q. One of my parish priests, after celebrating the communion rite, will ask members of the congregation to acknowledge their own birthdays for the week by hand-raising, whereupon he leads the congregation in a jubilant chorus of "Happy Birthday," and everyone spiritedly applauds. Visitors and anniversary observers are also acknowledged. Then the priest will move into the concluding rite, pronouncing the blessing and dismissal. I find this a crude and jarring intrusion that shatters the solemnity and holiness of the sacred ritual. Is this priestly performance permissible according to current liturgical law?

A. No, it is not, and you should be diligent in getting the man himself or those in authority over him to put a halt to it.

Intinction protocol

Q. Does a bishop have the right (or power) to establish a diocesan policy such as below? Is intinction allowed by a priest? Does not the wording "not encouraged by E.M." mean it can still be done? What about the Precious Blood that may drip off the host? How can we/they in the parish stop the practice?

Here is the notice from a neighboring parish bulletin this week: "Communion by intinction (the practice of dipping the host in the chalice by eucharistic ministers) is not to be encouraged. However, the practice of communicants dipping the host in the chalice is allowed."

A. The policy is wrong on several counts. First, Communion by intinction, that is, with the minister of Communion dipping the Sacred host into the Precious Blood, is a legitimate mode of eucharistic distribution, sanctioned by the universal Church. Therefore, no local authority can abrogate its use. Second, if that option is taken by the priest, the recipient may not receive in the hand. Third, under no circumstances may a recipient receive the host in the hand and then dip the host himself into the chalice; this is strictly forbidden by both universal and American norms.

Not demanded

Q. For years, my wife of forty-seven years and I have received Communion on the tongue while holding hands. This has meant a great deal to us as we head into our twilight years. My wife is a special eucharistic minister — not at Sunday or daily Mass, but when visiting the sick in hospitals, rest homes, etc. A few weeks ago, at daily Mass, we approached our pastor in the Communion line as usual, holding hands. He refused to give my wife Communion, whispering, "You are now a minister of the Eucharist, you take Communion in the hand." Period. We dropped hands, and she received Communion in the hand for the first time in her life. I continue to take it on the tongue. When our assistant pastor says Mass, we hold hands and receive Communion on the tongue. Is there a Church rule or regulation that states a minister of the Eucharist can only take Communion in the hand?

A. No, there is not. Your priest is completely out-of-bounds; you should speak to him about this privately and firmly insist that he drop this demand. By the way, I have been an *ordinary* minister of Holy Communion for twenty years and have never received Communion in the hand in my life.

Altar appearance

Q. In more and more churches, I notice the corporal unfolded on the altar even when Mass is not being celebrated. It seems that this practice defeats the purpose of using a corporal in the first place. Is this permitted?

A. No, it is not. We are told in the General Instruction of the Roman Missal that the corporal is to be opened on the altar at the time of the preparation of the gifts (offertory) and that it is to be removed after the Communion rite. You are absolutely correct that it makes no sense to keep a corporal on the altar around the clock and, from my observations, the practice has reached almost epidemic proportions, done in parishes that could be classified as both "liberal" and "conservative."

Loss of the sacred

Q. As an altar boy before the Second Vatican Council took place, we were not permitted to touch the chalice, other sacred vessels, or the linens. The Sisters taught us that this was based on the Mosaic Law, that is, what is brought into intimate contact with something sacred shared its sacredness (cf. Nm 17:3). Today, altar servers wipe the chalice with the purificator and haphazardly fold the corporal, this being done while the priest is distributing Communion. Last Sunday, I looked at the chalice, and there were still smears and droplets of the Precious Blood on it. I told the sacristan, and she simply put the chalice into a cabinet for use at some other time. Whatever happened to the "second wine" that was poured into the chalice before it was purified with water? Why aren't the vessels considered sacred anymore? By whose authority and in what writings is this new way permitted? Our respect in years past moved us to belief in the Real Presence.

A. You raise several questions, all of which are related but requiring some disentanglement at the same time.

The "second wine," as you refer to it, is optional in the revised rite of the Mass. I have never done it for the simple reason that I have never had a difficulty in purifying the sacred vessels without it, that is, the use of water alone has always worked fine for me. Its use was practical, not spiritual. I have never heard of altar boys purifying the vessels or folding up the corporal. The General Instruction of the Roman Missal indicates that an extraordinary minister of Holy Communion or an acolyte, that is, one formally instituted into that ministry, may perform these tasks. I cannot conceive of delegating a child or a teenager to do these things.

The chalice, paten, ciborium, etc. are still referred to as "sacred vessels" by the Church — because they are. Unfortunately, some folks in the International Commission for English in the Liturgy have attempted to drop all sacral language, speaking of such objects as cups and plates. Should they ever win the day with such jargon, we shall be even worse off than we are now in terms of preserving any sense of the sacred and, yes, any residual belief in the Real Presence of Christ in the Holy Eucharist.

Communion distribution

Q. In the book Vatican Council II: The Conciliar and Post Conciliar Documents, *the question of whether Holy Communion in the hand should be allowed is addressed. The vote by the bishops of the world is broken down as follows: Yes, 597; No, 1,233; Yes but with reservations, 315; Invalid votes, 20. A few paragraphs below that, it states, "the Holy Father has decided not to change the existing way of administering Holy Communion to the faithful." My question is: Since the bishops voted against giving Communion in the hand and the Holy Father decided not to change the way of administering it, how did we get to where we are today with all the churches giving Communion in the hand, as well as the faithful drinking the Precious Blood?*

A. You are right in identifying this as one of the most puzzling of post-conciliar developments. Of course, the document you cite goes on to note that Pope Paul VI, in spite of his determination to maintain the tradition of mandatory Communion on the tongue, did agree to allow episcopal conferences, where the practice of Communion in the hand was already in place, against the law, to allow its continuation if the bishops of that place voted to do so and had their vote ratified by the Holy See. Practically speaking, that would have meant no more than six or seven countries: Germany, Belgium, Holland, Canada, perhaps France, and one or two others.

Needless to say, this was the proverbial "camel's nose in the tent," so that countries that never had it [like the United States] began to harass Rome for the permission and eventually got it.

Renovation in question

Q. I returned to my home parish in the Midwest and saw the results of their recent renovation. The ambo and altar are side by side, sharing "equal billing" as it were, with the sedilia centered behind them. The pastor told me that this placement of altar and ambo was the "policy" for renovations in the diocese. Others have told me it is based on Vatican II. I suppose something is being read into Sacrosanctum Concilium *(Constitution on the Sacred Liturgy) that is really not there, concerning the building up of the Liturgy of the Word and its relation to the Liturgy of the Eucharist. It would also seem to parallel certain Protestant rearrangements after the Reformation. What do you think?*

A. Once more, we find people according to Vatican II things the Council Fathers never even dreamt of, let alone put into documents. There is not a single official position of the Church dealing with the matters you describe. Whoever is foisting this on parishes is doing it solely on his own initiative. On a theological level, there is no justification for suggesting the total equality of the Liturgy of the Word and the Liturgy of the Eucharist. In fact, repeatedly, we find ecclesiastical documents stressing that the Liturgy of the Word finds its fulfillment and culmination in the Liturgy of the Eucharist.

Correct call

Q. This past Easter, our Sunday School coordinators, together with our parochial vicar, wanted the children (ages three to seven) to serve as lectors and cantors at one of the Easter Sunday Masses. They wanted to use the Children's Lectionary and have the children perform cute little ditties (including the parts of the Mass) in lieu of congregational singing. As a member of the Liturgy Committee, I did not feel that this was proper. In fact, it is my understanding that Masses for Children (as distinct from Masses with children present) should never displace the regular Sunday Mass. Our pastor and the diocesan director of worship concurred with me. Now we are accused of not welcoming children into our church. I took offense at this, since my wife and I bring our young children to church all the time. Am I in accordance with the

Vatican II documents on this matter? The parochial vicar also told me that liturgical dance is permitted at children's liturgies. When I researched this point, I found that the documents do mention "gestures" as permissible. Can that be interpreted as permitting liturgical dance? One final question. Is it permissible for lectors and eucharistic ministers to gather around the altar to hold hands with the celebrant and one another during the Our Father?

A. Your pastor and you are correct; the parochial vicar is wrong on both scores. Finally, no non-ordained individuals ought to "gather around the altar," and no one ought to be holding hands, period. Why? Because the rubrics do not call for it.

Tabernacle luna door

Q. My friends and I are looking for liturgical directives on eucharistic adoration, particularly using a "luna door" in the tabernacle. This seems to be more common in Europe than in our country.

A. For any information about eucharistic adoration, I would refer you to: Perpetual Eucharistic Adoration; 660 Club View Drive; Los Angeles, CA 90024.

Church precepts, altar breads

Q. I have two questions. First, I have an older catechetical booklet (copyright 1975) put out by the Leaflet Missal Company entitled "Outlines of the Catholic Faith." In it is a short treatise on the six traditional precepts of the Church. Are these precepts still valid?

The 1983 Code of Canon Law seems to make void (by what is not said) the precept that attendance at weekly Mass and holy days of obligation is obligatory under pain of sin. If, as the name implies, a holy day of obligation is obligatory, but Sundays are not, something is amiss. Has the word "obligation" been dropped from holy day solemnities?

My second question is this: I notice many Latin-rite parishes have been using handmade breads for Holy Communion. There seems to be no concern for the many crumbs which fall on the ground and are trampled underfoot, or for those left on the corporal or altar cloth. Is this a sacrilege? Additionally, I have noticed some parishes purposely do not use water for the preparation of the gifts. Is Mass affected in any way by this irregularity? I leave such Masses more disturbed and angry than grace-filled. I don't even feel like a Catholic at these liturgies.

Because I am not in communion with what these presiders apparently believe (or don't believe) about the Eucharist, would it not be better that I simply not receive Communion, or even not attend? If the celebrant and those who assist him do not believe in transubstantiation, does he consecrate validly?

A. To answer your first question, my reading of Canon 1247 leaves no doubt in my mind as to the obligatory nature of Sunday Mass: "On Sundays and other holy days of obligation, the faithful are *obliged* to participate in the Mass" (emphasis mine). In other words, Catholics are required to attend Holy Mass on all Sundays and any other days of obligation which exist in a certain region. If your concern is that the word "sin" is not used, then realize that the Code of Canon Law is not a moral theology textbook; therefore, the discussion of sin is out of place.

The *Catechism of the Catholic Church's* treatment of Sunday Mass obligation sets the whole question within "the context of a moral life bound to and nourished by liturgical life," referring to this as "obligatory" and "the indispensable minimum" (2041-2042).

To answer your second query, bread used for the Holy Eucharist is not to be made in such a way that it crumbles readily. All the liturgical documents stress the great reverence and care that must be extended to the eucharistic species; failure to accord proper respect is indeed a sacrilege. Failure to use water in the preparation of the chalice is illicit but does not invalidate the sacrament. Although the Church does not hinge a sacrament's validity on the celebrant's personal worthiness, he must have the intention to do what the Church does; otherwise, the sacrament would not be valid.

If you have other options for worship, utilize them. God calls us to peace, not strife, especially within the celebration of that rite which is supposed to give us on earth a foretaste of the joy and peace of heaven.

Traveler's Mass aid

Q. I travel a great deal. I notice that, at many airports, chaplains offer Mass in Latin and sprinkle it with other languages as well. Are there any aids for the worshiper in these circumstances?

A. Liturgical Press has a most attractive booklet, called *The Ordinary of the Mass in Eight Languages.* In parallel columns, you will find the text in Latin, French, Portuguese, English, Italian, Spanish, German, and Polish. This is an invaluable tool for those who rack up frequent flier miles in foreign environments.

Mass postures

Q. Enclosed are copies of two letters from one of our priests requesting that everyone "stand throughout the Communion rite" of the Mass. Many parish priests in our western Washington archdiocese are encouraging this practice; some have even stopped the Mass until everyone is standing. It is my understanding that the American bishops and the Roman Missal state that we should kneel during the Consecration. Are we in disobedience if we kneel during the Consecration, when we know that the priest has requested that everyone stand? Please advise.

A. Your letter is somewhat confusing, especially when put into the context of your pastor's missive to the congregation.

Some of his material has the following statements: "I am aware of the struggle some of you have in adapting to the pastoral decision to stand throughout the Communion rite." "Choosing to kneel, during the moments immediately preceding and following Communion sets one apart from the unity expressed by the Church at prayer." "Receiving Communion is first of all a sign of the unity of the people of God who gather to be built up as the Body of Christ."

"This issue is not about the opinion of the pastor or of the Liturgy Coordinator, it is about the opinion of the Church. The directions on when to stand, sit and kneel are very clear in the Sacramentary."

Your pastor's immediate directive is in keeping with — or at least not in contradiction to — the General Instruction of the Roman Missal, as well as American guidelines. In the United States, the faithful are to kneel from the Sanctus to the conclusion of the eucharistic prayer. His instructions do not touch that part of the Mass; your problem seems to be confusing the eucharistic prayer with the Communion rite, which follows and is not part of it. If you have been told to do no more and no less than what is in the material you sent me, there is no problem, as such.

That having been said, I would take issue with a number of his statements and even the directive itself. Permit me to explain by beginning with his last comment.

Directions on standing, kneeling, etc., are generally clear in the

Sacramentary, but not always; the present instance is a case of some lack of clarity — probably deliberate to allow for local options, devotion and practice. And this was always the situation — even in the old rite of the Mass.

Second, the moments immediately preceding and following Holy Communion are not necessarily to be what your pastor envisions; the proof for that is that there are no comments in the General Instruction to support his viewpoint. Furthermore, one of the great post-conciliar insights was that unity does not imply uniformity. I think he is taking a far more rigid posture than the Church ever has or will.

Third, I mightily disagree with his assertion that "receiving Communion is first of all a sign of the unity of the people of God. . . ." The liturgical documents and the *Catechism of the Catholic Church* make it eminently clear that the reception of the Holy Eucharist is, first and foremost, the act of receiving the Lord's Body and Blood, with the community angle actually taking last place in the *Catechism* (1416).

Fourth, I agree with the pastor when he declares that liturgical norms are not to be the result of "the opinion" of either pastors or liturgy directors; he is less than accurate, however, when he says they are "about the opinion of the Church." The Church does not give us liturgical guidelines on the basis of her opinion but in conjunction with solemn teaching on the nature of the sacraments, which then brings about liturgical law.

After all this, what have I really said? That the precise matter under consideration finds your pastor correct, but having made an issue out of a non-issue. Far better, in my judgment, to have spent the energy instructing the parish on the essentials of Catholic eucharistic doctrine — which are probably poorly apprehended there if your parish is in any way typical of the whole American scene.

Out of place

Q. Our pastor was recently reassigned to another parish after eight or nine years of service. He was a wonderful priest in every sense of the word, and we were blessed to have had his spiritual guidance. At his last Mass in the parish, the organist played "Danny Boy" for our meditation song. Needless to say, I was jolted away from what had just taken place — Communion with Our Lord. I find this to be inappropriate and disrespectful since it takes our attention away from thanking the Lord for His wondrous gift of love. Granted, our pastor may have liked this music, and our organist wanting to please him, made this choice of music for this special moment. I believe our organist made an irresponsible choice. Am I out of line?

A. No, I don't think you are. Secular songs are always "out of line" for the sacred liturgy. I know that some claim that "Danny Boy" is not secular (because of the line about "say an 'Ave' "), but I don't think that case can be honestly made. Beyond that, even if it had some religious merit, it has no place as a post-Communion meditation hymn.

Forgiven venial sins

Q. How is it that the penitential rite of the Mass can absolve us from venial sin when the prayer of absolution, "Indulgentiam, absolution-em . . ." (which was in the Tridentine Mass) is not in the present Mass? Where is there a prayer of absolution?

A. The prayer that concludes the penitential rite (which was also in the Tridentine Mass) likewise petitions God for the forgiveness of sins: "May Almighty God have mercy on us, forgive us our sins, and bring us to everlasting life." However, a prayer of absolution *per se* is not necessary for the forgiveness of venial sins; indeed, the entire action of the Eucharist can accomplish that.

Feet-washing fiasco

Q. Approximately sixty years ago, when I was a Mass server in our parish, our good priest would have twelve altar boys on Holy Thursday. Father would explain to us that he would be washing our feet just as Jesus did to the Twelve Apostles at the Last Supper before He made them priests. I always thought of the ceremony as a cleansing of the soul for future priests. Now, judging from our parish bulletin, the ceremony has a very different meaning: "The ritual of washing feet is a sign of our willingness to be of service to others. It is not to be a re-enactment of what happened at the Lord's Supper when He washed the feet of the Twelve. Anyone who wishes to have his/her feet washed is invited to come forward and, in turn, you are invited to wash the feet of your fellow parishioners as well. We will begin with six washing stations in the body of the church with members of the parish council, worship commission, and others prepared to wash and dry your feet. As you approach, and if you wish, you may take their places to wash others. This will give everyone the opportunity to be of service." Is this the real meaning of this ceremony today? Most of the washers and washed were women and girls.

A. The French proverb asserts that "the more things change, the more they remain the same." Your pastor sixty years ago was wrong, as is your pastor today!

The Church never subscribed to the theory you attribute to your old pastor; it has always been understood that the ceremony was to be regarded as a dramatic re-enactment of the Lord's humble service toward His apostles and His way of incorporating them into His ministry. Indeed, more than a few scriptural commentators maintain that since John's Gospel lacks a narrative of institution for either the Eucharist or the priesthood, this gesture of Christ's actually supplies for the "ordination" of the apostles in St. John, which is the very reason why women's feet should not be washed on Holy Thursday.

Your present pastor, on the other hand, has turned the whole ceremony on its head and created a fiasco. The headship of Christ is lost in his rendition, as well as the association with the priesthood; it has become no more than some sort of celebration of democratic social service.

Given the politics of the moment, I have argued for more than a decade now that we should just consign this ceremony to the liturgical dustbin until a more sane era dawns. After all, for an optional rite, it has caused untold confusion and even outright theological harm.

Pro-forma prayers?

Q. I have enjoyed The Catholic Answer *for a long time. I remember that you went into detail about the proper use and timing of the various eucharistic prayers; the second seems to be replacing the old Mass for the Dead as it is shorter and the priest is many times too hurried. What is the correct way to use these options?*

A. Eucharistic Prayers I and III are ideal for Sundays and solemnities; the fourth option may be used on Sundays if there is no proper preface, since it has its own unchangeable preface; and option two should not be used on Sundays, and is most appropriate for weekdays.

Sacred services?

Q. I have three questions at this time. The first is with regard to the Mass we celebrate at the parish elementary school where I teach. For Thanksgiving, Christmas, and Catholic Schools Week, we had "programs" after the reading of the Gospel. The goal of these little programs is to involve as many of the children as possible, so there is singing ("Hail, Holy Queen," from "Sister Act"), a bell choir, little actors dressed up for many parts (little sheep crawling up the aisle, for example), and parents taking pictures everywhere. Of course, there is clapping, usually with the encouragement of the priest. The programs were in place of any homily. I am aware of the guidelines regarding dancing at Mass, but I would like to know if these programs are within the proper guidelines. Can you please quote the source or document?

My second question is with regard to something the assistant pastor, an older priest, told the nun in charge of our religious education program. He said, with regard to a child I am preparing for the sacraments, that the Church now accepts converts from the Mormon Church without Baptism. I have read your answers to the question of Mormon Baptism in The Catholic Answer *books, so I know the answer to that error. I am just shocked that a priest would say such a thing.*

A third question, if you bear with me, concerns my own parish, which has a Communion service two days of the week. At these services, some of the lay people that are doing the service read the Gospel and then make comments and observations about the readings. My understanding is that if this is incorrect during the Mass, it must be incorrect during a Communion service. Our priest has said that these comments are fine. When I am in attendance it sounds like a homily to me.

A. You sure like to get your money's worth!

Nothing you describe in the school Masses appears to violate the norms for children's Masses. However, I personally think much of it is unfortunate because it cheapens liturgy and lends an air of informality and entertainment, which ultimately leads to the destruction of the sense of the sacred. Over the longterm this does not help children; in later years, they are often turned off by the remembrance of such trivializations of the Church's worship life.

Recently, I have read exactly what your assistant priest has said on Mormon Baptism, but I do find it hard to believe. I have not yet been able to track down the document in question and would refrain from comment until such time. Laity conducting a Communion service may offer a reflection on the readings of the day.

I must say that I am opposed to the whole concept of such services for the following reasons: they separate sacrament and sacrifice; they confuse the distinctive roles of the ministerial priesthood and the priesthood of all the baptized; the use is generally dictated more by political considerations of giving lay people (especially women) the occasion to preside at liturgical functions than by a desire to have the Eucharist more readily available; and because they suggest that daily access to the Eucharist is more important than prayer for vocations and a genuine hunger for the Eucharist. In my judgment, these services will continue to spin out of control unless and until someone in authority decides to regulate them or ban them entirely.

New Baptismal pool

Q. While at Mass this past Sunday in a church I sometimes attend, I noticed that the side altar to St. Joseph had been removed, and nothing was in its place. I was astounded to find, during an investigation after Mass, a swimming pool gurgling away! I was told it is the Roman Church's new way of baptizing adults, with total immersion, once a year at Easter. Babies are still baptized weekly in this parish in the traditional way, using a baptismal font. . . .

The desecration of the sanctuary and the removal of the liturgical art was a grievous affront to St. Joseph as well as the parishioners, in my opinion. Replacing it with a bleak, undevout thing, which is a danger to small children and a distraction to all seems un-Catholic.

What are the Church's new regulations on Baptism by immersion, and the modification of churches to accommodate this mandate?
A. You deal with a number of different issues, so some "sorting out" is in order.

Whether or not one thinks that certain architectural developments in churches are good or bad (or neutral), I still think that fooling around with existing church buildings is nearly always disastrous for two big reasons: first, the original architecture won't bear the changes gracefully (e.g., re-arranging the sanctuary to sit sideways in a Gothic church, so that the building's lines draw attention vertically, while the liturgical action occurs horizontally); second, for better and for worse, people get used to a particular structure, and this type of tampering is generally offensive to their deepest sensibilities.

Honesty compels us to admit that few churches in this country before the council would ever be included among the most beautiful works of art; furthermore, were I constructing a new edifice today, I might well not build in the same manner, but I think we ought to deal from the deck we've been handed. In all too many places, the money spent on such changes could keep a parish school going for years to come.

Side altars had very little use in the old days, except for private Masses or to reserve the Blessed Sacrament when removed from the high altar for some reason. They were not and should not now simply function as pedestals for statues. Altars are places to offer sacrifice, pure and simple. However, if I were the pastor, would I remove those altars? No, for the reasons given above. If constructing a new church, would I have them incorporated into the plan? No. As far as poor St. Joseph is concerned, I think he bore sufficient affronts during his life on earth that the present one he'll consider "small potatoes."

So, what about your "once-a-year splash"? You surely realize that in the early Church all Baptisms were done by immersion. With the increasing frequency of infant Baptism, infusion or pouring took the ascendancy. While Baptism of adults should normally occur at the Easter Vigil, it could take place at any other time for serious pastoral reasons. Many parishes now baptize infants and adults alike by immersion, although I think that prudence might well dictate reserving immersion for adults for a variety of reasons. I also see value in getting the opinion of those to be baptized, since many adults express grave discomfort with the immersion option. Inasmuch as both forms of Baptism are valid, we don't need to be more apodictic than the Church herself on these matters. This leads to requirements for revamping to accommodate the immersion method. Since the form is optional, one can hardly claim that architectural changes are mandatory.

On previous occasions I have also noted that where baptismal pools are kept running constantly, parishioners often speak of attendant physical difficulties. Sometimes liturgists don't really live in the real world.

Minor irritations

Q. My husband and I appreciate the solidly Catholic answers you give in your magazine; however, there is one problem these answers have caused at home. We are both in our seventies and have had the practice of going to daily Mass together. Now my husband is often so irritated by aberrations at the parish — by both priests and parishioners — he now often refuses to go to daily Mass. He still goes on Sunday. The tabernacle is still in the center of our parish church, but the communion rail was removed, people are bowing in front of the Blessed Sacrament instead of genuflecting, and there is talking out loud after Mass. I have tried to say that even though there are these particular aberrations, the Mass is said correctly otherwise and so we should close our eyes and forget what others do, receive Holy Communion, and do our best. Please give us your advice.

A. Knowledge is a terrible thing at times, which, of course, is how we got the proverb, "Ignorance is bliss."

I agree with you, however, especially since you note that the Mass is properly celebrated. Pray hard that your own good example will motivate others to follow you in demonstrating reverence in our Father's house.

Liturgical dance

Q. In your article, "Liturgical Dance" [in a recent] edition of TCA, the answer seemed to forbid dance only during the liturgy. Would this also include the entrance processional and the recessional? Last year at the CCD conference, our bishop was led in and out by dancers. Was this appropriate or not?

A. The liturgy begins with the entrance hymn and concludes with the recessional; they are integral to the celebration.

All Souls' Mass

Q. I have been responsible for implementing a special All Souls' Day Mass in our parish for the past two years. However, since "no one, not even a priest, has the authority to change the Mass, except the Magisterium," I have had second thoughts about whether I am responsible for introducing illicit changes to this Mass.

During our evening All Souls' Day Mass, after the homily and before the Prayer of the Faithful, the celebrant sits down and a lector reads the names of those in our parish who have died during the preceding year. As each name is read, another person lights a candle for them, one candle for each deceased person. The candles are on a small table to the far right on the steps leading up to the sanctuary.

It seems to me that this ceremony is a conclusion to the homily and a lead-in to the Prayer of the Faithful. Are additions such as this legitimate? Does it matter if the candle-lighting is done before or after the Prayer of the Faithful? Does the placement of the table with the candles matter? I have seen other parishes do this ceremony on All Saints' Day, so that more parishioners would be in attendance. I believe that practice to be inappropriate and theologically misleading.

A. I have no difficulty with your adaptations. In point of fact, in the old days many parishes had a procession for the dead following the Mass; it also named the dead of that community for the past year. I agree that doing this on All Saints' Day is totally incorrect, since it would be tantamount to a decree of canonization.

Eucharistic adoration

Q. I have two questions concerning eucharistic adoration: First, is it in the regulations of the Church for the priest to give a lengthy homily during the time of exposition, so that there is no time for quiet meditation and adoration? With the prayers, songs, and homily there's less than a single minute of quiet before Jesus in the Eucharist.

Second, since eucharistic adoration isn't given much priority at my church, if I found a priest willing to have adoration — probably a retired priest — does it have to be exclusively in a church? Our pastor has also refused other priests access to our church because he said he does not want to be responsible for the visiting priest!

A. A homily is entirely appropriate during eucharistic adoration, but common sense ought to prevail. If you are not exaggerating, then your priest should revise his approach. A most important aspect of Holy Hours is precisely the opportunity to engage in quiet prayer and meditation; indeed, that is one of the principal attractions for so many adorers. I cannot conceive of eucharistic adoration taking place outside a church building, except for those extraordinary situations of eucharistic congresses and the like. Again, by its very nature, adoration of the Blessed Sacrament should be in a sacral setting, closely associated with the altar on which the Eucharist is confected.

As far as visiting clergy are concerned, your pastor surely has the right to determine who will or will not celebrate the sacred liturgy in the church for which he has canonical and pastoral responsibility. For myself, I can say that I am always most careful about who is invited or permitted to function liturgically because I do not want my people confused by improper forms of celebration or deficient preaching. If

that is your pastor's perspective, he is absolutely within his rights —
and should be commended on that score.

Baptism required

*Q. I went to a meeting at the seminary where a priest talked about
marriage. He said that if one of the persons was not baptized the
marriage was not legal. Is he correct? If so, could you explain the
meaning of "legal"?*

A. Either you misunderstood the priest or he misspoke. If a marriage
takes place within the laws of the Church, it is a valid marriage. If,
however, one of the persons is not baptized, it is not sacramental. Why?
Because a sacramental union demands that both partners be baptized.

Liturgical colors

*Q. What is the significance of the liturgical colors? Aren't they supposed
to be changed to conform to the season wherein the celebrant wears
the appropriate color vestments as well as using matching colors for
the altar covering, statue of the Infant Jesus of Prague, etc.?*

A. Let's take the last question first. The robe of the Infant of Prague has
no intrinsic connection to the liturgy. Now, if people want to change the
Infant's garments to correspond to the season, that's fine, but it is not at
all required. Similarly, altar hangings and the like may conform to the
seasonal colors, but need not; if not, they are always white.

The colors of the Roman rite are fixed thus: white (gold and silver
also), red, green, purple, black. White (for purity and joy) is for all
feasts and solemnities of Our Lord and Our Lady, as well as for
memorials of saints who were not martyrs. Red (expressive of the fire
of love and the shedding of blood) is used for martyrs' commemorations,
as well as for Palm Sunday, Good Friday, and Pentecost. Green
symbolizes hope and life and is the color for the ordinary season
throughout the year, those Sundays following Epiphany and Pentecost.
Purple connotes penance and sorrow for sin; in a magenta hue, it is the
color of Advent, while its darker shade is for Lent. Rose (not pink!)
may be substituted for the Third Sunday of Advent and the Fourth Sunday
of Lent to signify joy at the impeding conclusion of those seasons.
Black may be used for funerals and for All Souls' Day; for the same
occasions, purple or white also may be used.

The Eastern Church does not employ the same detailed color

scheme, maintaining only the distinction between "bright" and "dark" colors, but with the same basic psychology and symbolism behind them.

Self-communication and prayer postures

Q. Just what is self-communication, and is it now allowed? I have been given to understand that intinction is no longer permitted in our diocese, and we are being encouraged to receive from the chalice. The chalice is placed on a ledge where the priest stands holding the ciborium. He distributes to each communicant the host and says, "Blood of Christ" when/if someone takes up the chalice to drink. Right now I receive the host only, as I really do not want to receive from the chalice if this way (for me to pick it up) is not really allowed. Could you go into this?

Second, I have been told that the bishops are urging the joining of hands at the Our Father, recognizing this as the stance the ancient Hebrews took when beseeching the Lord for help. If the Holy See gives the permission for this to be done, could it be forced upon us? I am neither an ancient Hebrew nor a present-day charismatic; such externals are just not a part of my makeup. I really do not see how such outward actions can increase our devotion, love, and reverence for the Mass.

A. We really have a tangled web here, so let's try to unravel it.

First, intinction is a time-honored method of receiving Holy Communion — and the normal manner in the Eastern rites of the Catholic Church. It is one of three legitimate options in the Roman rite. No bishop can outlaw a practice sanctioned by universal law.

Second, self-communication is prohibited — and always has been. But self-communication is not what you seem to think it is. You may not take the host in your own hand and then dip it into the chalice; that would be self-communication. Nor may you approach the chalice and drink from it without the presence of a minister who says, "Blood of Christ"; that, too, would be self-communication. The procedure, as you describe it in your parish, is perfectly sound.

Now, on to the hands. Some liturgists have recommended that the faithful be permitted not to join hands with others at the Lord's Prayer but to raise their hands in the ancient *orans* position. While this was surely done in the early Church, that does not automatically mean it should be done today — we are not liturgical antiquarians. For instance, the early Church had public penance which went on for years, during which the penitent could not receive Holy Communion; do we want to return to that as well, simply because it was done for five or six centuries? I think not. Although there is obviously nothing doctrinally wrong with having a congregation raise its hands in prayer, we must take into account cultural concerns.

You are by no means in a minority when it comes to a kind of self-consciousness in regard to gestures. While the practice, if ever approved by the bishops, would be optional, I do not think we should put people in the position of feeling "odd" or "out of place." Actions or gestures intended for all ought to be culturally acceptable to all. That is not the case in the present instance.

Benediction

Q. In our diocese, many churches no longer have Benediction after the Stations of the Cross. Enclosed is a copy of our diocesan policy on this; it seems to say Benediction is forbidden under these circumstances. Would I be disobedient if I went to a church that continued to have Benediction, in spite of the diocesan guidelines?

A. I guess the first point to be made is that "guidelines" are not laws. If a bishop wishes to promulgate laws, he must do that. Guidelines are no more than suggestions.

In 1974, the Holy See gave us the document "Holy Communion and Worship of the Eucharist Outside Mass," containing norms for eucharistic devotion, etc. Therein we find the regulation that one may not simply expose the Blessed Sacrament for the sake of giving the blessing with the Eucharist; encouragement is given, however, to have frequent periods of exposition, which would include hymns, prayers, Scripture readings and time for quiet reflection.

So, for your precise question, I would answer thus: Stations of the Cross should take place as usual. At their conclusion, the priest could expose the Blessed Sacrament and lead the congregation in a time of prayer and meditation (ten minutes?), ending with the solemn blessing with the Eucharistic Lord. All that is completely in keeping with both the spirit and letter of liturgical law.

Improper practices

Q. I have two questions regarding practices during Mass at my parish: First, the gift-bearers bring the ciborium and the wine up to the altar. After receiving them, the priest gives back to these individuals the ciborium and the prepared chalice. They elevate them while the priest says the offertory prayers. I thought that the priest should receive the gifts at the edge of the sanctuary and that he (alone) should elevate the bread and wine. Please comment.

My second question involves the extraordinary ministers of the Eucharist taking handfuls of consecrated hosts and redistributing them among several ciboria prior to Communion. This seems harsh and irreverent, as if Jesus is being manhandled in order to even out the distribution. If even allocations of consecrated hosts are so important, why aren't the ciboria filled evenly beforehand? It seems just one more instance of disregard for the Eucharist. What do you think?

A. On the first matter, the practice can be justified in no way. On the second score, I agree that the action you describe comes off as irreverent. When hosts must be transferred from one vessel to another, it should be done by a discreet pouring from one ciborium to the next; after all, we don't even handle regular food so crassly, let alone the Bread of Life.

Divine Office query

Q. In the old liturgy, priests were permitted to anticipate the recitaion of Matins and Lauds the night before.

Can this still be done, especially if one is planning to take a trip the next day?

A. Lauds is Morning Prayer. If the purpose of the Liturgy of the Hours is to be fulfilled according to the mind of the Church, the "hours" are to be celebrated as closely as possible to the designated time, so that the goal of the sanctification of the whole day is achieved. Therefore, it would make no sense to pray Lauds or Morning Prayer at ten o'clock the night before, particularly since the prayers all speak of the rising sun, the new day, etc.

Matins is now called the Office of Readings; nothing in that "hour" is time-specific, hence an anticipation would not be out of place. It should also be mentioned that while the duty of clerics to pray the Divine Office is still viewed most seriously by the Church, she also gives priests greater latitude in dispensing themselves or in substituting alternative prayer forms if genuinely inhibited from fulfilling the obligation. In situations where that has happened to me, I have prayed the Psalms of the "hour" I could not celebrate at the proper time, either before or afterwards, omitting the prayers that do not fit because of the time of day.

Dancing at Mass

Q. While visiting my daughter, I attended Mass at her parish. I was shocked when four young girls came out and danced around the altar. My daughter said they were "liturgical dancers." She finds it beautiful, but I think it is sacrilegious — not to mention not approved of by the Church.

I turned to another column for an answer to give my daughter, but now I have a larger problem. I include that article, which suggests that I "encourage my own parish to consider using a liturgical dance that is both reverent and exuberant to the glory of God."

Please clarify whether or not this is allowed.

A. The Congregation for Divine Worship on April 27, 1987, indicated clearly that dance during the celebration of the sacred liturgy is strictly forbidden. That norm has also been re-stated by the Bishops' Committee on the Liturgy of the National Conference of Catholic Bishops.

Marian hymns

Q. Why is it wrong to sing a hymn in honor of Mary during the Mass? Isn't it true that there would be no Mass — as we know God's plan has unfolded — if it were not for Mary's fiat? The new Marian hymns seem to extol all of her human virtues, but never get to the heart of why we honor her.

A. You really have two questions. First, unless it is a Marian feast or the month of Our Lady, it is not appropriate to sing a Marian hymn during the celebration of the Mass, especially a Sunday Mass, which is preeminently given over to the Lord's resurrection.

On the second front, I think we must distinguish between good and bad Marian hymnody, both old and new. The greatest weakness of the old Marian hymns was that they tended to be very soupy, sentimental and pietistic, and the swooping melodies simply added insult to injury. Truth be told, I have very little time for most modern hymns — Marian or otherwise — and I rely on the analysis of an expert observer like Thomas Day in his brilliant work, "Why Catholics Can't Sing."

Hymns need to exhibit poetry and theology at one and the same time, so that they elevate the mind and heart alike. To extol Mary's human virtues is not wrong at all, but a very important aspect of Marian doctrine (that needs reinforcement continuously) is that Our Lady's gifts, prerogatives, virtues, etc., all are a result of divine grace (to be sure, necessarily involving her full cooperation). In this way, Mary stands out as God's finest work of grace and becomes an example to us all as to how we should respond to God's overtures of grace in our own lives.

Charismatic praise

Q. If a Mass is celebrated especially for a charismatic prayer group, is it permissible to deviate from the rubrics slightly, in order to allow for charismatic praise? This takes place at the time of the Gloria.

Also, liturgical musician David Haas mentioned that at his parish they greet the priest and one another at the time of the entrance and sing the opening hymn only after the priest has gone up to the altar. Are these changes permissible?

A. I have not celebrated or attended a charismatic Mass in many years, so I'm not thoroughly familiar with what is permitted or not. The last time I did so, the prayer group leader told me that their custom was to engage in spontaneous prayer during the post-Communion meditation. There are offices for charismatic renewal at the diocesan, national, and international levels, and I suspect that some guidelines have come from the Church on this type of thing. If any readers are aware of them, I would be happy to share them.

On the second matter, I must say I am most uncomfortable because it leads to a man-centered liturgy instead of a God-centered one. As wonderful and important as the horizontal dimension of Christian life is, that is not the focus of liturgy, which is and must be the worship of God.

Bizarre

Q. A few Sundays ago, there was a bizarre occurrence in our parish. A retired priest, eighty-one years old, omitted the eucharistic prayer at one of the Sunday Masses. My daughter attempted to tell him as he began to distribute the bread and wine that he had not said the words of consecration. The extraordinary ministers of the Eucharist did not want to say anything that would embarrass him! The pastor attempted to calm my daughter by saying that the priest had a good intention. Unfortunately, after Communion, hosts from the ciboria which were not consecrated were mixed with hosts taken from the tabernacle.

We thought this was the end of the incident. But two weeks later, the pastor said that everything was all right because an ex-priest was in the congregation with his wife, and when he noticed what was happening, he said the words of consecration before the people received Holy Communion. Is such a consecration valid? What additional advice might you give us in the event that this situation ever arises again?

A. "Bizarre" is surely the right word, on any number of scores.

First, fear of causing "embarrassment" can never hold one back when it is a question of sacramental validity. Years ago, I used the consecratory formula for the wine over the bread; immediately, a woman called out from the pew and alerted me to the error. Although I was embarrassed (see, you can be twenty-seven and not eighty-one to have something like this happen), I was most grateful.

Second, while a so-called ex-priest can indeed perform priestly functions in emergency situations, I have my doubts about the present case for two reasons: (1) I don't think this truly qualifies as a life-or-death incident, and (2) in order to consecrate validly, one must be in a certain proximity to the species being consecrated. Sitting in a pew a hundred feet away hardly seems to fill the bill.

Now some readers may ask about concelebrants at papal Masses, for instance, who are hundreds of yards away. But there is a critical difference: The principal celebrant is in direct contact with the species and, often enough, even the concelebrants are holding a ciborium that is to be consecrated.

Third, where was the pastor during the Mass? If he had been in the sacristy waiting for the time to assist with the distribution of Holy Communion, he could have nipped the error in the bud.

Fourth, while I doubt that people receiving hosts "consecrated" at that Mass did indeed receive the Holy Eucharist, I am sure that God still granted them the graces and blessings they would have received had it been a valid Mass. After all, the problem occurred because of human error and not malice on the part of anyone. Furthermore, we should always remember St. Thomas Aquinas's sage reminder that God "is not bound to the sacraments" to bestow His grace; the sacraments are definitely the normal channels of divine grace, but God — being the sovereign Lord — is free to act outside or beyond those instruments as He chooses.

Finally, should this happen again, let the priest know immediately, but also insist to the pastor that he be present when the retired priest celebrates Mass in the future.

Are changes mandated?

Q. Our parish is planning some renovations that I find disturbing. They want to install a "baptismal pool," adequate for the immersion of an infant or the pouring of water over the whole body of an adult. The plans also call for a movable altar-table. The statue of Mary is to be removed from the church entirely and placed in the school. Are these changes mandated by any Church authority? If so, why?

A. No, they are not. Some of them I would question on grounds of practicality or aesthetics. Others are harmful to the Catholic Faith and should be opposed.

I'm not sure what you mean by a "movable altar-table." But an altar should be permanent and should not give the impression of something flimsy or insubstantial. Indeed, it is the most important appointment in the sanctuary.

Banishing the Blessed Mother from the body of the church is just plain un-Catholic. Even Martin Luther insisted on retaining an image of Our Lady in his churches.

You will find that very often the only authority which can be cited for many of these so-called post-conciliar changes is the whim of individual "liturgists." They can cite no authority beyond themselves because there is no documentation to promote their agenda. And that is precisely the point on which they should be challenged.

Act of Contrition

Q. The last few times I have been to confession, the priests have not asked me to recite the Act of Contrition. Is this no longer done? Were my confessions valid?

A. The confessor should invite the penitent to make an Act of Contrition before he bestows absolution. The only exception to this would be in a communal penance service, during which the entire congregation would pray an act of sorrow together. If the priest neglects to ask you for this sign of repentance, be sure to do it later as you perform whatever penance he has assigned you.

I must admit that sometimes this gets confusing. Since my First Confession in 1958, the recitation or non-recitation of the Act of Contrition in the confessional (and/or aloud) has changed a half-dozen times. But in the final analysis, *when* it is done is not nearly so important as the fact *that* it be done.

Early exit is rude

Q. When out of town with relatives on Easter Sunday, we all went to Mass and Holy Communion. However, they decided to leave right after Holy Communion. Does that affect the hearing the full Mass and its validity? I am confused as to whether or not I fulfilled my obligation to hear Mass because of leaving before the final prayer, blessing and dismissal. Please advise me.

A. First of all, validity is not affected. Secondly, you appear to have been their "hostage," so it can hardly be laid at your doorstep. The real issue, of course, is why so many Catholics get "cabin fever" after Communion. I have been at hour-long Masses, and people feel compelled to leave after Communion: I have seen the very same people leave after Communion when Mass took less than forty minutes.

Preachers need to remind the congregation of the ignorance and discourtesy involved. Ushers should also be pressed into service to make such exits more difficult. (Ushers should certainly not facilitate the mass exodus by opening doors during Communion or by handing out bulletins to early leavers!)

Mass confusion

Q. This past Sunday we attended a parish other than our own; however, the Mass raised three questions in our minds:

(1) The priest omitted the Confiteor, Kyrie, and Gloria. In speaking to him after Mass, we found that it had not been simply forgotten. According to this priest, these may be omitted during the fifty days following Easter. Also, he mentioned that when there is no choir, as was the case on this occasion, the Gloria is omitted. We have concern that the Mass was invalid. Was the Mass valid? Was the priest's omission licit? (2) There were a number of handicapped and wheelchair-bound people in attendance at this Mass. When they received the Eucharist, they seemed not to know what to do with the Blessed Sacrament. What is the Church's view on the distribution of Holy Communion to those who do not seem to be aware of its significance? (3) This priest also said that if no choir could be found for the second Sunday Mass, he would discontinue it. Is this justified?

A. Once more, let's do this in order of presentation.

(1) No, his omissions were not justified. While not invalidating, they were grossly illicit. I would suggest you ask him to show you the

document that allegedly legitimates his practices. He'll not be able to produce one.

(2) I suppose by "handicapped" here you mean mentally handicapped. Furthermore, I guess you say they didn't seem to know what to do with the Sacred host because the priest apparently placed it in their hands.

The first criterion for admission to Holy Communion is the ability to distinguish the Eucharist from ordinary bread, and if that is absent, such a person should not be communicated. Second, I think it is rather irresponsible to place the host into the hand of someone who gives evidence of confusion, disorientation, etc. Beyond that, by using the traditional method of distribution, a priest might actually aid the person in recognizing this action as significantly different from consuming regular food.

(3) On the last point, as wonderful as it is to have a choir, how can one make this a *sine qua non* for celebrating a Mass? If the priest in question paid as much attention to the Church's real liturgical laws as he wants people to heed his made-up rules, things would probably go better for all.

Gospel proclamers

Q. It is my understanding that only a bishop, priest, or deacon can proclaim the Gospel at Mass. If this is so, it would seem that a "dialogue Gospel," in which lay people read different parts, is not permissible. On the other hand, there is the practice of having lay people read parts of the Passion on Palm Sunday and Good Friday. Can you please clarify this matter? I would appreciate a list of your citations.

A. Aside from the two days you noted, the only possible exception would be for children's Masses when they are permitted to take the "speaking parts," all the while the deacon/priest is clearly seen to be the principal reader of the Gospel. Citations cannot be given to prove "negatives;" in other words, the rubrics tell us what ought to be done, not what ought not to be done.

Those proposing something other than the traditional proclaimer of the Gospel have the burden of proof on them to demonstrate the contrary.

Tabernacle placement

Q. There still seems to be so much confusion regarding the correct placement of the tabernacle in our churches. The February 1995 edition of the newsletter Environment and Art *traces the development of documents permitting/recommending that the tabernacle not be kept on the main altar. It states: "The 1983 Code of Canon Law simply reminds us that the* tabernacle chapel *[emphasis in original] must be 'prominent, conspicuous, beautifully decorated, and suitable for prayer' (no. 938.2)." I thought that the Code was speaking of the tabernacle itself, not the chapel. Can you please offer some (further!) clarification?*

A. The citation is most intellectually dishonest. You are quite correct; it is interesting that the author manipulates the quote by offering his own expression ("tabernacle chapel," which does not appear in the Code) and then following it up with the rest of the material as it appears in the canon. The real text says the following: "The *tabernacle* in which the Most Holy Eucharist is reserved should be placed in a part of the church that is prominent, conspicuous, beautifully decorated, and suitable for prayer" (no. 938.2, emphasis added). I think that makes it quite obvious as to the mind of the Church, as well as the law.

Deacon's role

Q. When a deacon assists the priest at Mass, should he stand a step or pace behind the celebrant?

During the Lord's Prayer our deacon and servers stand at the altar and join hands with the priest as the prayer is said; is this correct?

At the Communion verse, the priest elevates the Sacred host and our deacon (right next to the priest) elevates the chalice. To me, it looks like the deacon is trying to "play priest." Can you please help me to understand the role of the deacon better?

A. Let's take these concerns in order.

(1) Yes, the deacon should be positioned in such a way as to make it clear that he is not a concelebrant (cf. General Instruction of the Roman Missal, no. 134).

(2) No one ought to be holding anyone's hands during the liturgy, for the simple reason that the rubrics do not call for it.

(3) By "Communion verse," I presume you mean the invitation to

Communion ("This is the Lamb of God. . . ."); there is no provision for holding up the chalice at this time (that is done at the doxology of the eucharistic prayer).

(4)The principal liturgical functions of the deacon are: To proclaim the Gospel; to offer the invocations of the penitential rite and the general intercessions; to prepare the altar and the chalice at the Offertory; to assist with the distribution of Holy Communion, especially the chalice; to perform the ablutions; and to preach the homily, when and where permitted.

Hail Mary at Mass

Q. At our parish it is the custom of the priest to have us say a Hail Mary after the Prayers of the Faithful. It's not a bad idea, but is it part of the Mass? I've never seen it done this way before.

A. This is a carry-over from certain Hispanic cultures. The liturgical norms do not stipulate the form to be used for the prayer that concludes the General Intercessions; therefore, there is a good deal of leeway here. If using the Hail Mary, I think it would probably be a good idea to lead into it by saying something like, "And now, let us entrust our prayers and petitions to the loving intercession of Mary, Mother of Christ and Mother of the Church."

Improper absolution

Q. During a retreat I recently attended, the retreat master did several strange things, but one especially stuck out. He said he would be hearing confessions individually, but would not be giving individual absolution. Instead, retreatants were to come to an afternoon Penance Service during which general absolution would be given. When I asked him if this was now permitted by the Church, he said that it had been approved by the bishops' conference, adding that I should not be so critical and trust him! Well, I don't! The last I heard, individual absolution was required for the sacrament.

Did I miss something?

A. No, you did not. And the regulations of the episcopal conference could not be any clearer: General absolution is to be given only in emergency situations. The diocesan bishop ought to be informed of the situation because the practice is wrong and harmful.

Prayer time after communion

Q. I remember being taught that the time immediately after the reception of Holy Communion was especially precious for prayer because Christ is physically within us until the species are digested.

I sing in my parish choir, and it is our practice to sing a hymn at Communion. This creates a problem for me because I cannot sing and still do the praying that I want to do (and was taught to do) at that time. The person in charge of the singing in our parish told me that my approach was "pre-Vatican II." I even suggested the use of an organ instrumental piece instead of singing, but this idea was also rejected. I am going to the parish liturgy committee about this; any additional information you could supply about this time during and after the reception of Holy Communion would be appreciated.

A. I regret that I shall not end up being much help for your point of view. Those who exercise specific roles within the sacred liturgy often have to sacrifice personal devotion for the sake of the total celebration. Imagine, if you would, if the priest said that distributing Holy Communion disturbed his own spirit of recollection and thanksgiving, and that he would prefer to meditate!

Nearly fifteen centuries ago, St. Augustine taught us that "he who sings well prays twice." In other words, singing is the highest form of prayer possible. Now, I do think some "quiet time" after Communion is appropriate, either during the distribution of the Eucharist or in the period following immediately.

I must note, however, that I found it somewhat amusing that while you don't want to be "disturbed" by having to sing, you don't seem to have a problem with allowing the organist to be "disturbed" as an alternative!

Wheat host allergy

Q. There is a person in our parish who is allergic to wheat bread. Whenever she is at Mass, the parish priest mixes wine and water in a small glass at the offertory and consecrates it in the course of the Mass. Then at Communion, while the other parishioners are receiving the host from the priest, she walks past him, goes to the altar and consumes that small amount of the Precious Blood, and then returns to her seat. Is this permissible?

A. Yes, it is. I would only add that she ought not be communicating herself. The priest should present her with the sacred species and say, "The Blood of Christ," to which she would respond, "Amen."

Epiclesis gesture

Q. Please comment on the acceptability and possible significance of the gesture in which the celebrant extends his outstretched arms in a broad sweeping motion over the people while praying the epiclesis during Mass.

A. One of the traditional keys to celebrating and appreciating the Roman rite is understanding an expression made popular by Pope Paul VI — "noble simplicity." In other words, exaggerated gestures are completely out of place.

In this light, we can see what Monsignor Peter Elliot has in mind when he talks about the use of hands by liturgical celebrants in his new and superb book, *Ceremonies of the Modern Roman Rite* (Ignatius Press, 1995); the greeting with the hands, for example, "should be smooth, never abrupt or mechanical. It should not be overly expansive, rather it should convey a sense of reverence and control. Such use of the hands never distracts the people but is an expression of peace and an invitation to prayer and recollection" (p. 69). This logic would apply to all hand gestures.

In the instance you cite, however, more than taste is at stake; the celebrant could have a theological agenda he is trying to push, namely, that the people present are the Body of Christ as much as the eucharistic species. This is thoroughly false, and I have dealt with this problematic view of the Real Presence on numerous occasions in these pages.

Having alluded to Monsignor Elliot's work above, let me make an even more serious pitch for it here: His book is "just what the doctor ordered" as an antidote to the liturgical nuttiness we see around; if it gains sufficient currency, the worst of the abuses will be over and, more importantly, a new era of liturgical sanity and true renewal will have arrived, as the Fathers of Vatican II envisioned. This is really an essential text for all priests, seminarians, church musicians, etc.

Mass words changed

Q. In Eucharistic Prayer IV, it says that Christ was "a man like us in all things, but sin." A priest I know says "a person like us." To my understanding, that is not sound doctrine because Jesus was a Divine Person. If there is no doctrinal problem with his formulation, could you please explain why?

A. The first and most basic point to make is that a priest has no right to change the words of the liturgy. And the principal reason the Church is so loathe to have personal additions and subtractions is precisely because of the potential for heterodoxy to slip into the Church's rites.

You are right in asserting that Jesus was a divine Person, not a human person, that is, He was a divine Person (Second Person of the Blessed Trinity from all eternity) with two natures — human and divine. For a thorough treatment of this cardinal tenet of the Catholic Faith, review the *Catechism of the Catholic Church* 464-478.

Mass bread invalid

Q. The Catholic chaplaincy of my university has a beautiful new chapel which is now big enough to accommodate the public. The campus ministry department has invited neighbors and friends to help them with various "ministries," one of them being the making of the eucharistic bread. The recipe for this bread calls for flour, water, honey, and oil. I know that more than one person has inquired about this recipe's compliance with Church regulations, but the chaplain goes on with his recipe, and nobody seems to care. What is the proper way to respond if one is asked to help make the bread, or if one attends Mass there on Sunday or any other day? Should one receive Communion?

A. The Code of Canon Law states it with abundant clarity: "The bread must be made of wheat *alone*" (emphasis mine, Canon 924.2). Additives like honey and oil render the matter invalid. If talking to the priest has done nothing, your diocesan office of worship and/or bishop should be contacted for so serious a violation of liturgical law.

Baptismal sponsors

Q. My husband and I attended a Baptism for the baby of a friend. There were several things about this Baptism that disturbed me.

First of all, our friends had selected one godfather and two godmothers! There was another family present for the Baptism of their child with the same situation. Still another family had chosen five godfathers and six godmothers for their child. I have never seen anything like this before; it was a circus.

Later, I was talking to one of the godmothers and she told me that the godfather wasn't even Catholic. I distinctly remember our parish priest telling us that the godfather and godmother — one of each — had to be practicing Catholics. Is it now allowed to have more than one godparent of each sex and that they don't have to be Catholic?

A. Your concerns are valid. The Code of Canon Law says the following: "Only one male or one female sponsor or one of each sex is to be employed" (Canon 873). Those chosen must be at least sixteen years of age, must have received First Holy Communion and Confirmation, and must live according to the teachings and discipline of the Church (Canon 874). A non-Catholic may not function as a sponsor but may stand in as a "Christian witness," says the same canon, provided there is at least one practicing Catholic who is the sponsor.

All that having been said, certain cultures (like that of the Filipinos) have traditionally employed several sponsors or witnesses, as a way of stressing the communal nature of the Sacrament of Baptism, and thus, the responsibility of all for the Christian upbringing of the newly baptized. I do not think the Church's law wants to eliminate that type of practice, so long as it is clear who has the ultimate and canonical responsibility and, of course, so that the "circus" element you cite is obviated.

Index

108, 171, 179, 195, 205, 217, 220, 224, 240, 244, 246-247, 255, 269, 270-271, 274, 288-289

Baptismal pool, 270-271, 281

Baptismal sprinkling, 205

Basil, St., 108

Benedictines, 15

Benediction, 30, 207-208, 249, 276

Bible, 27 *et passim*

Birth control, 181, 212; pills, 160, 178

Bishop, 13, 21-22, 36-37, 44, 45, 71, 74, 79, 97, 110, 117-118, 148, 166, 197, 202, 211, 225, 243, 246-247, 259, 272, 275-276, 283, 285, 288

Bishop Sheen Prayers Leaflet, 51

Bishops' Committee on the Liturgy, 204-205, 211, 278

Blaise, St., 10

Blessed Mother, see Mary, Blessed Virgin

Blessed Sacrament, see Sacrament, Blessed

Book of Job, 136

Borromeo, Charles, 158

Boy Scouts of America, 23

Boys' Brigade, 23-24

Bread of Life, 104, 277

Breast augmentation, 181-182

Broken body of Christ, 77, 93-94

Brown, Father Raymond, 110

Bunson, Margaret, 15

Bunson, Matthew, 15

Burial, 72

Byzantine-rite Catholic, 254

Canon Law, 16, 29, 42, 44, 52, 56, 58, 83, 120, 165, 171, 185, 205, 241, 248, 258, 263-264, 284, 288-289

Cardinals' titles, 63

Case, Thomas, 96

Catechism of the Catholic Church, 29, 40, 49, 60, 71, 72, 75, 82, 83, 98, 109, 110, 112, 114, 116, 119-120, 122, 124, 128-129, 138, 143, 153, 167, 172-173, 174-175, 176, 180, 182, 184, 185, 190, 191, 194, 207, 222, 224, 227, 228, 246, 255-256, 264, 266, 288

Catherine of Genoa, St., 90, 122, 158

Catherine of Siena, 158

Catholic bookstores, 34, 49, 74

Catholic Mission of Northern Alaska, 13

Catholic doctrine, 14, 34, 71, 82, 83, 84, 92, 102, 115, 118, 130, 173, 251, 266

Catholic Faith, Catholicism, 7, 10, 20, 34-35, 44, 46, 49, 52, 54, 55, 72, 74, 77, 84, 85, 93, 94, 96, 97, 102, 104, 118, 158, 172, 180, 183, 219, 222, 263, 281, 288

Catholic moral vision, 92

Catholic salvation, 94

Catholic-Jewish wedding, 253

The Catholic Woman, 98

Catholics, 7, 21, 23-24, 27, 41, 43-45, 48-49, 53, 60, 64, 67, 69-70, 74, 76, 88, 90, 92, 94, 114, 122, 125, 130, 132, 142, 149,

Our Sunday Visitor's

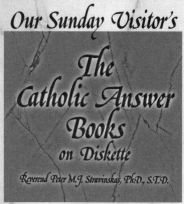

The Catholic Answer Books on Diskette

Reverend Peter M.J. Stravinskas, Ph.D., S.T.D.

Instant Answers to Age-Old Questions

From history to doctrine to just plain fascinating facts, you'll get instant answers to age-old questions with *The Catholic Answer Books on Diskette*.

The most-frequently asked questions from Father Peter M.J. Stravinskas' column in *The Catholic Answer* are now available on computer diskette. Just type your question and the answer appears on your screen! Ideal for research, study, or personal enrichment. Comes complete with printing and Boolean search capabilities. Requires Windows 3.0 or better, 2 megabytes of hard disk space, and one 3.5" high density disk drive.

The Catholic Answer Books on Diskette
By Rev. Peter M.J. Stravinskas, Ph.D., S.T.D.,
Designed by Pat Burke
No. 0-87973-768-9, 3-disk set, $15.95

Available at bookstores. MasterCard, VISA, and Discover customers can order direct from **Our Sunday Visitor** by calling **1-800-348-2440**. Or, send payment plus $3.95 shipping/handling to **Our Sunday Visitor**.

Our Sunday Visitor
200 Noll Plaza
Huntington, IN 46750
1-800-348-2440

Your Source for Discovering the Riches of the Catholic Faith

Our Sunday Visitor...
Your Source for Discovering the Riches of the Catholic Faith

Our Sunday Visitor has an extensive line of materials for young children, teens, and adults. Our books, Bibles, booklets, CD-ROMs, audios, and videos are available in bookstores worldwide.

To receive a FREE full-line catalog or for more information, call **Our Sunday Visitor** at **1-800-348-2440**. Or write, **Our Sunday Visitor** / 200 Noll Plaza / Huntington, IN 46750.

Please send me: __ A catalog
Please send me materials on:
    __ Apologetics and catechetics   __ Reference works
    __ Prayer books   __ Heritage and the saints
    __ The family   __ The parish

Name_____

Address_____Apt._____

City_____State___Zip_____

Telephone ( )_____

A73BBABP

Please send a friend: __ A catalog
Please send a friend materials on:
    __ Apologetics and catechetics   __ Reference works
    __ Prayer books   __ Heritage and the saints
    __ The family   __ The parish

Name_____

Address_____Apt._____

City_____State___Zip_____

Telephone ( )_____

A73BBABP

Our Sunday Visitor
200 Noll Plaza
Huntington, IN 46750
1-800-348-2440
OSVSALES@AOL.COM

Your Source for Discovering the Riches of the Catholic Faith